Candles
in the
Darkness

A True Story of Faith, Hope & Friendship

Sally Fugazi & Debbie Harwell

This book is a work of non-fiction. Names and places have been changed to protect the privacy of all individuals. The events and situations are true.

ISBN: 1-4140-5125-5 (e-book)
ISBN: 1-4140-5124-7 (Paperback)

Library of Congress Control Number: 2003099420

This book is printed on acid free paper.

Printed in the United States of America
Bloomington, IN

Photographs: © 2003, Unique Images, Humble, TX
www.uniqueimages.com

1stBooks – rev. 02/27/04

What Others Are Saying About "Candles"...

— *"I'm enjoying every joy, every pain, every tear, the light and dark times..."*

— *"I truly believe it will minister to others 'on the journey'."*

— *"Laughing... sense of humor...outstanding—I must admit I smiled more than once... I laughed out loud—growing skin, chin hairs, adjoining rooms in the nursing home, etc."*

— *"Fantastic—thank you!"*

— *"I was captivated and at times spellbound"*

— *"Thank you for sharing your feelings and thoughts"*

— *"Thank you especially for giving God the credit and hope to all those who dwell in the darkness."*

— *"Yes, I found it fascinating!"*

— *"...even when discussing something quite serious you were able to find something humorous."*

— *"You had me giggling, smiling and a little tearful as I read of your journeys and your blossoming friendship."*

— *"It was very therapeutic for me to read your book..."*

— *"...an open, free flowing communication about the everyday, mundane, yet often extraordinary parts of a woman's journey..."*

— *"Oh my gosh! It was all I could do to not stay home today and finish it—or bring it to work and incorporate it in amongst my #1 Priority work pile."*

— *"...a poignant and touching jewel created by two wonderful spirits."*

— *"...by page ten I was hooked! At first it felt a bit voyeuristic—somewhat like peering into the bedroom windows of [their] hearts but in a short time I stopped feeling I was violating [their] privacy—and began to feel I was welcome to "pull up a chair and join the conversation." So every night I would "run" to my little bed, hop in and open the pages to see what was the latest topic among the "gals."*

Dedication

To
Bob and Tom

For keeping the flames alive

Contents

Literary License

The reader will note some misspellings and not-so-perfect grammar in the correspondence contained in this book. A minimum of grammatical editing has been done in order to preserve the authenticity of our e-mails. This book is a non-fiction, casual exchange between two friends (who were not always on their best behavior).

Enjoy the grammatical errers. Nobody's perfect!

Prologue

*

My Turn — August 10, 2001

Who's Who

*

Fugazi & Harwell

Prologue

Subj: *My Turn*
Date: *08/10/2001 1:14:40 PM Central Daylight Time*
From: *sarahjf50@hotmail.com*
To: *debbiesb13@aol.com*

On you and I putting our e-mails into book form—
       I may get ill, no, wait...:
       How embarrassing, no, wait...:
       Do we have to? no, wait...:
       Are you crazy? no, wait...:
       Is God behind this..............? wait...
That last question above I have no response for, Deb, but you do: Let me just recap: August 9, 2001, you had a calling: You were on your daily walk, strolling through the greenbelt (do you take a pooper scooper for your dog?) and you felt the call and urge to compile our e-mails—inspired to do this with a strong feeling that we need to share our ministry of two friends with millions. I have not had a similar calling...should I feel insulted? Maybe I should just feel saner than you...

I have not received this same "share our story, help somebody" book calling yet...I just keep writing to you, informing, interrogating, laughing, crying, overreacting, underreacting, and sympathizing. Maybe when I do reread our e-mails I will feel the urge, as you have, to share our gift of friendship and spirituality with others.

Of course, in order to reread the e-mails, I will need to have some help: the cat wet all over the printed copies you mailed me, and then, the two discs you sent me won't boot up on my computer...I, being a spiritual person, am always looking for signs from God, and I have attributed my inability to reread our "story" to one of the following signs being posted in my heart:
       1)   Don't go there (signed, God)
       2)   Don't go there (signed, Satan)
       3)   Don't go there (signed, the cat)
or, my favorite sign, and the one I will most likely plant in my garden:
       "In order to pick a rose, you must first negotiate the thorns..."
       —sarah j., August, 2001. (inspired by God, thank you)
Translation: does it have to be this hard, Lord?

The real story of our relationship, which begins just a year ago, began with our introduction to one another at our husbands' company conference. That was simple enough. You, Deb, were a nice, new, refreshing addition to our corporate wives circle. We wives have a special bond as we all reside in different regions of the US. We decided, as a group, to exchange e-mail addresses to keep in touch as two years is a long time between conferences.

Oddly enough, I did not keep up an e-mail conversation with any of the other wives except you...I didn't even know you well...I knew the other wives much better... but something (?) encouraged you and me to continue our friendly trade of e-mails. Do you ever marvel at divine intervention where God quietly takes you by the hand and says, "Go this way..."

We progress to a polite friendship: enjoyable, entertaining and all done via e-mail—how bizarre—but how practical for friends who live hundreds of miles apart. Then we found ourselves wading into deeper waters with the development of your devastating depression, and my fledgling attempt to guide you through the darkness with two tools: God's light and the knowledge of my own previous experience with the terrifying, hopeless and lonely condition of anxiety and depression. Actually, my most valuable contribution was to show you the options available for treatment...and my most profound contribution came in the call I received to bring God into your world...Me of all people: the original unbeliever for the first 40 years of my life.

Ah, but our story is not just about depression and our sharing of spirituality and healing!

LIFE IS TOO SHORT TO BE MISERABLE!

We have shared many other hilarious and tragic vignettes through our e-mails, and gifted each other with philosophy appropriate to the day: We are two women in the midst of our lives, homemakers, wives, mothers, and now!: grandmothers. We are also caretakers of elderly widowed parents, and we have both just recently lost a beloved father. We have hormonal/menopause issues, we have physical disabilities and we deal with these all with a maturity that fluctuates between ages 10 to 52...: we're not perfect. Yes, our thighs are flabby.

Oddly, our two backgrounds are so different, I am amazed we had the opportunity and ability to ever connect. You are a born Texan, I am an Air Force Brat (emphasis on the brat). We both went to college, you finished with honors, I didn't (finish). But probably our most obvious difference is that you are a blonde, and I am a brunette: that keeps us from being confused on who is who in our photos...No, I am not a shallow person!

I truly believe there are only two reasons our friendship and "candle in the darkness" ministry have flourished and endured: God and e-mail. What do you think?

Okay, I am looking forward (gag...) to rereading our daily e-mails, which are full of all those profoundly trivial and irreplaceable daily experiences that we celebrate/suffer through... Your e-mails, Deb, are interesting; mine, I think, will be embarrassing for me to read, rather of the classic, "did I really say that?" genre...

But, bottom line: I can't ignore the calling you had on August 9th...if you think we should share this pile of blah, blah, blah with other lovely women, then we will. Can we help the readers get though their own daily trials? No.

But God can.
May Grace be tangible for you today.
Love, Sal

4

Who's Who?

The Blonde:	The Brunette:
Deb	**Sal**
Native Texan	Air Force Brat
At the time of this story	At the time of this story
<u>her family credentials included:</u>	<u>her family credentials included:</u>
Wife of Tom, 20 years	Wife of Bob, 30 years
Mom of Travis & Austin	Mom of Tisa, Andrea, Gina,
Stepmom of Tracey & Tiffany	and Anthony
Mother-in-law of David	Mother-in-law of Dave & Stephan
"Grandma D" to Tristan	"Nana" to Zachary, Lyndsey & Julie
Daughter & caretaker of Irene	Daughter & supervisor of Nonny
Home: Kingwood, Texas	Home: Trophy Club, Texas

Fugazi & Harwell

I

The Lull Before the Storm

*

Kindred Spirits and Caregivers

Wheaties and Wine

Hospice and Hope

Summer Storms from the Veranda

Domestic Schizophrenia

Parents and Children

*

Fugazi & Harwell

Kindred Spirits and Caregivers

Subj: Hi Sally!
Date: 6/12/00 3:05:17 PM Central Daylight Time
From: debbiesb13@aol.com
To: sarahjf50@hotmail.com

Hi Sally –

Hope all was well when you got home from World Golf and you missed out on the Dallas area flooding. I was so glad to get home, but have to admit it would have been fun also to have another day or two after getting to know people better. Besides we never even made it to the pool, which is probably a sin in Florida!

I was paying some bills for my mom today and thought I'd send you the phone number for AARP customer service in case you still want to inquire about insurance for your mother. They're very nice and one of the few places I've dealt with that don't give you a hassle when you are not the person named on the account.

Well that's about it from here. Keep in touch.

Take care, Debbie

Subj: Re: hello in Texas!
Date: 6/14/00 9:34:45 AM Central Daylight Time
From: sarahjf50@hotmail.com
To: debbiesb13@aol.com

Good morning Debbie!

Thanks for the AARP number—I will use it. I am up to my ears in liquidating my widowed mother's assets, getting all legal paperwork done etc. etc., but these are all things that when in place, will not have to be done again.

We have had lots of rain, but not to the point of flooding in our "neck of the woods," just to the point of refilling the reservoirs and have an abundance of green growing things...rather like a tropical paradise. Any rainy/cool day we have now, is one less day to be hot this summer. My roses are growing well and producing some lovely little flowers—this first growing season for them will not produce a lot of big gorgeous blooms, as the plants need to acclimate to their new environment, but the fragrances are lovely.

It was really nice to meet you and spend some time together. Our next conference/whatever, will be more enjoyable as we can look forward to visiting. I feel like we are kindred spirits!

Hope your boys (including Tom) are enjoying summer in your new home in Houston. You live in a lovely area.

Well, time to pack (again!!). We're off to California and Wyoming for a vacation. I will be glad to come home and just stay here for the rest of the summer... Hasta Luego! Sally

Subj: how was your trip?
Date: 6/21/00 2:56:11 PM Central Daylight Time
From: debbiesb13@aol.com
To: sarahjf50@hotmail.com

Hi Sally!
How was Wyoming? Beautiful and relaxing, no doubt. Things have been busy here.
You and my friend Trish are getting me quite interested in growing roses. I love the fragrance, but have always thought them too difficult for my meager (OK, non-existent) gardening skills.
At the conference you mentioned your daughter Tisa has an ultrasound soon. Hope all goes well with that. You must be so excited at the prospect of another grandchild!
By the way, how did your mother and your son Anthony manage together while you and Bob were away on vacation? That would NEVER have worked with our boys Travis and Austin. Even being teenagers, my mom wouldn't let them cross the street.
It was great to spend time with you at the conference and I also feel like we are kindred spirits. It's just too bad we didn't know sooner, I had the travel Scrabble in my suitcase!
Well, time for me to pick up Austin and fix us some dinner.
Take care, Debbie

Subj: *Tune in tomorrow...*
Date: *6/30/00 2:13:02 PM Central Daylight Time*
From: *sarahjf50@hotmail.com*
To: *debbiesb13@aol.com*

Hi Debbie!
Jackson Hole, Yellowstone and surrounding areas are absolutely beautiful. On the sad side, we saw Bob's parents in Monterey and they are really both suffering with the pain of Bob's mother's radiation therapy. If she survives this it will truly be a miracle. It does not look too promising.
Saw all our friends from college days, and they look so much older than I do (yuck-yuck!). It was so nice to catch up on everyone's lives.
Now we are home and life here is like a soap opera. We have a wedding in our home next weekend for our youngest daughter Gina. Wedding arrangements have been hasty as the couple, who have been engaged since December, were a

little too ambitious in their quest to "become one" and now they will soon be "three!" Yes, that makes two grandchildren to be born in December.

The good news is that our two daughters are sharing all their pregnancy woes with each other and have formed a strong support unit.

Am slowly but methodically getting my mother's affairs in order, and after the wedding we will seriously start looking for a place for her to call her own, nearby. With all the stuff going on in our family right now, I know she is looking forward to a little less excitement.

I thank God for his blessings that I can smile, while in the midst of family issues. On any given day I am dealing with four generations, frequently all under the same roof. Time for me to get a job...what do you think? I think it could be my salvation! That, and a good sense of humor!

Speaking of roses, if you do take the plunge into roses, I'd be happy to give you advice via e-mail, as I grew roses in Houston for 14 years. Have fun! Let me know if you are going to plant and I'll e-mail you a little maintenance schedule, which will guarantee lovely flowers. If I can do it, you can too!

Must go, time to finalize flowers and cake for wedding—Good Lord! It's a zoo around here! Will keep you posted on the "Young and the Pregnant"—

Wouldn't it be nice to be sitting on a veranda somewhere right now, sipping wine and playing a good game of Scrabble?
Love, Sally

Subj: the world turns here too
Date: 6/30/00 4:15:37 PM Central Daylight Time
From: debbiesb13@aol.com
To: sarahjf50@hotmail.com

Hi Sally!

Just came up to the computer to kill some time waiting for Tom to get home and got your e-mail. Nothing like a smile to brighten the day.

We are leaving this evening for four days in San Antonio/New Braunfels. It'll be our first family vacation in two years as all the trips we planned since then have been cancelled due to my parents' various illnesses. It won't be long, but it will be family time and it will be relaxing (picture the tube floating lazily down the Comal).

Glad to hear you had a good time on your trip. Sorry though to hear about Bob's mom. I can certainly sympathize, but it doesn't ease the pain. I'll be keeping her in my prayers.

Sounds like you certainly have your hands full. A wedding at home is an ambitious undertaking! Good luck!!

This last week or so has been a little trying. My 87-year-old mother, Irene, who is in an assisted living facility, is insisting that I am somehow keeping her from seeing my dad. She refuses to accept the physical aspect of his passing away and wants to see him face to face. She knows in her heart this isn't possible, but somewhere between denial and dementia she can't always sort it out.

Fortunately, even though my dad has passed away, the hospice chaplain, Nancy still comes by to see my mom. My mother confides in her much more comfortably than with me, and Nancy is helping her to sort things out to some extent.

I finished this week with liquidating the last of their assets. It was a relief and sad at the same time. When we get back next week I have to get the neurologist to come by to see her. She also has been destroying her medicine since she found out we were taking a vacation.

If you ever need anyone to blow off steam to about the frustrations of caring for your mom's finances, medical needs, etc. you know where to go. Hopefully you and your mother will be able to have fun finding her a new home and getting it all to her liking when things settle down. It's good that you are looking for a place near by, as it will make life much easier on you in the long run. When we moved here from Florida, my parents moved into a nearby apartment that had a large seniors group with activities several times a week. They loved it! Heaven forbid you would even suggest missing the card games on Tuesday and Thursday! Anyway, it gave them something to look forward to and have their own life so to speak.

I had to laugh at what you said about getting a job to reduce life's challenges. I've gotten to be friends with one of the ladies who runs the food service at the Rosemont (Mom's asst. living). That's exactly why she's working. She's our age, two kids in high school, and got tired of everyone in her immediate and extended family turning to her to do all their errands etc. because she wasn't working. She swears she has more free time now (although I really doubt that). Actually, I think you hit the nail on the head with the good sense of humor.

Thanks for the rose info. We have a great place behind the garage as you suggested that gets plenty of sun.

If you ever come to Houston for a visit it would be great to get together if you have time. We don't have a veranda, but we do have a deck, wine and Scrabble. The Harwells could even cook dinner if you were so inclined!

Well, Tom just called and is on his way home. I'm so excited! Four days, just the four of us - it's been too long. Good luck with the wedding and keep that sense of humor.

Love, Deb

Subj: Re: life is beautiful?
Date: 7/10/00 7:07:46 PM Central Daylight Time
From: sarahjf50@hotmail.com
To: debbiesb13@aol.com

Hello!
*   I looked at the date on your e-mail and am sorry it takes me so long to answer…we were in high gear last week with the wedding. I had to put my mother's affairs on hold, tell my daughter I couldn't come to visit my grandson, and counsel our son on how to break up with a girl who wants to marry him (he's sixteen…) plus plan a wedding in less than two weeks.*
*   The wedding did happen, it was very nice, and hopefully Gina and our new son-in-law, Stephan will live happily ever after. We met his family, who are from Germany and they seem very nice.*
*   Meanwhile, Gina and Tisa continue to grow and expand. They are lucky to share their pregnancies. Makes throwing up more fun!*
*   Your mother sounds like she's going through some very typical emotional symptoms for one who suffers from dementia. Sounds like you have her in a nice place with good people to care for her. My prayers are with you as you work with all the details of her life. And yes, it is comforting to talk to someone who has a similar situation of care giving. Isn't it interesting how once you become a caregiver for your parents, that you realize that there are a lot of people out there experiencing the same situation!*
*   At times I feel so stretched between four generations and there is no time to think about important things like painting my toenails…or taking a day to just do whatever comes to mind. On the other hand, I do realize my life could be a lot worse (don't even go there) so I count my blessings (which are many—thank you, Lord) and keep plodding on.*
*   I really have had enough crises this year to last the next decade. The interesting thing is that none of these issues are generated by Bob and I. They are coming from the generations that orbit around us. I guess that is what some people refer to as the golden years? That must apply to people who never had children, they were orphans and had no siblings. As for the rest of the world, our responsibilities seem to be multiplying instead of diminishing. I can see the future now, I will be living in squalor, going in and out of consciousness due to strokes and Alzheimer's, perennially giving advice and attempting to cook dinner for someone.*
*   Think I'll start my new* Harry Potter *book tonight. Have you read these books? Total fun and fantasy. A literary vacation.*
*   Speaking of vacations, hope you had a wonderful time in San Antonio & New Braunfels! Great places to have some fun!*
*   Take care, stay in the shade, and enjoy these long days of summer,*
Love, Sal

Wheaties and Wine

Subj: well, mostly beautiful
Date: 7/12/00 10:26:19 PM Central Daylight Time
From: debbiesb13@aol.com
To: sarahjf50@hotmail.com

Hi there!

Things are good here tonight as I managed to find what I am sure is the perfect dress to wear to my stepdaughter Tracey's wedding, and ate an enchilada dinner. This was after being frustrated all day, from Tom's telling me he did not like the first dress I had planned to wear. I hate looking for a dress when you NEED one — nothing fits, or it requires extra accessories like a boob job. Isn't it nice to be amused by such simple pleasures?

We had a terrific time in San Antonio and New Braunfels. Best of all, I felt like we truly reclaimed ourselves as a family. It is difficult to describe, but I suspect, you understand.

I also came back feeling relaxed and ready to return to the challenges of parenting my parent. She has started an anti-depressant, but it is too early to see any improvement.

I made a commitment to Tom that I would also start taking time for myself (since my parents' health began to decline a year and a half ago, I have been an almost daily visitor). This sounds great, but my mother is a master at manipulation a la guilt. I'll have to be stronger — what do you think, Wheaties or wine?

You are right about the generations around us. Sometimes I think we are traveling in a bumper boat, and just when we get headed in the desired direction, someone rams us from the side and we go shooting across the pool. We are truly the "sandwich generation" although some (as in four generations) have more layers than others. Daddy always said, "It's hell to get old." My reply was always the same, "It's hell not to." As with many other things in life he will probably prove to be right in the end. But in the meantime, I plan to go along in my "boat" blissfully believing I will regain control of my course at some point.

So, how is *Harry Potter*? I haven't read these books, but did buy the first one the other day. All the hype for the latest book really drew my interest. I assumed the beginning was a better place to start than book four. Yes?

Well, it is time to put the dogs out and go to bed. Hope you are enjoying your pool (it was 108 on the car thermometer when I left the mall at 8pm!)
Love, Deb

Subj: Re: wheaties AND wine!
Date: 7/13/00 7:48:05 AM Central Daylight Time
From: sarahjf50@hotmail.com
To: debbiesb13@aol.com

    Let's enjoy our prompt e-mails while they last! As we know, we have lulls in the madness, and it's nice to recharge with a friend! Especially a friend who understands.

    Tell me more about Tracey's wedding: dress, cake, flowers, people—it's a whole mini series on its own! This is Tom's daughter?

    Buying a dress when you need one: the rule is you will never find the right dress. However, you will find the perfect dress when you don't need one or when you don't want to spend the money! But the latter is a lesson we learn, right? Just buy the dress when it looks fabulous (even if you have to eat hot dogs for a week) someday it will pay off. I never follow this advice, however!

    Harry Potter? Enjoy! I am reading the fourth book—yes, do read them in order, and this book is as fun as the others. The boys will remind you of your boys. Just fantasy with a heart.

    On the home front: the two pregnant daughters: both get ultrasounds at the end of the month, and if the babies cooperate, the girls can start decorating the new nurseries soon.

    On your vacation, I understand what a wonderful feeling it is to rejuvenate a family, and feel back in synch again. So many things pull the family apart—As mothers and wives, this is what we strive for: family harmony—sometimes it is beyond our reach, but sometimes, like on your vacation, an opportunity arises to grab them all back in the fold again, happily. Very satisfying for you, I imagine. Enjoy and celebrate!

    Must go, have banking with Mom and financial planner coming over today, plus my speech therapy (my voice is beginning to waver).
Auf Wiedersehn, Sal

Subj: zwei dunkle biere
Date: 7/13/00 5:28:21 PM Central Daylight Time
From: debbiesb13@aol.com
To: sarahjf50@hotmail.com

Hi Sal!

    You mentioned previously, your new in-laws are from Germany. I visited Europe once right after college with a friend who was studying the organ in Switzerland. I learned to drink cheap French wine, order two dark beers in German, and sneak mugs past security at the Hofbrau. On the whole a very productive trip!

    I'm surprised you are going to a speech therapist. I didn't notice any wavering in your voice, and we obviously talked enough in Florida to realize there was a lot more we had to say to each other. Did they tell you what has caused it? Is it a sort of Katherine Hepburn waver? I have always thought she sounded very regal and self-assured.

Hope everything went well with your mom's financial planning. This will make life so much simpler for you both in the future. Tom and I begged my parents so many times after they sold their house to do the same. "You'll never have to take care of us," my mother would say. She was actually an astute money manager successfully running her own business. But unfortunately, as dementia began to set in, her more recent "investments" were all lottery tickets and fraudulent contests. By the time I took over their finances there was only enough left to last through this past spring. Now we are working on the little bit of my dad's life insurance money.

You asked about Tracey's wedding that's coming up in August. She and David have planned every detail themselves and done a great job! Her dress is simply gorgeous and she will carry a bouquet of star-gazer lilies. The ceremony will be held in the atrium of the hotel in front of a waterfall. She and Tom will "enter" by coming down the glass elevator. Should be beautiful!

Austin called me "middle-aged" today. CAN YOU BELIEVE THAT!? I was so insulted. Our grandson, Tristan can call me grandma, but I will NOT be middle aged! Wish we were on the veranda with the wine and Scrabble game.
Love, Deb

Subj: *Re: di-say-bility*
Date: *7/20/00 10:24:40 PM Central Daylight Time*
From: *sarahjf50@hotmail.com*
To: *debbiesb13@aol.com*

Preparing for Bob's 50th birthday party tomorrow. Kids are buying him a new electric guitar...he gave his old one to our nephew. Bob was in a rock band in college when I met him. Even wrote some songs and recorded in LA—to no avail.

Speech therapy. I have a strange condition called spasmodic dysphonia. It is simply that my vocal chords will spasm involuntarily, making it only possible to speak in a strangled voice pattern. It is a condition which appears when people reach their 40's—which happened to me—an increasing tremor in my voice, sort of like one would speak under great strain—except I had no great stress. Caused by a neurological glitch, in the same family with facial tics. Cure: none. Treatment: injection of botox (botulism toxin) into the vocal chords—thru the neck—once every 6 months. This keeps my voice smooth for about 4 months, then it starts to quaver and I need to use my speech therapy to help me maintain a voice until my next injection. But with injections and speech therapy, I keep it under reasonable control...my mother says it is a travesty for someone like me who is such a motor mouth—sounds like a mom, yes?

Harry Potter, I will repeat it...have some fun and begin reading. I am almost done with this newest book. It is good.

Must go to the kitchen with my recipes—much rather be on the veranda with Scrabble, wine and a nice lady! Do you do the Jumbles in the newspaper? Love, Sal

Hospice and Hope

Subj: sending you an owl
Date: 7/23/00 9:35:12 AM Central Daylight Time
From: debbiesb13@aol.com
To: sarahjf50@hotmail.com

Good morning!!
Hope you've had a good weekend. How was Bob's party? Was he surprised about the guitar? I bet it was fun dating a "rock star." Sometimes I think we could do with a little more of the "age of aquarius-peace-love-flower power" music for this generation.

The injections you take for the speech difficulties sound painful!! I hope it's not as bad as it sounds. Isn't botox the stuff they give people to control their wrinkles?

You are 100% right about *Harry Potter*. I love the books! Finished the first one last weekend, bought the rest on Tuesday, and am already ¾ of the way through book 2. My family thinks I'm nuts, but so what.

To Dr. Sal: *Harry Potter* has been a wonderful place to "hide." I mean that literally. My mom reacted badly to the anti-depressant. In fact she became overly sad, hostile, and belligerent. Even after stopping the meds it has taken days to get her back to "normal." On top of this, her doctor [who comes to the assisted living] has been a no-show for his appointments since end of June. We switched doctors on Thursday. I really like the new one who is a woman and shows more compassion. She is doing new labs etc. to start new treatments.

I was not however, prepared for her to tell me my mother should be put under hospice care. To say I was overwhelmed would be a gross understatement. Even telling you this now, is making my heart beat fast and my hands tremble. I wanted to scream, "It is too soon! I'm not ready yet!" Of course, she is ready. She will be 88 September 1, has a non-malignant brain tumor, and can no longer walk or stand. In addition, since December, she has lost a sister, her husband, a sister-in-law, and three dining companions.

Despite "hiding" all week, I have given this a tremendous amount of thought and prayer. The conclusion, I will confess to you - it is not losing her I fear most, but the journey. Does that make sense? Is it too selfish? I hope you do not take it as a lack of love for her on my part because I do love her. It's just everything with my mother is always complex (with Daddy, everything was always simple). I will spare you the volumes on that topic.

On a lighter note: Tom bought me a Mr. Lincoln rose bush yesterday. It is not the greatest specimen - mostly a stump with two little twigs coming off of it, but am sure it has potential (like Charlie Brown's Christmas tree).

Yes, I always check the Jumbles although I rarely have the time to work through the whole thing.

Can't tell you how much it means to feel there is a friend with so much understanding on the other end of these e-mails.

Must go. Promised Austin I'd let him have a turn at the computer. I think I need my own laptop — what do you think?

Love, Deb

Subj: *Re: summer with the Dursleys*
Date: *7/26/00 6:11:36 PM Central Daylight Time*
From: *sarahjf50@hotmail.com*
To: *debbiesb13@aol.com*

Harry's summer vacations, yuk!

I have been rushing through this week—tore down a side fence yesterday, rebuilt it and installed a gate—ruined my hands. But I like the look of the gate, I designed it a little different than most, of course I messed it up, too! But if there's one thing I do well, it's hide my mistakes...sort of. Anyway, it's coming along—I like to work with wood—I did not say I was good at it, just enjoy it. And I have the basic tools so it is fun. Bob just winces when I get out my power tools—yes, they are my tools...he rolls his eyes and mutters things about sawing off my fingers and tackling jobs way too ambitious...but, hey! he doesn't have the time to fix a fence. His masters program has robbed him of time for the last 1½ years and he's not done until December. So I am the Bob Vila of our home.

Anyway, sat down to read your e-mail, and my world slowed down when I got to the part about your mom. I understand how difficult this must be for you. I understand that we both have different issues with our moms versus our dads—being with my dad was like dancing, we always followed each other's steps.

Making the decision to put her in a hospice may be something to talk over with a hospice professional. When we were handling my father's illness, we learned so much from speaking to the hospice coordinator. They are the professionals of dying. Their one mission is to make the final days, months, and years as dignified and as comfortable as possible for the patient. This would include good drug therapy. It is probably the best quality of life (and death) your mom can be offered at this point. She will have support there that you cannot provide for her, just because you are her daughter and you have such emotional issues connected with her.

I did not realize your mom had lost so many people this year. No wonder she's depressed. And she's probably very angry—I would be. Too much of a bad thing. Talk to the hospice people, Debbie, ask questions, tour the facility—maybe you have already had personal experience with the hospice world and don't need any add'l info—in that case, ask yourself what your mom would want if she was managing her own life (when she was in her right mind)—she would not have wanted you to be suffering because she is suffering. I will keep you and your mom in my prayers.

Glad you're enjoying Harry! *I think your inner child has to be alive and well in order to enjoy these books. I am refreshingly immature for my age (just ask Mom) and plan to stay that way—if only to bug my mom—just kidding—*

Have we discussed the Mitford *books?*

I really am enjoying our friendship. In a world which robs us of personal time, it is so nice to know we can still talk and share our lives and be refreshed by a friendly word of encouragement and let's not forget the humor! Kindred spirits...a treasure.

Love, Sal

Subj: defeating the dementor
Date: 7/29/00 5:34:52 PM Central Daylight Time
From: debbiesb13@aol.com
To: sarahjf50@hotmail.com

Hi Sal!

The timing of your email could not have been better (ESP?). Actually read it on Thursday morning. Something just said, "check it." Your words of encouragement on hospice were confirmation I was doing the right thing.

My mom had been sent to the hospital Wednesday night for another possible stroke. After hours in ER and getting admitted, she seems to have had a TIA (mini-stroke) and Bell's palsy (pressure on nerve causing one side of face to droop). I decided then we were NEVER coming back to the hospital again (the fact that she told me I should be ashamed for bringing her didn't hurt either!). So on Thursday morning, we enrolled in a hospice program and by the evening she was back at her assisted living: no more MRI's etc.

I feel really at peace with this decision and in fact as if a weight has been lifted from my shoulders. Too bad I could not see last week that this was the path of least resistance. I am using the same hospice we had for my dad, so she will already know all the nurses, social worker, etc. In fact she and I both have still maintained regular, but separate visits with the chaplain, Nancy. Plus, now she can stay where she is and should not have to go to a nursing home as her condition declines in the future, as the hospice service comes to her. All in all for the best.

I am very impressed you can build a fence and gate!!!!!! I remember Tom telling me Bob had told him you do all the yard work yourself. Tom would never give up the yard - he says it's his therapy.

Went to the neurologist Monday for my back update. Still have degenerative discs and arthritis but one disc is bulging causing my current problem. Good news - I am not bad enough for any radical treatments - surgery. Bad news - must continue to grin and bear it (translation - take more drugs). Of course he told me to lose weight and add swimming to my daily routine, which already includes exercises and a 2-3 mile walk. Of course then my back will feel better, but the day will be gone. Doctors are so practical.

We have not discussed the *Mitford* books. In fact you'll need to fill me in as I'm clueless as to who that is.

Perhaps it is the inner child that is the key to our kindred spirits. (My mother thinks my Eeyore watch is ridiculous.) In my twenties I thought surely I'd mature in my thirties, then forties. After 40 I realized it was just never going to happen and that was a good thing. Makes having to ACT like an adult a lot less painful.

Well must go, hospice has brought my mom an electric bed, so I'm going with Tom to get her old bed out of the way, plus check on her progress. Hope you have a great weekend. Let me know what's up with you and yours, and thanks again for the smiles and encouraging words.
Love, Deb

Summer Storms from the Veranda

Subj: *Re: Dumbledor means "bee"*
Date: *7/29/00 10:52:08 PM Central Daylight Time*
From: *sarahjf50@hotmail.com*
To: *debbiesb13@aol.com*

Hi!

    Let's thank God and celebrate that we have these storms in life, but we also have something more powerful: the strength to endure them. Just look at Harry: he is a normal little guy, full of normal flaws but he is faced with incredible darkness and evil, yet, in the midst of turmoil, his inner sight gives him the key to survival. And then he wins. Yes.

    We too, shall survive and triumph...through situations with aging parents...and teens...and cellulite...and hormones...and loving husbands (they are adorable but they can get to us like no one else)...and......

    Oh, my! Your arthritis sounds painful! I have been going to a therapist for bioenergetics, which is a combination of yoga and circulation, and breathing. Will ask her for some exercises to help your condition.

    Tell Tom YES, that I understand fully what he means by working in the yard is therapy...it is an issue of having control over your own space, solitude, a work out for anger, a place to think, a visual accomplishment; it satisfies our need for creativity but no one gives you a report card or job review. A sanctuary.

    I have done many things to improve this house...some have been good things, some have been disasters! I lack the sense to stop myself. I will try anything...Bob just shakes his head. The gate I planned first by using all my chopsticks (I can't eat Chinese food without wooden chopsticks so I keep a supply on hand) to build the three dimensional fence to determine the support joints, etc. Rather an unorthodox and sloppy craftswoman, but the end product is usually passable. Bob wants me to get a job—a real job—probably so I will stop trying to build things at home. That's okay, too, once I get my mom settled.

    Here's the good news, Debbie! THE GODS ARE WITH US. You have found a haven (the hospice) for your mother (good for you, by the way) and I have found an apartment for my mom, nearby. We found a nice condo, which is surrounded by golf course and creeks, in our neighborhood, in the complex she wanted and she can move in August. (None too soon for her as Bob got an electric guitar for his birthday and Anthony has started playing it—rather loudly)—

    Will send first Mitford *book with Bob to give to Tom. There are five* Mitford *books written by author Jan Karon. Get ready for a lovely ride with Father Tim, the Episcopalian priest who is the main character of these five books. These books would be good to pick up after you have finished the last* Harry *book. When you are in withdrawal pangs from the world of Hogwarts and wizards, thinking you can't wait until the fifth book emerges next year, settle in with* Mitford *and get ready to relax for a while.*

In closing my prayers are with your mom, that she will find peace and understanding.
Love, Sal

Subj: it does?
Date: 7/30/00 9:54:12 PM Central Daylight Time
From: debbiesb13@aol.com
To: sarahjf50@hotmail.com

Hi! Dumbledore means "bee?" Is that in another language or in book 4 and I haven't gotten there yet. I think Debbie means the bee. Is that significant? Am I missing something?

Congratulations on finding a place for your mom! Sounds great with the golf course and creek. My neighbor and I were talking this evening that the mother daughter relationship must be the most complex on earth. Like mine, her mother acts unappreciative for any assistance given - we never do anything right. Sometimes I think it is more a product of our generation vs. theirs. We just don't look at things the same way.

I don't get the impression you have that type of relationship with your daughters. I can see you being loving and accepting even if things are not always how you hoped they might have been - concerned more with their finding their own way to happiness rather than yours. With me for example, it has only been the last year my mother has stopped telling me how much better a person I could have been if I hadn't dropped out of law school - twice. Her dream, not mine. Too many judgments!

My mother, by the way, is not speaking to me now except for answering a few yes and no questions. Says she isn't mad, but chooses to close her eyes or read the newspaper when I visit. This too shall pass.

Meant to tell you before - the single sentence about your dad said so much. He must have been a wonderful man. I bet our fathers may have been kindred spirits as well.

You can eat with chopsticks?! There is no end to your talents! So what is your next project?

Are you serious about the job? Any ideas yet on what you'd want to do? I had said when Austin started to high school I would go back to work part time, but now that the time is here - probably not, especially not with my mother's health being questionable. Plus I still enjoy my volunteer work for the Houston Junior Forum and high school (gave up all the PTA when Daddy was sick). I work in the college room at the high school two Tuesdays a month and at the Houston Junior Forum's resale shop in the Heights two Thursdays a month during school.

The *Mitford* books sound good. I'll look forward to reading them.

Do you really think it's possible to survive parents, children, and hormones in the same lifetime? Maybe with good friends and inspiration like Harry.

'night.

Love, Deb

Subj:　*archaic English*
Date:　*8/4/00 8:54:43 PM Central Daylight Time*
From:　*sarahjf50@hotmail.com*
To:　*debbiesb13@aol.com*

Yes, Dumbledor means "bee" in archaic English. Read that in an article in USA Today *about Harry Potter.*

This week while Bob was gone, I painted all the cupboards and wood work in the kitchen. It was that old yucky oak color and I changed it to a mottled ivory with taupe.

I have so much to tell you but I must go for now. Will write more tomorrow. It has been quite a week! But before I go, let me just say that your relationship with your mom sounds like it's been rather difficult. From the little I've known of you, if you were my daughter, I would be thanking God for the intelligent compassionate person that you are. There are some very unhappy women in the world. How sad for them. Rather like PMS on a permanent basis...the question is, what made them this way? How were they hurt?

Hasta la vista, mi amiga!!

Sal

Subj:　the Harwells are in-laws!
Date:　8/7/00 2:22:42 PM Central Daylight Time
From:　debbiesb13@aol.com
To:　sarahjf50@hotmail.com

Hola! Como estas?

We had such a great weekend! Everything for the wedding was wonderful!!! Tracey was a beautiful bride; Tiffany was a gorgeous bride's maid; Travis and Austin looked like grown men in their new suits. Tom was such a proud "father of the bride" and even danced. It was all very touching (especially grandson Tristan at the alter with a big bag of goldfish). We all had a grand time!!!

With regards to my mom - she is a dichotomy - "the best of times, the worst of times." She is loving and generous to a fault, and at the same time prideful and difficult. It took me up until a few years ago to figure out it was not my fault she was dissatisfied with life. Her glass was and is always half empty. I read once people like this have some sort of brain chemistry thing that give them this outlook on life, but who knows.

In Barbara Bush's autobiography (highly recommend it if you haven't already read it) she said essentially she realized from watching her own mother that you can choose to be happy with your life or not, and Barbara Bush chooses to be happy. Her mother was always waiting for "her ship to come in" never realizing it had. This is my mother and I exactly. Sad for my mother, but it helped me stop striving to please her, and just let knowing she loved me anyway be enough.

I told her recently I was content and felt blessed with my life just the way it is. She could NOT understand this concept at all. Of course having Tom there to support me has played a big role as well because things said can still hurt no matter how "intellectually" you look at life.

Isn't it amazing how the time gets away from us? Read in *USA Today* last week that women deal better with stress than men because they share their thoughts with other women. Must be why we're so well adjusted.

Be of good cheer –

Love, Deb

Subj: the days of our lives?
Date: 8/13/00 6:43:49 PM Central Daylight Time
From: debbiesb13@aol.com
To: sarahjf50@hotmail.com

Hi Sally!

I'm assuming you are super busy with kids, possibly moving mom, etc. and hoping all is well otherwise even if hectic. Thought maybe you could use a friendly hello in the middle of the madness. I can remember what a job it was moving my parents into the asst. living. Hope it goes as easy as possible for you getting your mom situated whenever that may be.

This was an up and down week for me - you can of course guess the single source of my mood swings - mom, not hormones. On Tuesday and Wednesday I gave serious consideration to running away from home for a few days, but did not have the nerve. Things improved later in the week. It is very interesting in dealing with professional caregivers how they can have such diverse views on the mind set of the same individual. This of course leads directly to immense frustration - do not pass go, do not collect $200. So, I am trudging on.

Have thought all week how nice it would be if we ever actually do get to sit on the veranda watching the summer storms roll by as we enjoy a glass of wine and a game of Scrabble. Sometimes it keeps me going. Hang in there with whatever you've got going - there will be another lull in the madness eventually.

Love, Deb

Domestic Schizophrenia

Subj: *dog days of our lives?*
Date: *8/15/00 8:45:55 AM Central Daylight Time*
From: *sarahjf50@hotmail.com*
To: *debbiesb13@aol.com*

Hello!

Our e-mails: they're like a drink of cool water in the dog days of August!

The situation with your mom sounds like a bunch of professionals are trying to deal with a very complex woman—and it probably is not easy to get a straight, consistent answer out of her concerning her feelings, etc. Then they probably try to sum it up into some kind of analogy about your mom and it sounds like a potpourri of conditions. How confusing and frustrating for you, as it is hard to help her without some solid diagnosis. At least you have her in the best place for her condition(s) and she is receiving the appropriate attention—my prayers are with you as you trudge on...if it helps, I'm also in my combat boots trudging a parallel path, with somewhat different circumstances. It's rather like having triplets in midlife.

Just finished reading World of Pies *[by Karen Stolz] that you sent me. The pictures evoked by the book are lovely—wish we were there. The girl is the same age as I was: 12 in 1962. I built a tree house that summer and sat up in it spitting on the cows that would meander below.*

Did I tell you Tisa is having a little girl? Gina finds out on Sept 1 (if baby cooperates) what they're having.

Ah, Deb, life goes on...(praise God) and we are slipping gracefully through this summer. I have times when I suffer from domestic schizophrenia: sometimes I want more time for myself and pursuit of my own goals, and other times I am so glad that I can provide my family with a safe haven when they need it. I just keep praying to do the right thing, and not to dwell on the grass on the other side of the fence. Also helps immensely to share and to talk to you, dear friend!

What do you think: a couple of white wicker rockers on the veranda, a lovely wicker table set with Scrabble and graced with frosty glasses of ice tea...a little lemon and mint to compliment the drink...maybe some lovely instrumental in the background: Mozart or some new age strain...Someday!

Love, Sal

Subj: veranda – our haven from the storms
Date: 8/17/00 4:45:21 PM Central Daylight Time
From: debbiesb13@aol.com
To: sarahjf50@hotmail.com

Sounds like you are really on the move!!! Will look forward to getting the *Mitford* books as the one I just finished was on understanding hospice patient mentality - lighten up, please!!

Domestic schizophrenia has got to be the most perfect phrase I've ever heard. You have such a way with words! I understand this feeling completely.

So where did you live with cows? Just that summer or on a farm or what? It does not surprise me you were already building things then - it must be a life long passion with tremendous gratification in the finished product.

I was 10 in the summer of '62 and spent a great deal of time in a tree minus the house. My parents along with 4 other aunts and uncles bought our "farm" that year, 10 acres near what is now Intercontinental Airport, with a house, stable, woods and horses. For five years of my youth, I spent a good part of almost every weekend in the biggest pecan tree. No one could see me - my own private retreat. I loved it at night there - all you could hear were cicadas and crickets - no cars - and the stars and moon were so bright!

We recently toured the new Mormon temple. They have a place called the "Celestial Room" that is an opulent living room with Strauss crystal chandeliers and gold leaf inlays. It's absolutely beautiful!! For me though, heaven on earth is the outdoors, and possibly Brennan's bread pudding souffle (sp? I am a terrible speller).

Your veranda description is fast becoming that ideal spot for peace of mind, a bit of heaven on earth - the ultimate dream - the calming place to go when life is unmanageable. We need a setting - how about looking out over a green meadow, dotted with wild flowers, large oaks nearby laced with Spanish moss, and just the subtle hint of jasmine in the breeze? Someday ... without a doubt!

Vaya con Dios!
Love, Deb

Subj: *Re: dirty books*
Date: *8/21/00 3:04:54 PM Central Daylight Time*
From: *sarahjf50@hotmail.com*
To: *debbiesb13@aol.com*

Hello friend!

I sent the first two Mitford *books back with Tom. They have been read by four different women in my family, and they are a mess (hence "dirty books") but this means you can take them anywhere, eat, drink, drop them in the pool, run over them with the car, and ultimately, throw them away. So enjoy reading them, then, throw them in the laundry or something.*

Gina has been feeling a little under the weather. She is supposed to put her feet up, but I think she went to work today. She has been very concerned about losing her very girlish figure and I think she may have overdone the exercising. Please keep her and the little one in your prayers.

The cows and I lived outside of Dayton, Ohio, in 1962. I was fresh back from three years in Germany. I was so shy and didn't talk much, so the kids thought I didn't speak English. Got over that quick: I soon was back in my motor mouth mode (much to my teacher's dismay).

In response to your thoughts defining "heaven on earth": I, too, feel that God is present within us and any elaborate trappings would actually be contrary to the true spirit of humility before God. He asked Moses to take off his shoes because he was on holy ground. He did not say hire a decorator and create a simply fabulous tent so we can commune in style...

Life is good, when viewing it from the veranda: I see a meadow with wildflowers, I feel the cool breeze with the fragrant memory of an afternoon thunderstorm, and don't forget the little babbling brook, with sun drops, sparkling like thousands of tiny diamonds, bubbling over the smooth stones and skipping around and through the tall grasses. In a cool, dark, still pool, suspended in a few inches of sapphire water, is a small, iridescent rainbow trout, secure in her quiet corner of the brook. She rests patiently, knowing she will be rewarded with a lovely little bug at sunset...What do you see?

Must go, take care,
Adieu, Sal

Subj: peaceful coexistence
Date: 8/21/00 10:01:56 PM Central Daylight Time
From: debbiesb13@aol.com
To: sarahjf50@hotmail.com

Hi there!

Will definitely be keeping Gina and her baby in my prayers. Please let me know how she's doing! Tell her not to worry about her figure - Tracey went right back to a 4 or smaller after Tristan was born and is still that size. It's easier when you're younger I guess.

My mother and I are temporarily peacefully coexisting. She is no longer discussing unearthing my father's grave and raising the dead in my presence. I am therefore not being as "argumentative." She does however still get furious if anyone tells her to do something because "Debbie wants you to." This sends her on the warpath for hours. The truce is due mostly to Nancy (hospice chaplain) counseling with her.

Must brag for one moment - we saw our son Austin march for the first time Friday in a preview show. It was such a thrill. I was so proud of him because he has really worked hard with his music. It is almost 11 hours from the time he leaves in the morning until he is through practicing marching and he still comes home and wants to play his trumpet.

How interesting you added a brook. I had thought about the brook, though definitely not as artistically as you did. Thought maybe after we finished playing Scrabble we'd wade in the water. Can you feel the water splashing over your feet like it does the stones? I can feel it cool and relaxing, but at the same time warming our very souls.

Be of good cheer my friend.

Love, Deb

Subj: *Re: daily blessings*
Date: *8/22/00 8:56:30 AM Central Daylight Time*
From: *sarahjf50@hotmail.com*
To: *debbiesb13@aol.com*

I was struck by your notes of happiness in your e-mail about your son and the welcome peaceful respite between you and your mom.

If it weren't for the tough times, we wouldn't treasure the good times so much.

It must have been so heartwarming to watch your son and feel he is finding some fulfillment during those tough teen years. It sounds like your sons are very active and participating in different areas of school which is so important as it will temper their success as they move into adulthood.

Let's give the hospice counselor a rose! Sounds like she's helping you in your effort to plug along with your mom.

Enjoy the Mitford *books and I will think about my other favorite books! I am up to college age in the* Pies *book, which you sent me. A very real story! Enjoying it immensely.*

Love, Sal

Subj: riddikulus
Date: 8/23/00 10:15:53 AM Central Daylight Time
From: debbiesb13@aol.com
To: sarahjf50@hotmail.com

Good morning!

Tom brought home the *Mitford* books - thank you much! I only read the first 16 pages but know I'm going to love it already - I'm sure Father Tim's taking the toast to the dog - my kind of guy! And the early descriptions of the town sound quaint and beautiful.

Maybe it is a "riddikulus" spell, a la *Harry Potter*, I needed for my mom this week. Oh, if only it worked that way! I can't tell you how many times I have left my mom and had a good cry all the way home. People tell you all this comforting stuff: she doesn't mean it; you can handle it; you're doing such a good job. The intentions are good, but it doesn't mean shit. It still hurts, it still frustrates me, it makes me feel guilty and rips me up inside. So what do I do? I give into emotion sometimes, and get up the next day and hope it will be better - some days it is, some days not. I certainly don't think of myself as strong and don't think I've been through any more stuff than you have - we have both been on the roller coaster just at different parks. I hope this doesn't sound all gloom and doom because that is not my intent - only honest. We may be super women, but cannot expect ourselves to be "Superwoman."

Sharing and talking with you through our e-mails has done much to brighten my spirits and my "dog days." What if you hadn't asked for my e-mail address? (Let's don't even go there!!!)

Walking helps me a lot. It is the one time every day I take for myself no matter what. It is just me, my dog and I. It is great meditation and prayer time and is a MUST for my back. Did a really stupid thing today. Lifted up on the back of my mom's wheelchair to go around a chair. Don't know what I was thinking - OK, I wasn't thinking!!! So now my back is killing me again. Hopefully it will be better tomorrow after a night's rest or Tom will be furious with me again for pushing her. Oh well, won't be the first time.

How is Gina doing?

Hope you have a great day today. Kingwood has a restaurant called "The Veranda," - haven't eaten there, but hear it's good. Maybe someday we can try it.

Love, Deb

Subj: Re: Russians know how to live (if they have money)
Date: 8/24/00 5:03:05 PM Central Daylight Time
From: sarahjf50@hotmail.com
To: debbiesb13@aol.com

Hello!

Taking a break before I rev up for dinner:

Did I tell you I am going to look for an office job? I have been planning on this for years, as soon as our son Anthony began driving. Bob said he would help me with connections. Okay...here's my perfect job: get to wear really nice clothes, work in a beautiful office, close to home, do all sorts of research and data entry, organize files and have a fabulous boss who loves my work. Reality: I will probably end up at the local discount store as a "customer service specialist." Who wants to hire a middle-aged professional housewife (who was supposed to be a queen)?

Wow! You are a great walker! I'm inspired. I will start up again. Sorry to hear about your back, will ask my friend Julie for some exercises.

We went to the Kimbell Museum exhibit of the Stroganoff collection. Stroganoff's were a very powerful family (from 1570-1918) with a fabulous art collection and palaces. Stalin auctioned and dispersed their priceless collection in 1931 after the family had tiptoed out of Russia during the revolution. The descendant of the direct Stroganoff line has begun a foundation to renovate their palace and reclaim the lost art—most of the things we saw today were taken by the revolutionaries and put in public museums during the revolution. The rest disappeared, most likely sold to finance the Stalin regime. The art includes pre-Colombian art, Van Dykes, Ming vases, Botticelli paintings, Reubens...it goes on and on. The icons are literally priceless and the embroideries are exquisite with gold thread. I could retire on the proceeds from one of their dining candelabra.

Have a lovely weekend and enjoy Mitford...*it will grow on you. There are three more books after the first two. We're going to the Mesquite rodeo this weekend.*
Adios, Sal

Subj: you'll be living like a Russian with your dream job
Date: 8/26/00 11:48:22 AM Central Daylight Time
From: debbiesb13@aol.com
To: sarahjf50@hotmail.com

Hi Sal!!!

Hope the weekend is living up to your expectations - meaning fun of course. The museum exhibit sounded great - wonder if it's coming here. How was the rodeo? When Travis was about 4, he wanted to be a bull rider and wouldn't go to bed on Sunday night until the Mesquite rodeo was over. Wouldn't be caught dead now doing anything remotely rodeo related. He's thinking about going to UT. Where did Tisa go to college?

In caring for my mother, Nancy asks me all the time, "Are you sure that you are giving yourself time to grieve and not just taking care of mom?" I probably haven't, but am trying. I hope you are giving yourself whatever time you need, but think that maybe daily life gets in the way for you too.

I'm still trying to sort out my mother's mental health issues. Do you think our parents' generation had some sort of phobia about the stigma of mental health treatment? When I was 26 (lived at home for cheap rent and bought sport's car) I definitely needed some professional help, but my mother would not allow it because it would "follow me for the rest of my life." What ever that means. Don't know if it was depression, panic attacks, both or what, but it was how I reacted to a suicide at the hotel where I worked. Eventually went to some osteopathic doctor that gave me medication to stop me throwing up after every meal and got over it in time. Now people have so much more of an open, honest, unashamed attitude about seeking mental health care.

You mentioned about the job: Sally, I was "discount shopping" today and the blue vest is definitely NOT your style!!!!! Go for the dream, girl! Just picking out the wardrobe will be half the fun. Need more details: boss - man or woman; research - on computer, library, marketing, legal, or none of the above; fulltime or part time; salary - big enough to live like a Russian? You'll have to keep me posted on your quest when it gets started. Any company would be lucky to have someone as energetic, intelligent, and organized as you are. Have you checked any job websites yet?

On families: I miss the family meal time. I cooked a REAL meal once all summer. Real meaning - four people, same table, same time, no one rushing off, no convenience foods, everyone eating the same thing. Tom and I had a "date" last night. It was so nice just to sit and talk leisurely for a change. Seems like the weekends have just been too busy!

I'm thoroughly enjoying Father Tim and all the people of *Mitford*!!! It is almost Christmas in the first book. In typical male fashion Tom asked, "Is that a chick book?" I gave him the appropriate "look." Some times there is entirely too much testosterone in a house full of guys.

Love, Deb

Parents and Children

Subj: *Re: life after sadness*
Date: *8/27/00 10:06:02 PM Central Daylight Time*
From: *sarahjf50@hotmail.com*
To: *debbiesb13@aol.com*

Rodeo was great fun!

You talk about grieving, I am coming to terms with the grief for losing my dad. I find that caring for my mother fills up the empty space left when my dad passed away.

Mental health: I suffered from depression years ago. I found, that for me, cognitive therapy was an effective method for treating my depression. It deals with giving the patient tools to work with the symptoms at hand and teaches one to understand oneself, rather than a Freudian approach which seeks to dissect your childhood and your past psyche. Cognitive therapy is very effective, efficient, and goal oriented. I was educated about depression, how it affects me and how to deal with it if it occurs. I was lucky to happen upon a great Christian therapy center. And let's not forget my faith: the source of my strength and salvation.

Finished Pies *today! Good reading and so true to life! Thanks, will wing it back to you. Also received the other book today. Hey, I feel so grungy...you send these lovely books, in pristine condition, and I send you books that look like they've spent the summer on the floor of my car (humm, maybe they have...) I will take good care of them.*

Tisa has her degree from Texas Women's University. She loved it there and she loved teaching elementary school. She will go back to teaching when her two little ones are school age. Gina is going to Tarrant County College and is in her second year. Wants to be a teacher too...will be hard to go to school and have an infant, we'll see!

Wow, a date with your husband! What a lovely concept. Helps to remind us of the reasons we fell in love with these men and is so necessary. Yes, you do have a house full of testosterone! I find it overwhelming when it's just Bob and Anthony and they start teasing me...Good luck in holding up your end of the hormonal tug of war. I know you're up to it! They are putty in your hands (they just don't know it!)

I would like to work into office management of some sort...think I could do it with my skills: typing, computer, organization. However, I could end up at a home improvement store with a tool belt and plumber's butt—never know!

Have a great Monday and enjoy this last week of August, it's getting cooler (let's be positive!)
Love, Sal

Subj: moving on
Date: 8/28/00 4:36:12 PM Central Daylight Time
From: debbiesb13@aol.com
To: sarahjf50@hotmail.com

Hi there!

Can certainly understand your feelings on grieving. Also know you are strong and will make it through, with your faith and humor.

How can you say your *Mitford* books are grungy?!! These are not dirty books — they are LOVED books. They are soft and comfortable when you hold them, they can almost cuddle. I have to say I haven't read anything in a very long time that has touched me as much as this first book which I'm still reading. You have brought it to me at a time when it was much needed. When I'm done, I'll return them to you without going thru the laundry (will also be looking forward to next three!). Do you like historical fiction about real women?

Tip of the day: Do not ask, "How are you?" of anyone on the way out of a senior living facility unless you have an extra ten minutes to spare. Somehow I can never remember this.

Tomorrow night will be the last meeting of our little group of four women at the "wineless-wine-bar" (not it's real name; sometimes they are out of wine) since my best friend from that group, Trish is moving. I'm really going to miss her tremendously! In all our moves, I have never figured out which is harder — being the one to stay or go.

I have given so much thought recently to the roles our friends play in our lives and how we turn to different friends for different needs. We have friends who come and go as quickly as a summer storm; others stick by us in good times and bad for decades; and others are the first ones you want at a party, but you wouldn't dream of telling them a secret. Find it interesting that in not even four months I have shared things with you concerning my faith and the challenges of caring for my mother that I have not even thought about sharing with others.

Your friend, Deb

Subj: Re: tomorrow, tomorrow, I love ya, tomorrow.
Date: 8/29/00 9:14:15 AM Central Daylight Time
From: sarahjf50@hotmail.com
To: debbiesb13@aol.com

Ah, little orphan Annie was so prophetic...or rather like Scarlet O'Hara: "tomorrah's anothah day."

It is interesting how our conversations flow easily and we understand each other without having to spell it out.

Anyway, yes, I do love historical fiction, and the girls and I pass books back and forth. Some are rather "racy" and I do believe all three of my girls furthered their sex education when reading these novels in high school...but at least they learned to read!!! Anyway, love books about queens of England (I was supposed to be one...) and Scotland!

> Must go, have lots of papers to shuffle for my mother.

Love, Sal

Subj: wound too tight
Date: 8/30/00 9:13:24 AM Central Daylight Time
From: debbiesb13@aol.com
To: sarahjf50@hotmail.com

So which queen were you supposed to be - not one of Henry VIII's I hope! So you let your girls read racy books. Sally, I'm shocked!! (ha! ha!) Would have been fun being your daughter. I read *Lady Chatterley's Lover* about six times in high school. My mother would be scandalized to this day. Never know what you might learn from a book!

I'm going to enjoy my day today, I have only to pick up something in Humble and go visit my mom. Think I'll take the rest of the day off so to speak. Tom says I don't relax enough. Guess that is true as I can only remember feeling truly relaxed those few days in San Antonio. Do you feel that way? Even when you're "relaxing" you never really seem to unwind? I never used to be that way. I could be efficient, and organized but still be laid back. Now I will admit to being a rubber band wound too tight.

Love, luck, and thanks, Deb

Subj: *caregiver chronicles*
Date: *8/31/00 4:57:40 PM Central Daylight Time*
From: *sarahjf50@hotmail.com*
To: *debbiesb13@aol.com*

> *Took mom to Wal-mart super store to get her first big load of groceries for her new home. Had our grandson, Zachary with me—Tisa at OB doctor—it was interesting as Zachary and I had a great time for 2½ hours that mom shopped around. Zachary, at age 2 and just being potty trained, was a prince.*

> *So-o-o-o-o-o, life goes on, and I am getting more at ease with the responsibility of my mother.*

> *Thank heavens for my family. They are such a lovely balance to the stress we endure on a daily basis.*

> *How's your mom doing? Know you were going to see her yesterday.*

> *Must go, will write more later. TGIF!!!*

Your pal, Sal

Subj: short, but…
Date: 9/1/00 3:30:26 PM Central Daylight Time
From: debbiesb13@aol.com
To: sarahjf50@hotmail.com

Hey Sally!
    Today's my mom's 88th birthday. Spent the day with her, but we are having family party tomorrow.
    More to tell, but probably won't have time till Sunday. Have a good weekend!!!
Love, Deb

Subj: thank heavens for little girls!
Date: 9/1/00 3:37:53 PM Central Daylight Time
From: sarahjf50@hotmail.com
To: debbiesb13@aol.com

*   I am in the middle of my usual Friday housecleaning, laundry stuff, but had to sit down and share this with you…*
*   Gina and Stephan are having a little girl. Gina is happy because she has wanted to dress a baby girl ever since she had 50 baby dolls. This will be one fashionable little lady. It is so nice that the tiny granddaughters will be so close in age—nice for Tisa and Gina too!*
*   Must go, time to get back to vacuuming!*
Love, Sal

Subj: trying again - electronic frustration
Date: 9/3/00 10:43:57 AM Central Daylight Time
From: debbiesb13@aol.com
To: sarahjf50@hotmail.com

Hi Sally!
    I had just finished writing you a long email when the thing closed for no reason and disappeared. I'm really pissed!!!!! Will try to start again, but will probably not have the same feeling.
    I was so excited to hear about your little girls. There is nothing more joyful than a new baby in the family. I could feel the pleasure in your heart and am so happy for you!!! And what a wonderful connection for the two darlings growing up together.
    Will your mom be cooking a lot for just herself when she moves into her own home? My parents were obsessed with eating out, going twice a day at least. They would keep their lunch leftovers for dinner, go out again instead, and then I

would have to clean out the to-go boxes with mold about once a week. It's a wonder they never got sick.

Aren't we blessed to have men in our lives like Bob and Tom who are willing to take on these family challenges we bring and yet be most concerned with our welfare. I really don't know where I'd be without Tom.

Tracey, David and grandson, Tristan, are coming over tomorrow with the proofs of the wedding pictures. Can't wait to see them - meaning kids and pictures. Tristan loves to come here - alternates between playing outside in the sprinkler and the pool table in the game room. He likes to play video games with Austin too, but sometimes Austin expects him to compete like he's 15. Cannot imagine having a granddaughter. It was fun having stepdaughters Tracey and Tiffany when they were growing up, and it is very fun now watching Tracey grow as a young mother.

Well, guess that about covers everything. Hope you enjoy the your weekend.
Love, Deb

Subj: Re: thank heavens for little boys!
Date: 9/4/00 10:27:48 AM Central Daylight Time
From: sarahjf50@hotmail.com
To: debbiesb13@aol.com

Today is the day. Mom wants to move into her new home. She told me at breakfast. Thank you Lord, for giving her the strength, peace, and willingness to start a new home and life.

In answer to your question, she enjoys cooking and will be cooking for herself. It sounds like you really had your hands full with your parents and their leftovers.

On the home front: our son Anthony is now working at a fast food restaurant and brings home these Winnie-the-pooh toys for Zachary. Ever since Zachary was a week old he has had this thing for his uncle Anthony. It probably helps that Anthony is 6'2" and sort of stands out in a room, but Zachary could not take his eyes off Anthony when he was a newborn...he would just stare at Anthony and follow him around. Anthony has always been great with him, carrying him everywhere (Zachary has always reached for him to hold him). Anthony will put Zachary in the stroller and wheel him around the mall while we shop, which is so nice to see a boy his age not caring about being seen pushing the stroller. I think part of that comes from the fact that Anthony has always been tall for his age, and doesn't need to prove he's a tough guy, he already looks the part (heart of gold—kisses his dog) but not someone another guy would try to push around.

When Anthony was born, I was afraid he would go off to kindergarten wearing a dress and toting a doll as a result of the influence of his three older sisters. However, I discovered by his first birthday that he was a different breed, and he conducted himself on an entirely different (testosterone pumped) plane than the girls. What a surprise!

Gina just called, sleepy voice, she and Stephan will also join us for lunch. Stephan bought his little daughter-to-be an outfit for coming home from the hospital...like I said, this child will be a fashion plate. Tisa's little girl will be like Hermione in Harry Potter. *We'll see. Must run.*
Love, Sal

Subj: snails and puppy dog tails
Date: 9/5/00 3:57:13 PM Central Daylight Time
From: debbiesb13@aol.com
To: sarahjf50@hotmail.com

Anthony sounds like a terrific uncle. Zachary will really appreciate having him even more when his little sister arrives on the scene. Our boys would probably never be found pushing a stroller or bringing home Winnie the Pooh toys. They will go to Chuck E Cheese, however. How terrific Anthony has that kind of confidence. Travis really enjoyed holding Tristan when he was a baby. Austin would not even touch him, let alone hold him, until Tristan was about 1½ years old. A few months after Tristan was born Austin wrote a paper for English about a special day: the day he became an uncle.
          Take care.
Love, Deb

Subj: Re: 2 hours
Date: 9/5/00 5:18:18 PM Central Daylight Time
From: sarahjf50@hotmail.com
To: debbiesb13@aol.com

I have been alone in my house for two hours now. I had a piece of bread and butter and watched a gardening show. Wonder how Mom is doing in her new nest?
Your boys sound like normal boys when it comes to babies! Anthony had three older sisters and I know they indoctrinated him over the years. Said they were raising him to be a good husband...toilet seat down, appreciation for PMS, probably told him a man's place was by his wife's side with the diaper rash medication...
Must go. Have to run some stuff over to Mom. Have a good evening!
Love, Sal

Subj: that's a start
Date: 9/6/00 7:56:13 PM Central Daylight Time
From: debbiesb13@aol.com
To: sarahjf50@hotmail.com

Will be praying for your mom as this is a difficult transition. I really enjoy my bit of time home alone each day even if it's just an hour or so. Never really realized before, but Tom is never actually home alone. Wonder if that bothers him.

Perhaps now that a "cool front" has passed through, we'll all be more comfortable. (Who would have ever thought we'd be grateful for the relief of temps in the high 90's!) How are all your plants doing by the way? Especially the roses. We have at least had a few days of rain the past couple of weeks.

Stopped by my mom's on the way home today and ran into Nancy. Guess she and my mom were having a heart to heart as my mother pointedly let her know they would continue their private conversation next week. Fine with me as she has started up again on the denial stuff that we don't handle well together. Thank you God for Nancy. Maybe my mother needs more birthdays as she was in wonderful spirits those two days (hmm, maybe…)

Well, guess I ought to go start some dinner. Would really rather take a nap than cook - long day.

Have a great evening - Love, Deb

II

Women of Strength

*

Rough Spots

I Have Been Where You Are

Women of Strength

Coping Tools

Anti-Depressants and Therapy for Beginners

A Frustrating Search for Help

Sleep Tight (Yeah, Right...)

Facing an Angry Rottweiler

*

Fugazi & Harwell

Rough Spots

Subj: not feeling so good
Date: 9/8/00 4:17:59 PM Central Daylight Time
From: debbiesb13@aol.com
To: sarahjf50@hotmail.com

Hi there!

Hope all is well with you. Has been busy here - some very good, some frustrating.

Told my mother last night I could no longer discuss my father with her. It's just too painful for me on her terms. She can't understand it, but I am sticking to my guns no matter what. Told her I will help her with anything else but cannot do that.

Have also spent some time back at the doctor's this week as the dizziness and pain/numbness in my face have been worse. Still seems to be a vertebrae problem so I'm now on steroids (no muscles or chest hair yet) for a short period and have to go for more tests. Tom thinks this may be from trying to lift my mother's wheel chair. It definitely stressed me to the max and sent me into a period of feeling sorry for myself, which I'm trying to overcome with prayer and humor. Works sometimes, sometimes not. Today has been good. Better go for now.

Have a great weekend.

Love, Deb

Subj: afternoon tea
Date: 9/12/00 10:28:04 AM Central Daylight Time
From: sarahjf50@hotmail.com
To: debbiesb13@aol.com

Good morning!

Just read your e-mail and sounds like you had some rough spots last week. I'm sorry and I really don't think it's fair of God to give the tough assignments to those He knows can handle them...your mom is so lucky to have you as a daughter and from what I can assume, she had a wonderful husband.

Unfortunately, people who are unhappy inside themselves, cannot see beyond their gray curtain to the bright day outside. They see everything through this haze and the world (and the people in it) will always be grimmer for them. I understand your frustration with her attitude. And you're absolutely right in stopping the discussion with her—it is pointless and hurtful to go there for both of you...

Wow! Let me know how your tests come out on your back—sounds like a pinched nerve. Looks like you will have to rest and read some good books until you're feeling better.

I've been curling up in my window seat reading books, watching the oak tree out the window. Made a big comfort food dinner for the Sunday Horde (girls, husbands, grandson, whoever wanders in on Sunday gets a great meal). This time I made real southern fried chicken, noodles from scratch (old family tradition), mashed potatoes, beans and corn. Everyone had plenty to eat and left with a look of comfort on his/her face.

Zachary and I were walking at the park (we go over after dinner sometimes so the guys can throw the football and Zachary can play in the playground) and Zachary said, "Guess what, Nana?" I asked, "What?" And he said, "I love you," and just toddled away on his little bike...what a lovely moment.

Well, time to do some paperwork...let me know how you are feeling! I get my vocal chord injections tomorrow to smooth out my voice—unpleasant experience but worth it!

Take care of yourself,

Love, Sal

Subj:	having a little difficulty
Date:	9/13/00 2:48:53 PM Central Daylight Time
From:	debbiesb13@aol.com
To:	sarahjf50@hotmail.com

Dear Sally!

I am taking one of my few lucid moments to reply to your e-mail. Did get the *Mitford* books. Thanks so much.

Thanks for the card. It was a cheerful respite. The steroids I was taking sent me over the edge so to speak — translation major anxiety attack. Should have seen it coming I guess as I was so stressed and had lost 5 pounds in the last two weeks, but didn't. Then I had to finish the damn things anyway and could not get started with any help until yesterday. Am now on anti-anxiety and anti-depression meds, which are helping but not fast enough to suit me. Tom has been really wonderful and understanding. So I feel the Lord is currently giving me more than I can bear. I am scared to death that I'll be like this forever but also trying to be determined knowing that the help is there if only slow and that I can be strong. Phil. 4:13.

Have thoughts on other things in your e-mail, but don't feel up to it now. Please keep me in your prayers and you know you are in mine. Your strength is an inspiration.

Love, Deb

I Have Been Where You Are

Subj: Love you
Date: 9/14/00 6:15:33 PM Central Daylight Time
From: sarahjf50@hotmail.com
To: debbiesb13@aol.com

Dearest Deb,

Hang in there. I have been where you are, on anti-anxiety meds and anti-depressants. They never seem to work fast enough, but they do work in time.

Know this: you are feeling very anxious and hopeless, this is a symptom of a chemical imbalance. You cannot control it, the meds must control it. Think of it like diabetes: it is a physical condition, and will respond to medication. Your job is to stick your tongue out at your feelings of anxiety and say, "Feelings are not truth, they are a response to something." In your case, they are a response to many months of stress both physically and mentally. Ouch.

Let your mind and body hurt, it needs to recover, just remember, it is a healing process and every day is a step in the right direction. You will have good days and bad days. As time goes on, more good days in a row, until you are healed.

The good news???? This will make your faith stronger. God never picks the good times to bring us closer to him.

Am sending you a care package, dear friend, so look for it in the mail next week.

Hey, I am as crazy as you are! I have been the whole route of anxiety attacks, and conquered the pesky things. Want to know how? If you feel one coming, just start deep breathing and say, "God, I trust you." Get mad, think of the attacks as attacks from Satan, trying to keep you from living a life of peace, trusting in God. Anxiety attacks will fade and you will not fear them once you are educated in how to control them.

Must go, time to make dinner. Will keep close by both in e-mail and prayer. You are an amazing woman (just ask Tom) and you will get through this.
Love you, your kindred spirit, Sal

Subj: TGIF!!!!!!
Date: 9/15/00 9:10:41 AM Central Daylight Time
From: sarahjf50@hotmail.com
To: debbiesb13@aol.com

Dear Deb, Good morning!

Am going to start my usual house cleaning here in a minute. Wanted to wish you a more peaceful day, remember, you need to be kind to yourself and realize that you are convalescing from an assault on your body. Give your body and mind the permission to heal at slow, but strong and steady pace.

You live in an era where anxiety and depression are treated well and not dismissed as a mental weakness. Your condition is totally curable. You will come out of this stronger, I promise you.

In the meantime, if you feel up to it, write and tell me how you're feeling, you can bitch, whine, complain or count your blessings. Just use me as a sounding board, as I have used you. We will get through this together.

I have some news for you, but will close for now and let you get back to your book. Will write later.
Love, Sal

Subj: one small step
Date: 9/15/00 11:37:48 AM Central Daylight Time
From: debbiesb13@aol.com
To: sarahjf50@hotmail.com

Dearest friend — Cannot even remember what day I first wrote to you about this but am feeling better than when ever that was. Yesterday and today feel at least that I'm moving in right direction even if it is slow. I actually put on mascara today. Your words of encouragement mean more than you can ever know. This is just so scary, but I am, as you said, putting my faith in God who has brought me you, Tom, and my family doctor (a very understanding woman).

Mornings seem to be the worst, but this one seemed to get a little better a little earlier than the one before. I still feel that pressure to be up making lunches and breakfast even though things seem to be going along fine without that.

If you don't mind my asking — how did you explain this to your kids? I'm not sure Tom has told our boys what is happening with me, and I certainly haven't been up to it. Maybe later.

Looking forward to your news. Also wanted to tell you how much I loved your story about Zachary. What a very special moment!

Will go for now. Wanted you to know there is at least something in the way of progress, and how much I appreciate your help and e-mails. A truly kindred spirit......
Love, Deb

Subj: Re: one small step
Date: 9/15/00 2:04:25 PM Central Daylight Time
From: sarahjf50@hotmail.com
To: debbiesb13@aol.com

Hey there, good to hear you're feeling better! Just remember to treat yourself to things that make you feel good: walks, reading, whatever. That is also good medicine.

What did I tell my kids...the truth...that my brain chemistry was imbalanced and I needed to take medication to correct the situation. I told them the symptoms were sadness, and anxiety, and it was physical response to stress, and I needed medication. They were really not all that interested or concerned, once they understood I was not heading for the loony bin...

I did seek therapy, however, because I wanted to know how to deal with this rather complex problem.

Have you seen the USA women's soccer team—they are awesome! Enjoy the Olympics—go for your own gold, Deb! You will do it, I know!
Love, Sal

Women of Strength

Subj: *books*
Date: *9/16/00 10:22:26 AM Central Daylight Time*
From: *sarahjf50@hotmail.com*
To: *debbiesb13@aol.com*

Hello!
     I am sorry I've been so tardy in thanking you for the books on pioneer women!
     Hey, did you see the opening ceremonies of the Olympics where the torch was brought into the stadium? Did you see the relay that took place between the previous women gold medal winners from Australia? It made me cry. They ranged in age from their 40's to 75 and they ran with the torch held high. The final hand-off was to the young female aborigine athlete, who lit the cauldron. Go women! They all had gray or white hair, some were overweight, they were real women. And they were pumped.
     That's you and me, Deb! Strong, real women. We have obstacles in life, but because of our strength and training, we run the distance. We even win sometimes!
     Must go, time to take Mom to get her prescriptions. Enjoy the gorgeous, cooler weather today!
Love, Sal

Subj: you're good medicine
Date: 9/16/00 1:28:52 PM Central Daylight Time
From: debbiesb13@aol.com
To: sarahjf50@hotmail.com

     Sal, thanks so much for helping me through this ordeal. Yesterday afternoon and evening were so much better, I don't understand why mornings have to suck so much. It's such a beautiful day here today — cooler, blue skies but it took me till after 9 to drag my butt out of bed and another hour to stop feeling sick at my stomach. This is so frustrating as I am normally a morning person. On the bright side, I did just get back from a short walk, which I went on by myself. How stupid does that sound from someone who is used to walking 3+ miles alone daily? Very peaceful. Today was the one-mile circle that's just my neighborhood. Oh well, I must try to be more positive, right?
     I missed the part of the Olympic ceremonies that you were talking about. Wish I hadn't. Do you remember the movie *A League of Their Own* about the women's baseball teams in the 40's? It has a part at the end where they show the real ladies playing now. Last year at a collectibles show, Tom asked one of the

women, Pepper to autograph a movie poster. She did and it is a center point of our game room. Since you like women in sports so much, I'm going to send you a baseball card she autographed and sent to me with the poster. You don't have to like baseball cards to appreciate it, only the achievements of women in an arena and at a time when they were given no credit at all.

I can't say I feel like a very strong woman today, but do feel there is a time I will again. It just takes too long. We have tickets for the Astros game tonight. I want to go so bad, but am honestly afraid I'm not yet ready to cope. It is difficult to know when to force myself to do something and when to give in to the anxiety and not put pressure on myself. Any advice on this one?

I haven't seen my mom in a week. She is still confused about my problem. Yesterday she called and said, "How are you? Did someone from your place come and throw away my newspapers?" Gee, thanks Mom. (She has a thing about not throwing away the old papers because she's still going to read them).

As this time has passed, I'm felling a little better. Thank you, Sally, so much for being there for me — for listening and encouraging. You are part of my prayers of thanks every day. Hope you have a glorious day.
Love, Deb

Subj: went to doctor today
Date: 9/19/00 4:32:46 PM Central Daylight Time
From: debbiesb13@aol.com
To: sarahjf50@hotmail.com

Hi Friend!
Wanted to let you know how things are going. But Sal, I want you to tell me honestly if all these emails are too much. I don't want to ever add any burdens to you, nor do I want you to feel that you can't still bitch back to me because I can't handle it. I can. Plus it gets my mind off my own crap.

Tom by the way has been a saint. Sometimes he is a little unclear on why I can't just take charge on my own, but he is so patient. Maybe Bob can offer him some support. Have told him you are being a tremendous source of encouragement and support for me.

Today has been one of the toughest and best days. I went to the doctor earlier by myself. I was totally stressed. After having a really good day yesterday, I thought I couldn't cope when I got there, but just kept praying and made it. I felt more relaxed after our visit and even better now that a few more hours have passed. (Of course I'm in the safety of my own home. It will get better.) I'm supposed to increase the anti-depressant med in a few days.

Another friend who has been through a similar circumstance suggested I ask the family doctor for a clinical psychologist. The doctor will call me tomorrow with names. I have also asked the hospice people for therapist referrals. Interestingly, one of the names I got is that of a therapist who is the wife of the minister who assisted with my dad's funeral. So tell me what you think about the difference between a psychologist vs. therapist and how to go about choosing the right one. I, like you, would not want someone dissecting my childhood. My parents loved me. I wasn't deprived or abused or neglected. I just can't cope with my current issues.

I sent you that card from the baseball lady in yesterday's mail. And I'm still looking forward to hearing about your life, which I know has been busy and probably both wonderful and frustrating accordingly.

Thanks for listening. And I meant what I said earlier — you tell me.
Love, Deb

Subj: *good morning!*
Date: *9/20/00 6:48:40 AM Central Daylight Time*
From: *sarahjf50@hotmail.com*
To: *debbiesb13@aol.com*

Hi, Deb!

Love getting your e-mails and hearing how you are doing. Sounds like you are gracefully slipping into a routine, accepting that this is your time to heal.

As for whether or not you should go and do things if you do not feel up to it, I would say if you don't want to, don't. Right now you need to have as little stress as possible so you can regain your strength. That is not to mean that you couldn't handle something if you had to. You know you could. But if you have a choice, just take it easy. Rather like nursing a sprained ankle. You need to allow time for your medication to do some chemical therapy on your brain.

I have been carrying around a little box for you in my car—hopefully will have time today to mail it!

Must go, will chat this evening! Hope you have another strengthening day, and remember, if you can't think of what to do, just ask yourself what God wants you to do.
Love, Sal

Coping Tools

Subj: *I'm here*
Date: *9/20/00 6:57:58 AM Central Daylight Time*
From: *sarahjf50@hotmail.com*
To: *debbiesb13@aol.com*

Dear Deb,

I am reading your letters and hoping that you know the answer is yes, continue to tell me how you're doing. I am walking with you and understand. Sometimes it is helpful just to write or talk about it, even if the reader/listener has no great solutions. So talk all you want.

On the subject of therapy, by all means, do it. A Christian therapist is definitely a good idea for you, as it was for me. And it needs to be someone who understands your need to learn how to deal with/manage your anxiety first, then later go into more in depth therapy on your relationship with your mom (or whatever), if you feel you need to.

I have so many thoughts on all of this and will write more this evening. Take it easy and remember you are walking down the right path and are making progress! Go, girl.
Love, Sal

Subj: walking through the storm
Date: 9/20/00 2:17:34 PM Central Daylight Time
From: debbiesb13@aol.com
To: sarahjf50@hotmail.com

Dear Sally,

OK, here is my exciting news — I went to the bank, grocery store and cleaners this morning! And I only got really goofy once at the bank, but managed not to walk out. (Kept praying and reminding myself of your email this morning and visualized writing you back about my success.) I really actually felt quite comfortable in the grocery store. At first it felt a little surreal, but then it just got to be so normal. I still feel semi-stupid getting so excited over something so ordinary. Can't imagine how it will feel when I'm not afraid to do something outside the protection of my immediate family. Today has been encouraging. My neighbor had called this morning for me to go to lunch with her, but I wasn't ready to cope with that.

It is pouring rain here, thunder and lightning. Our poor dog Betsy is shaking and hiding under the bed. She has anxiety from storms since that episode in May. Not sure if I told you before, but she and I were stepping onto the patio about 15' away, when lightning blew the crown off our chimney. It was incredibly loud and the brightest thing I have ever seen! I'm still so thankful not to have been hit or that one of the small fires we had didn't burn down the house.

I did finally see a rerun of part of the opening Olympic ceremonies and they were very touching. (I'm glad to know I'm not the only one who cries at that kind of stuff — speaking about my normal self, not the current self.)

Even though I'm feeling better today and have had at least a minor victory I still want to hear your thoughts on therapy, coping, or anything. I know there is still such a long way to go before I can face the normal life I was living just a week ago, and further still: to face it without anxiety. That's probably enough rambling for now. Think I'll go read for a while and then really need to pick up this house. Now there's a really overwhelming agenda! Hope you had a great day!
Love, Deb

Subj: *life is good, really!!!!*
Date: *9/21/00 7:18:07 AM Central Daylight Time*
From: *sarahjf50@hotmail.com*
To: *debbiesb13@aol.com*

Good morning!

It's early, Bob just left for an early breakfast with Tom and company. I am off to take care of Zachary this morning while Tisa has her doctor's appt.

Wanted to add a couple of tools to your bag when it comes to anxiety. You are dealing with concern for physical symptoms when you venture out to the store, etc, right? I may be off base here, write and tell me what you fear when you go places. But I can help you with physical symptoms, for example, if panic attack is an issue, then, listen up:

Panic attack is a physical reaction to stress. It causes your chest muscles to tense up, constrict and makes breathing more difficult. Also makes your heart pound. You begin to hyperventilate and feel dizzy, is that true for you? First, hear this, you will not die from this, you are just tense and fearful.

If you feel one coming on, take a slow, deep breath, down to your stomach. Hold that breath for 4 seconds, let it out slowly. Do this until the panic subsides (maybe ten breaths). Then go into a deep breathing, relaxing pattern (inhale slow for 4 counts, exhale slow for four counts).

You just filled your body with more oxygen and expanded your chest to ease the tension. Say a prayer while doing it, thanking God or your guardian angel for standing beside you, knowing in your heart nothing can hurt you, not even death, if God is by your side. That prayer is the basis of your courage.

The deep breathing is something you need to do as an exercise three times a day for about 10 minutes. Lie or sit down, get into a relaxed position, deep breathe and think lovely thoughts, pray, whatever. It is your 10 minutes to rehab your mind so do not allow any unpleasant thoughts to enter. This will train your body to relax on command—therefore, no more panic attacks. You can practice breathing anywhere, actually, but the breathing with the mind rehab should be done in a peaceful place. You probably won't be too good at the lovely thoughts at first. It all takes practice. But I promise you it works and will change your way of dealing with all kinds of stressful events.

Okay, enough instruction! I hope this was of use to your situation. Another tool, quickly: journal, journal, write down your thoughts. Make a list of your fears and over the coming days, watch them fade away. It will happen. And remember to breathe! Have another good day,
Love, Sal

Subj: nothing to fear but fear itself
Date: 9/21/00 12:45:11 PM Central Daylight Time
From: debbiesb13@aol.com
To: sarahjf50@hotmail.com

Hi Sally –

Want you to know how much I appreciate the effort you are taking to keep me on track even so early in the morning. Can't even begin to tell you, but know you understand. You are a blessing. I feel like I'm letting you down on my end of our friendship for now — relying on you and giving nothing in return, but I promise you I'll get back there.

I have been awake since three this morning when the rain woke me up and I couldn't go back to sleep — not anxious or fearful, but just like my mind was in hyper-drive. So if I seem incoherent you can add another reason to the list. This has made today a bit of a step back, but know it will get better again. It is just difficult to not have more immediate results. I WANT TO FEEL NORMAL AGAIN!!!!!

Your breathing tips are a big help and right on target. I have already done the exercise once this morning. As to panic attacks — yes, I have had them as you described, but the ones now are more subdued. I feel this intense need to get out of where ever I am before I can't take it and "lose it." It is the fear of the fear I would say. And for now I definitely cannot handle having to be scheduled for something, even like lunch with my neighbor, for fear of not being able to handle it at that time.

Yesterday I felt so confident that I planned to go shopping for some pajamas today while the cleaning service is here. But this morning I just couldn't relax until I decided not to go. Partly from the lack of sleep, but as much from the pressure of having to go at a certain time and having these people in my house. So they are here and I'm hanging out talking to you and feeling better.

Your journal idea is good as well. As for writing my fears for now I would feel a little like Charlie Brown being told by Lucy I have the fear of everything, but that's really not true of course.

I'm dealing with my mother much better via phone, but know that I must return to see her at some point in time. Plus she is really starting to feel hurt.

You know, when you start looking for a job it should be something helping people. Sally, look at what you have done for me in just such a short time. I cannot imagine the good things you have done for friends you have had for years — not to mention your family!!!

Well, Travis is home now, and the ladies are about done cleaning, and I've said so much I'm worn out. Have a great day. Will be breathing.
Love Deb

Subj: *little gift coming*
Date: *9/21/00 9:43:51 PM Central Daylight Time*
From: *sarahjf50@hotmail.com*
To: *debbiesb13@aol.com*

Hi there, Deb!

FINALLY mailed your little gift today, watch for it probably early next week. Just a little something to help you along the way!

Another tool: do you listen to Christian radio? It has some great programs and I have received more good counsel and affirmation from the Christian radio than anywhere else. It's on 24 hours, by the way, so in the middle of the night, you can listen to great ministry! Some programs are not going to appeal to you, most likely, but there are lots that address daily living and are very helpful. Give it a try, if you haven't already. It will help.

Hey, in listening to your very, very good descriptions of your feelings I want you to know that I have been there and felt exactly the same...just not up to anything. Feeling stressed, walled in if you feel you have to do something or go somewhere. Let me tell you the solution: don't do it if it stresses you. It's only a temporary feeling (are you sick of hearing me say this?) and you will get back into the rat race soon enough.

I understand totally the brainstorming you have going on—why can't our brains work like that when we WANT THEM TO? I know it feels like your brain is on overdrive: very normal symptom, by the way. How about this? Marvel at yourself that at your advanced age, you can still think 1000 words a second...what an achievement! Now if you could just use them constructively...Hope you don't mind my "sick humor"—I am not laughing at you—like I said, I have been there and it's no fun, but I'm along with you for the ride and we might as well giggle a little!

You're doing all the right things, taking your meds, beginning your breathing exercises, considering therapy, journaling and talking about your journey. One thing I would try to stay away from, if you could, is trying to figure out how all this happened to you. Right now, it's too much to have to work out. Your brain and emotions need a rest from all that junk—and that is what it is JUNK. Anything that has hurt you enough to make you sick is JUNK. When you are stronger, and with a therapist you trust, deal with the JUNK. But don't let it hurt you anymore right now. DON'T MAKE ME COME DOWN THERE! I mean it, the trash that has hurt you is going to have to wait in line until you are strong again—

Hey, here's something that was a true miracle for me: the meds actually worked. I couldn't believe I could come out of the funk, but I started feeling better and better—it was such a surprise to me to watch myself come back into my own brain again—I had been so busy trying to figure everything out on my own, when the miracle of meds is what I needed. And, as time goes on, you will taper off the anti-depressant and anxiety meds and be strong on your own. God bless medical research!

Must go, Bob is home and we have to talk about Anthony, who is going through a disobedient moment.
Take care, Love, Sal

Anti-depressants and Therapy for Beginners

Subj: *TGIF!!*
Date: *9/22/00 8:33:25 AM Central Daylight Time*
From: *sarahjf50@hotmail.com*
To: *debbiesb13@aol.com*

Good Morning, friend!
     Thank you so much for the baseball card! I will cherish it. I like your note about what the card stands for, and you're right, she is an inspiration.
     A little note about friends and depression: When I was going through my tough times, I always had friends close by that stood by me. It was very important to me, even though I didn't feel like doing anything fun, just to talk to them. They were of great help to me. As I walk this path with you, I think it is my turn to help, instead of being helped. Some day you will meet someone who is going through the same thing as you suffer from today. You will be able to help that person because you understand their pain. Have you told your friends about your pain? I hope so. You may even find, like me, that they have gone through something similar. Everyone has tough times.
     It's Friday—On Friday evenings we usually rent a movie and I make one of our favorite dinners—salmon frequently. We look forward to this simple pleasure on Fridays!
     If you haven't already, please call for an appointment with the therapist. You will feel so much better, I promise, speaking to someone who deals with your kind of issues all the time. The first thing my therapist told me was to treat my illness like a broken leg. It is a physical disability (it's just in your brain rather than your leg), but totally curable, and you must treat yourself with kindness and patience.
     Enjoy all that rain, you lucky Houstonians!
Love, Sal

Subj: Yes, TGIF!
Date: 9/22/00 10:16:23 AM Central Daylight Time
From: debbiesb13@aol.com
To: sarahjf50@hotmail.com

Morning Sally —
     Will be hoping and praying for you some rain. Heard on the news it's been almost 3 months since you had any. Unbelievable! We have not started the rose garden yet — Mr. Lincoln is still in the pot, but Tom has it all planned out. I'm going to call it the Lincoln bedroom. (Thought of that at a happier time.)

OK - here's the bad part. Yesterday went from bad to worse than worse. My mom called in the afternoon and asked me to explain what was wrong. She started on the issues I can't handle, denying my dad's death and accusing me of lying about it. I tried to get her to stop but couldn't short of hanging up on her. Should have in retrospect.

Needless to say I totally lost it. I cannot face her. Felt like I went back to square one in coping with my anxiety. It took hours to regain my modicum of composure. About two hours later I called one of my aunts (a truly genuine person who has faced more adversity in life than any one person should have to bear) and told her I needed her help to be more communicative with my mom.

I called my doctor, who said take more of the anti-anxiety med. I talked to Tom for quite awhile. Finally, was able to settle down and sleep till about 4:30 AM. The doctor increased the dose of the anti-depressant last night and I am praying it will work at double speed. Going to start today on the therapist quest.

Did find your e-mail before going to bed last night — sometimes it's like you know when I really need someone to pick me up. The words of encouragement are always so helpful and your humor as well. I think that was probably the only happy thought I mustered all day.

Your Friday nights sound ideal. What a pleasant way to unwind from a hectic week. Have a great day and thanks so much for improving mine.
Love, Deb

Subj: *break time!*
Date: *9/22/00 1:40:51 PM Central Daylight Time*
From: *sarahjf50@hotmail.com*
To: *debbiesb13@aol.com*

Hey there!

Therapist: most important thing to look for: does this therapist believe in NOT focusing on blaming other people? Does this therapist believe that the focus should be on strengthening your own self, regardless of what antagonists you have to deal with? Also, you want cognitive therapy, which deals with the problems you have today. And finally, don't dismiss the fact you may not like the therapist, you'll know right away. If so, find another. And please don't forget to look at Christian therapists. That would be the first place I would go. As far as meds are concerned, only doctors (psychiatrists, MD's) can prescribe them, so most of your therapists (psychologists, MA's) will have knowledge of meds but will not deal in recommending/prescribing certain brands.

We all have these painful things, don't we? Sounds like you are really angry, and I don't blame you. I have trouble expressing anger...when I do it's very difficult, but I'm working on it!

Tisa is doing fine. Baby is long, says her doctor, will probably induce a week before term, due to her emergency c-section last time. Zachary and I went shopping and I bought us each a new pair of athletic shoes. Then we went and got happy meals, went home and watched cartoons then played outside. We both wore our new shoes. He's just too cute!

Must go, break time over, time to vacuum! Have a good weekend, dear friend,
Love Sal

Subj: POSITIVE NEWS
Date: 9/22/00 4:52:43 PM Central Daylight Time
From: debbiesb13@aol.com
To: sarahjf50@hotmail.com

Now there's a surprise, huh?

Just got off the phone with the hospice social worker discussing various aspects of therapists for me. Have made a therapist appointment. I feel so much better than when I wrote to you earlier today!! I feel hopeful that a step has been taken in the right direction. Must just keep headed there.

UPS just came with your package!!!!! You are so unbelievably nice! I will cherish and enjoy both of these books [*Simple Abundance* and *Rise and Shine*]. Thank you so much!!! I'm really over whelmed.

Hope you check your e-mails one more time so you know that it did in fact turn out to be a better day. Hope you have a great evening and weekend.
Love, Deb

Subj: can't get it right
Date: 9/23/00 11:17:23 AM Central Daylight Time
From: debbiesb13@aol.com
To: sarahjf50@hotmail.com

Brief note - having trouble with increased dose of anti-depressants. Can't stop shaking since taking them last night. Doctor no help till Monday. Will write when feeling better. Still love my books.
Love, Deb

Subj: Re: can't get it right
Date: 9/24/00 12:29:46 PM Central Daylight Time
From: sarahjf50@hotmail.com
To: debbiesb13@aol.com

Dear Deb,

Sorry to hear about your anti-depressant causing tremors. What is the name of the anti-depressant? When you talk to your doctor, tell him you are having trouble sleeping and lots of anxiety which means you need an anti-depressant that slows you down for awhile so you can rest while waiting to feel better. A thought: ask the hospice chaplain to recommend a psychiatrist you could see right away. The reason being that a psychiatrist is the professional in prescribing medications for mental conditions.

Maybe you can learn something from a little of my history: I went to my family doctor, who prescribed an anti-depressant, which did not help and made me jittery. So he recommended a tricyclic anti-depressant. This new medication began to show positive results in me after about three weeks. I was going to a therapist, at the time, who decided to take me off of this anti-depressant because I was feeling "too good." Big mistake. She also recommended in depth psychoanalysis and group therapy for me. After two months of this "in-depth" counseling and suffering from no medication, I was more depressed and anxious than before. I, amid threats from this therapist, stopped the counseling sessions. I moved on from her.

I went, almost crawled, to a Christian counseling center. Their system is to give you a long personality test on the computer, look at the results to help the therapist determine your issues, then they send you to their staff psychiatrist to have him prescribe medication. He also ordered complete blood work (with my family doctor). Results of personality testing: very high intelligence but very severe depression. Again he put me on the tricyclic anti-depressant, beginning at 25 mg, increasing to maintenance dose of 75 mg/day. Because it does make you sleepy, you take it at bedtime.

It saved my life. As a lot of my anxiety was due to lack of sleep and waking in early morning hours agonizing over everything. With this medicine I slept all night—that was the first big improvement. Side effects: I was very tired for the first couple of weeks and gained a little weight, as it slowed down my metabolism. But for me, after roller coaster emotions, it was all a welcome vacation.

I still functioned driving four kids to soccer and tennis, volunteering at school and church. In fact, not many people knew I was screaming on the inside. As for lifting the depression, easing the anxiety, that took me around four weeks to see a marked difference, but it did work. Also, I continued therapy for a year to really come to understand my illness and not only how to handle the symptoms but how to handle these tendencies that could pop up again in the future. Important education! That was in 1992. I stayed on medication for 5 years, then asked my family doctor if I could try going off of it. He agreed, cautioning me that I might do fine, but I might be one of those people whose brain will always need medication to keep the chemistry balanced.

I did okay, until this last Christmas when the illness and death of my Dad caused everything to come crashing in. So, I went back to the doctor. He put me back on the tricyclic anti-depressant, knowing it does help me to stabilize the depression/anxiety, and once again, it was effective.

Managing a depressive, anxiety disorder is all about finding the appropriate drug and getting a therapist who will give you tools to deal with the symptoms. I have come to know myself so well, and progressed from the ashamed, embarrassed and frightened patient to the informed, responsible and careful manager of my condition. I know the warning signs of a downward turn and I know what to do to prevent myself from lapsing into the depressive state. Very empowering feeling, believe me!

    VERY IMPORTANT:

    It is not a sign of weakness or mental instability to suffer from depression/anxiety. It is merely a physical glitch in your brain, possibly (but not always) caused by stress, but nonetheless a physical glitch—TOTALLY TREATABLE WITH THE RIGHT MEDICATION. THIS IS NOT ABOUT YOUR INABILITY TO COPE WITH DAILY LIFE. You can cope just fine, you are a strong woman, but your brain has shown you it has physical limitations and you must respect its need for medical help.

    I know one of your concerns is if Tom understands your condition. If you think it would help to better inform him, let him read this e-mail. I think he and Bob touched on this briefly on Friday, but I'm sure Tom is as perplexed by all this as Bob was in the beginning.

    This letter has been long enough for now, but I will be e-mailing you again as I have another tool for you, it has to do with a little book you need to get by Emilie Barnes, Fifteen Minutes Alone With God. *This book is a wonderful way to bring more of God and his power into your life, which I always need! This book has helped me many times over the years in my quest to bring God into every aspect of my life. There is one chapter on prayer, which is invaluable.*

    Okay, must go, having Sunday dinner of roast turkey in "Thanksgiving" for cool, rainy weather!

    Let's both count our blessings for the rest of today, everywhere we look, there's a good thing.

Love, Sal

Subj: sometimes it's who you know
Date: 9/24/00 5:07:41 PM Central Daylight Time
From: debbiesb13@aol.com
To: sarahjf50@hotmail.com

Dear Sal,

    Cannot tell you how much I appreciate your advice and totally honest history of where you've been. I can appreciate it even more knowing how difficult this struggle can be. You are my true inspiration that I can lead a normal life and control this problem if or when it should occur in the future.

    After my frustration caused by getting three differing opinions from three different on-call doctors, I was an even bigger basket case this morning. At the end of my rope, I called the hospice nurse who contacted the hospice social worker who, even though today is Sunday, got me an immediate evaluation at a hospital. It's the same facility where the therapist I'm supposed to see on Thursday works. Result — my anti-depressant med was wrong for me as well as the way I was taking it. The anti-anxiety med, though working initially, was not the best choice. I go in the morning for an evaluation by psychiatrist for meds, blood work, etc. I think it sounds way better than the road I was on, and a lot closer to what gave you positive results.

I don't really care right now if I had to be on anti-depressants forever if I could just get back to feeling normal. That will be a goal I can work on later. Thank God I received this help today. It was none too soon.

When we met in Florida, I remember being so impressed with the peacefulness that is a part of your demeanor and shows readily on your face. I figured out sometime ago in our friendship that this comes from your faith and the confidence it gives you. My faith is strong, but I have not yet found that type of confidence. I'm working on it though and will get there eventually.

Will try to let you know how tomorrow goes, but I may be too tired. It'll be my longest stretch out of bed in what seems like ages.

Hope you had a nice family day today and you enjoyed the cooler weather. One thing I haven't lost sight of, is even when I'm feeling so low, there are blessings in life. Thanks for being one.
Love, Deb

Subj: *You're on the way!*
Date: *9/25/00 10:04:31 AM Central Daylight Time*
From: *sarahjf50@hotmail.com*
To: *debbiesb13@aol.com*

Wow, Deb! It's always darkest before the dawn...you did the perfect thing in not settling for the family doctor treatment, especially when it was not working.

I will be anxious to hear how today goes for you, but I know you will have a great sense of relief because you are seeing the true professionals for your condition now. You may still feel bad but hey, you're in the right place and things will really start moving in the right direction.

I am going upstairs in a few moments to sit in my window seat, light my rose candle and pray for peace in your life to come soon.

Someday, when we're sitting on the veranda, sipping iced tea, watching the birds flutter around the feeders, I'll tell you the story of my discovery of my faith. I don't tell many people how it happened, how I came to discover the presence of God in my life. But sometime I'd like to share it with you.

I know this is a big day for you, and I'll be thinking about you. Take care, friend, have a better day!
Love, Sal

A Frustrating Search for Help

Subj: You aren't going to believe this
Date: 9/25/00 4:06:12 PM Central Daylight Time
From: debbiesb13@aol.com
To: sarahjf50@hotmail.com

Thanks so much for the kind thoughts. And I would consider it an honor for you to share the story of your faith with me. I know it is an incredibly personal thing.

As for my day—I never saw the doctor. In fact the day was nothing I had been told to expect. In fact it was more of more different people saying more different things. The doctor who never saw me told me on the phone to keep using the med that's making me nauseous. This is the same med his nurse said I should have stopped taking over a week ago. The good news was I was so mad, I became quite normal, even ate a hamburger (have lost 12 pounds since we met, 7 of it in the last 3 weeks).

My therapist appointment was cancelled as she wants me to first see a psychiatrist to prescribe the proper meds, but she doesn't know one to recommend with openings any time soon. Have called the therapist who is the minister's wife, but not heard back. Have called my ob/gyn but the guy he liked has retired. Have called friend at MD Anderson as well but not heard back. This is just TOO DAMN FRUSTRATING!!!!

Your experience on the other hand sounded positive, and that they really do thorough evaluating before jumping into things, so I was wondering can you give me the name of the clinic you went to. I assume it's in Clear Lake, which would be an hour drive, but it can't be worse than this. I really wanted to call you and talk about it but was not sure if that would be OK as it is not our normal mode of communication.

Anyway, I'll look later to see if you've had time to answer and if some of these people have called me back. Hope you had a wonderful retreat today. It sounds ideal.
Love, Deb

Subj: *deja vu*
Date: *9/25/00 5:33:03 PM Central Daylight Time*
From: *sarahjf50@hotmail.com*
To: *debbiesb13@aol.com*

Okay, I'm starting to get pissed. You need help and you need it yesterday. Some bozo's don't understand what it's like to live even one day in your shoes...I do, it's crappy. We must get aggressive. Look at the sources below and call every one. Boy, Deb, you and I really have some parallels when it comes to trying to get good help! But it will happen.

Yes, call me at home! I will try to help in any way.

The clinic that I used was called the Samaritan Center. Our Catholic church and many churches in the area supported the Samaritan Center. It was very well respected. But look for a branch clinic near you, because you need to go frequently and don't want to hassle with the traffic.

Another source: contact your church, or any church and ask for a referral to a local Christian counseling center.

Another source: There is also a number I remember from a radio show, which will refer you to Christian counseling centers around the country. I think the number is

1- (800) NEW-LIFE.

Another source: you can call the Christian radio station and they should be able to give you some referrals to counseling centers. The station is on 24 hours a day, so if you're up in the night, tune them in!

You may have noticed the definite leaning to Christian counseling. This is not to say that they are going to lay hands on you and evoke a cure. They won't even pray with you unless you want to. It's just that their values are so reinforced by biblical text on family and living that you feel you are going down the right path with the right people.

Loved your comment about losing weight. Same thing happened to me! I never looked better or felt worse! Same deal: lost 6 pounds in three weeks. Just not too hungry—no appetite. Don't worry, you'll be back to munching soon!

Will go and send this info to you. You're right to get mad, and to have some junk food! Feels good to be mad, right? Kind of letting off steam? Go ahead, and write it down, you'll feel better. Journal this experience, because someday, I promise, someone will benefit from your experience and knowledge.

Let me know your progress!

Love, Sal

Subj: GOOD MORNING!
Date: 9/26/00 11:55:26 AM Central Daylight Time
From: debbiesb13@aol.com
To: sarahjf50@hotmail.com

Hi there Friend!

OK, I'm still smiling and running on fumes because I only slept about four hours last night, the day still had me so charged up. Really enjoyed getting to visit with you on the phone last night. It would have taken ages to cover all that ground by e-mail! Plus it was fun to actually talk and share experiences.

So much has happened already this morning. Here's what I have definite – an appointment tomorrow morning (fortunately there was a cancellation) with a psychiatrist in Humble who was recommended to me by Mary Jo, the therapist who is the wife of the minister I told you about. Then after that is set, I can go to Mary Jo for therapy whenever I'm ready to start. And yes, she is a Christian therapist.

Also called Samaritan Center. They were the only other place where I spoke to a real human who acted like they cared at all. Their doctor is not accepting new patients at this time. I have made a couple of alternate psychiatrist appointments around town for next week as my MD Anderson contact advised which I can always cancel if I find the right doctor beforehand. And still waiting for three offices to call back with availability.

You know it's no wonder there are crazies out there killing people all the time. It's next to impossible to talk to an actual human, and the doctors' offices don't open till 9 or 9:30, and then they tell you to WAIT A MONTH. And don't even think about having a problem on a weekend!

Talked to Nancy, the hospice chaplain a few minutes ago. I have told her from time to time about the importance our e-mail discussions and friendship to my life. I told her this morning how I had written you before I went yesterday that God had answered my prayers. As it turned out the prayer was not answered in exactly the way I had anticipated in the morning. It led me in a new and better direction for today and tomorrow. Anyway I feel hopeful, if it doesn't work out right I'll just go to the next thing (OK, I will admit if I lose it again because of another adverse reaction to the medicine I will be really pissed!!!!!)

Speaking of meds, did they tell you anything about how those hormones could affect you in terms of depression/anxiety?

I also was glad last night being able to talk about what a stressful year this has been for you. I was unsure if you had been leaving those things out of your e-mails because they were too troublesome for you, or were afraid they were too troublesome for me. Anyway, it was good.

Well, think I'll go fix some lunch now. Yes, eating! Will let you know how it goes in the morning. Hope you have a really great day!
Love, Deb

Subj: *Good Evening!*
Date: *9/26/00 5:34:58 PM Central Daylight Time*
From: *sarahjf50@hotmail.com*
To: *debbiesb13@aol.com*

Well it seems like you are finally getting some results with appointments! I think seeing the psychiatrist in the morning is excellent! One thing you need to stress is the level of anxiety and sleeplessness and loss of appetite you experience. That gets you into a different realm of medication than those classic medications, which just deal with depression. As far as taking hormones and anti-depressants at the same time, I would think it depends on the meds...something your ob-gyn should check on. Mine was compatible.

I will be in and out tomorrow, going to be with Mom while she has an interview for her long-term care insurance. But I'll be waiting to hear how your appointment goes!

It was great to talk to you on the phone! Yes, we did get a lot accomplished. I have committed myself to a serious prayer time with the help of Emilie Barnes book, 15 Minutes Alone with God. *One of the tasks she suggests is to keep a prayer journal and also acknowledge in that journal when God answers your prayers. I have had some startling results already, in the ways that I petition the Lord and during the day he answers me. The great and uplifting moment is when I see an answer to my prayer and I write it down. The process of writing my prayers down, then later going back over those prayers and acknowledging answers has been very valuable in my development of a new relationship/dialogue with God. I feel like I have stumbled upon a very valuable gift.*

Am going to go for now, as it's time to make dinner, but will e-mail later! Have a nice evening!
Love, Sal

Sleep Tight (Yeah, Right!)

Subj: there' so much to keep in mind
Date: 9/26/00 6:34:12 PM Central Daylight Time
From: debbiesb13@aol.com
To: sarahjf50@hotmail.com

Hi! Thanks for tips on stressing needs. There's so much to remember. Think I will take some time tonight and make some notes.

Very smart to be getting long term care insurance for your mom!!!!!!!!! Can speak from personal experience how nice it would have been to have it. Got my mom's bill today, which had an extra $115 for doing her personal laundry, which I usually do. You may already know all the ins and outs, but be sure it includes different care options. Like assisted living, not just nursing homes for example. My mom's bill for a private room is about $2800 a month and it would be higher if some of her services were not done by hospice. And even then there are expenses insurance doesn't cover that can be high like meds, Depends, Ensure, etc. I think golden years means somebody else strikes it rich on you. Good luck with it.

On the phone we discussed how it can be so difficult when someone you love a great deal says things that are so hurtful. And even forgiving, it is sometimes hard to forget the hurt. Sometimes I even get confused and wonder if not forgetting means I haven't truly forgiven, but I don't think so. Even giving the anger to God sometimes it is still so difficult to empty your brain of the thoughts. It is a long process to move on and establish an almost new relationship. Am sure you find success on this issue with your prayer journal. What a great idea by the way.

I think we are going out for dinner somewhere tonight. The anticipation still creates anxiety, so I'm trying not to think about it too much although food is settling better these days. Tom was very insistent this morning about having a night of the four Harwells being more normal. Now I wonder what that meant.
Buenos noches and hasta luego, Deb

Subj: Hola, mi amiga!
Date: 9/27/00 8:05:11 AM Central Daylight Time
From: sarahjf50@hotmail.com
To: debbiesb13@aol.com

Buenos Dias!

Yes, you do have a lot to remember for the doctor and it is a GREAT idea to write stuff down! I never think of the appropriate questions to ask until I get home...

Hope you had a nice time at dinner! Don't be too hard on Tom if he makes comments that you think are rather insensitive to your condition. Bob did the same thing. I spent (rather, wasted) time trying to get him to see things from my perspective, especially about not feeling comfortable about going some places—but he just didn't quite understand. When I told him I just could not make the Hawaii trip (with his parents) he was very disappointed (ouch!) and his mother was horrible about it. She still talks about it, but in a nicer way now…Anyway, your therapist would be a good one to educate Tom about your condition, along with suggestions for him as to how he can help you with your recovery, if you feel the need to.

Thanks for tips on long term care insurance, and yes, hers does include options for assisted living and home care.

Must go, have to make the big guy some hot chocolate. Still a boy in so many ways.

Have a great day with the doctor and let me know what happens!!! I'm on the edge of my seat to hear the next chapter in "Deb's Quest for Peace."
Love, Sal

Subj: next installment
Date: 9/27/00 6:13:58 PM Central Daylight Time
From: debbiesb13@aol.com
To: sarahjf50@hotmail.com

Hi there!

What a day!! I am only just now getting home and left before 10 this morning (under normal circumstances OK, but…)

The psychiatrist is very knowledgeable on meds and explained in detail the chemistry behind all the actions and reactions of the steroids and anti-depressant to my system. I felt really good about that part. The only real negative was that she was running way behind schedule and looked at her watch a few times which bugged me. She did not however in any way short-change any of my questions or her explanations so I guess I shouldn't complain. She wants to change the anti-anxiety med but will wait until I go back next week to have the overall med progress evaluated.

She said it is common for people who have reacted as I have to meds to panic at the thought of how the new med will work (I could have done without having that thought planted in my brain, but I guess forewarned is forearmed) so to leave the one I know is working in place for now is better.

We discussed three possible anti-depressants. The one we ended up with is a tetracyclic anti-depressant that is relatively new. I think it must work similar to yours. I take it at night, should make me sleep good, and increase my appetite. I start with a low dose for now and will increase it next week. Statistically speaking she said I should expect to be on it at least a year, but that's not really an issue for now. She ordered tons of blood tests for thyroid, liver, CBC, etc and an EKG. I had all those done this afternoon on my way home and assume she will discuss the results of those next week.

On the whole I feel like I'm on the right track, but for some reason have found it difficult to feel relaxed since leaving there. Of course that may be because I had several errands to do while in that area. Then there was the blood work stuff, grocery store, and picking up Austin. Normal running, but today it felt like too much.

Hope all went well with your mom today.

Well, think I'll go start some dinner (catfish) and put up all the stuff I bought today. Never did make it to the mall for pajamas so got some cute zebra ones (pictures of zebras with crosswords and stuff, not stripes) at Target. It will do for now, something between summer gowns and winter flannel. Have a great evening!

Love, Deb

Subj: *sleep tight!*
Date: *9/27/00 9:43:58 PM Central Daylight Time*
From: *sarahjf50@hotmail.com*
To: *debbiesb13@aol.com*

Well, it sounds good! You have talked to a professional and are moving forward! A good night's sleep sounds like a great thing, I'm sure! I'm not familiar with your anti-depressant. Like I said, I took one of the dinosaurs of anti-depressants! Did she say how long she estimated it would take for you to start feeling normal again? Just sleeping through the night will be a big plus!

Also, was impressed with all the shopping activity and traveling you had to do. You're still in the game, Deb! Your jammies sound cute! Target has some great stuff.

Mom passed her interview for the long-term care insurance with flying colors.

Must go, I'm really beat! Nighty-night, sleep tight, dear friend!

Love, Sal

Facing an Angry Rottweiler

Subj: still among the living
Date: 9/28/00 3:38:12 PM Central Daylight Time
From: debbiesb13@aol.com
To: sarahjf50@hotmail.com

Hi Sal!

Tom was disappointed in my pajamas. "I thought you were going to get something sexy." So what's not sexy about cartoon zebras?

Have had a reasonably good day today. Did wake up VERY sleepy. Did get up by 7 though. Cleared all the junk that has been piling up on the little kitchen desk for what feels like years and finally went for a walk around 10:30. It's so nice to have it cooler now so I can walk at a later time without heat stroke.

When you were starting your anti-depressant and it made you sleepy did you get more sleepy as the first few days went by and then it got better, or was the first day the most sleepy? It took me till about noon to feel somewhat awake and still feel fairly dull. But it is so much better than feeling nauseous!!!!!!!!! I'm trying not to get too excited just in case this doesn't work as planned. And of course thanking God it is a beginning.

You know, it is that guilt/responsibility syndrome (domestic schizophrenia) that sucked me in to where you have been coaxing me out of today. The doctor yesterday drew an interesting analogy. She said if you go outside and see a rottweiler, your mind is on heightened alert until the danger passes. She said my last two years have been to my brain like facing that dog continuously. I never got to turn off the alert so to speak.

Well, must go for now. I'm going to call the therapist for an appointment.
Love, Deb

Subj: sleep is good
Date: 9/28/00 5:02:37 PM Central Daylight Time
From: sarahjf50@hotmail.com
To: debbiesb13@aol.com

When I started the anti-depressant I was sleepiest the first week, and it tapered off as time when on. However, the whole time I took it, I slept like a log at night. At one point when I complained to my doctor about not being able to get up easily he said take the pill at dinner instead of bedtime, to set back the reaction a bit. I've always been early to bed, early to rise and the groggy mornings really threw me.

I really love the analogy of you facing a rottweiler for almost 2 years. That is so true and helps you to understand that enough is enough (says your brain) even if you try to keep plugging along, handling everything.

I have had a pack of rottweilers this year, I swear there has been a curse put on my family. It began with my birthday last year, Oct. 30th when my parents didn't call me to sing their traditional serenade of the birthday song. Dad was heading downhill fast suffering from senile dementia, and abruptly passed away. We helped our mother cope with this difficult change in her life. In our immediate family, one child was having serious financial problems, another child became pregnant and married, another child also became pregnant and her husband is looking for a new job, and another child is having serious relationship problems with the current love interest.

Would you like to hear the sequel? Every crisis has been handled as well as our family is able. We just keep moving forward, together, hopefully learning from the past. I have told the Lord enough is enough. This has been the worst year of my life, truly. I have designated Oct. 30, 2000, as the day the crises stop, we are going to go back to the normal day to day irritations we live with all the time.

The good news is my faith has become so strong and I have moved so much closer to working with the Lord on crises, rather than imploding (which used to be my favorite way of handling stress). I pray, journal to God and read appropriate scripture to guide me. It is so powerful. 10 years ago, a year like this one would have had me devastated, beating myself up, getting furious but not letting it go. I would have made it through, but without severe damage to

Subj: Re: still among the living
Date: 9/28/00 7:20:32 PM Central Daylight Time
From: sarahjf50@hotmail.com
To: debbiesb13@aol.com

Oops, hit the send button by mistake in the middle of a sentence. Anyway, long story short. I'm a stronger, better Christian today, which is a blessing.

Try taking the pill a little earlier in the evening, see if that helps your tiredness in the morning. Enjoy the rest you're getting you need it and your body will strengthen up quickly! The depression/anxiety will most likely start to fade in 2-3 weeks, beginning with having more good days than bad, until most days you feel normal, 4-6 weeks after beginning medication.

Think you're on your way, Deb. I know it probably seems a little too much to hope for, that the medication will work, but it will.

Just talked to you! And I just got your pictures! Great to see all your boys! Also Tracey's wedding looks like it was quite a beautiful one, and a lot of work!— but fun, right? Your backyard is lovely! Tell Tom he does a lovely job in his landscape planning, he definitely knows what he's doing! Thanks so much for giving me a glimpse into your world, will send you some of our world here! What a

cutie you have for a little grandson, and Tom looks quite the distinguished grandpa.
What does he call you and Tom?
   Will go for now, and do something important (ha-ha). Sleep well, dear
friend, and have great dreams!
Love, Sal

Subj: "praise the Lord and pass the biscuits!"
Date: 9/29/00 10:24:36 AM Central Daylight Time
From: debbiesb13@aol.com
To: sarahjf50@hotmail.com

   Think that's the way it goes — Friar Tuck in the cartoon version of *Robin Hood*. Anyway, good morning, my friend! Thought I'd write early in case you're cleaning and take a break later. Why is it lately I never seem to know where to begin? It's like my brain is overflowing with all this information overload. Plus I think I started last night sometime after about 8:00 on this sort of stoned-high-euphoria that is really interesting.

   I'm still reeling from all the major things you have had happen in your life in such a short time. You are such an incredibly strong person, Sally. I think your pack of dogs has got mine beat by several litters and look where I ended up — the padded cell at the kennel!!! You were so right though about how these challenges in life can strengthen your faith in God rather than turn you away.

   Earlier in the summer I had gone to my dad's grave just to reflect. The cemetery I chose for him is a beautiful, peaceful place with huge old oaks and azaleas. While I was there a lady pulled up, got out a lawn chair, and walked over to a grave just past my dad's. I remembered it as having been new at his funeral. She asked me who I'd lost and if it had been recent. She had lost her mom three days before my dad. Then she said, "This is my daughter here beside her." I didn't know quite what to say except a feeble, "I'm sorry." She said, "Oh, no. God has blessed us." I was so totally blown away. I couldn't even say anything. Here was this lady sweeping the dirt from her daughter's marker, planning to relax in a lawn chair and counting her blessings at the same time! Sometimes I'm still not sure I could do that — I mean be strengthened at the loss of a child. But then I would have never thought the last two years would have brought me to this point either, meaning mentally, emotionally, physically, and spiritually. And certainly not that I would have ever discussed it with anyone.

   When this collapse began another friend sent me a book called *Balcony People* and told me she would be one for me. It's a wonderful book. It reminds me a great deal of our friendship so I got a copy for you the other day when I was running those errands. After hearing all of your challenges this past year I thought you could use it now. You have definitely been a "balcony person" for me and I want you to know I will always be one for you as well. Like you told me a while back, it is not that there are answers always (though you had many for me) it's having someone who will listen no matter how mad, sad, happy, or long-winded you may be.

I prayed today for Oct. 30th.

Here's our weekend plan — you'll be impressed — we're going to the KW game tonight at Deer Park to watch the band so Austin will know Mom can cope and does still care after all. Then tomorrow morning is the homecoming parade, shop for some plants, and Sunday lunch with friends. Am not sure I'm really ready for all this. At least it sounds like our old normal life.

Glad you like the pictures. Will look forward to getting some from you. Tristan calls Tom Grandpa. He loves to come to the hotel to visit Tom. He was calling me Grandma, but this got confusing during the wedding stuff because that is also what he calls David's mom. So he started calling me Debbie like Tracey does. It really shouldn't matter what he calls me. But actually, it bugs me because my mother would never let our boys call her any grandparent names because of her age hang-up. So they were always Irene and Frank. Tom and I hated that.

Oh forgot to tell you — just started reading *Mitford 3*. One thing you can do home alone with anxiety is shop the hell out of amazon.com!

Have a really good day today.

Love, Deb

III

Spiritual Conference Call

*

The Lord Works in Mysterious Ways

Southern Christians

Bookworms in Recovery

Peaks and Valleys

My Skin Is Growing Longer

*

Fugazi & Harwell

The Lord Works in Mysterious Ways

Subj: *Loved that movie!*
Date: *9/29/00 12:25:39 PM Central Daylight Time*
From: *sarahjf50@hotmail.com*
To: *debbiesb13@aol.com*

One of the kids' and my favorite Disney movies is Robin Hood!

Ah yes, it's time to take a break from the laundry, etc! Thanks for the great, newsy, letter! Your weekend sounds great, and if you get tired, then take a break, you are still recuperating from a long battle with a rottweiler, you know!

Your poor mom is a very unhappy person and sounds like she's been that way for a long time. How hard for you to live with her negativity. That's why we have a sense of humor, to balance out those dark forces in our lives. Did you tell her that your kids would always think she was old, just because she was beyond 30?

When Tisa turned 13, she started looking at me as if I was old and ugly, and this progressed so that each of my daughters, when entering adolescence had the same reaction. Then, as they matured, by their late teens, they began to see, I was still old, but sometimes I really knew what I was talking about, and may still have some value in their lives...a mom can't take it personally. We all did the same thing at their age.

Tisa and I started talking about prayer and she told me how she had been doing a prayer journal and how she had developed this new relationship with God and was really seeing her prayers being answered and signposts in her path. She said before she prays for something, she asks herself what she really needs, and what would God want for her or her loved ones. She, like me, goes back over her past prayers in her journal and writes down the answers and signposts that have popped up. It was exactly the parallel experience I was having, with my journaling, in that I have seen this pattern of my prayers being answered right and left, in God's wisdom. Both of us marvel at the new relationship this kind of prayer develops between God and us, and how it spills over into all aspects of our lives.

There is one important factor in life, a gift God has given us, to cherish and use for his glory, and that is friendship. I know it is no mistake that you and I met when we did and we had the inclination to start up the e-mail relationship. Then for us to have so many parallels come out in our lives...God does have us taking care of each other, with his guidance. The second greatest commandment is "love your neighbor as yourself" and I feel we achieve that very easily!—wish I could do that with more people.

As for the past year, it has been hard, but look what I've gained. Strength and trust in the Lord and a new best friend. Could be worse! Your story about the cemetery and the woman who had lost her mother and daughter was very interesting. One of God's signposts in your life, Deb!

This weekend I'll cut my mom's hair and give her a perm, and I will fertilize my roses. They all look very well, and the blooms are really coming on strong, which is so impressive as this is their first year in the ground and they've been through such a brutal summer. I love roses, gorgeous and tough!

Got together some pictures for you, will mail those off today or tomorrow.

Have a lovely Indian summer weekend!

Love, Sal

Subj: prayerful thoughts
Date: 9/30/00 12:02:57 PM Central Daylight Time
From: debbiesb13@aol.com
To: sarahjf50@hotmail.com

Watching the band last night and this morning was fun. But will admit to being tired.

I really enjoyed your sharing the stories of yours and Tisa's prayer journal. I'm sure it brings an even greater impact and realization of the glory God gives to our lives. Plus sometimes you forget as time passes (sometimes even minutes) the small prayers that have been answered. I will admit to not being the best at the overall journal concept yet, but am putting forth an effort. I remember reading in *Simple Abundance* it takes 21 days to make it into a habit – I will assume that means in a row.

I am so looking forward to my first meeting with the therapist on Thursday. I asked her quite directly about what role if any her Christian beliefs and prayer play in her counseling. She told me she prays privately for all her patients (or did she say clients) whether they ask her to or not, but that we would feel this out together as we go along. So we will see how it goes.

You are right about the unique friendship that has developed through our emails. Even having lived in the same cities twice in the past with husbands in the same business we had never met before that I can remember.

One day soon, I'm going to write you a separate e-mail to share some thoughts on God's role in our lives, (the sort of story you mentioned telling me on the veranda some day, but without waiting THAT long).

I'm impressed you can cut and perm your mom's hair. I can barely handle a curling iron on my own!!! Guess that comes with practice with your girls. I have cut Travis and Austin's hair for a couple of years now (when Travis wanted the buzz, he wanted it every week, and I was too cheap to pay $12 for a weekly haircut). Of course cutting theirs, as you can see from the pictures, is more like mowing the grass. You really can't make too many mistakes!

Well, it's time to make some lunch now. Have a great weekend and enjoy your family.

Love, Deb

Subj: a signpost
Date: 10/1/00 3:30:28 PM Central Daylight Time
From: debbiesb13@aol.com
To: sarahjf50@hotmail.com

Reading *Mitford 3*. I will admit to having lost some short term memory recently, but I'm almost positive I sent you an e-mail last week about not being able to get things right. Have to share this one part with you.

Father Tim is doing a lot of introspection about his life and tells Cynthia he can't get it right.

She responds by telling him that when she was going through her own difficult times that God spoke to her heart in a way He hadn't done before, and in turn, she was able to listen in a new way. She tells Father Tim the experience taught her that getting things absolutely right is God's job.

Wow, huh?

Love, Deb

Subj: straight from the heart—signposts
Date: 10/2/00 8:09:12 PM Central Daylight Time
From: sarahjf50@hotmail.com
To: debbiesb13@aol.com

Your quote from Mitford *has to be acknowledged, as this is how God made his presence known in my life: He spoke in my heart:*

In the early, dark morning hours of December 1990, I was lying in bed, so depressed and so anxious I had even lost the ability to cry. I wished I could just evaporate (never been into the suicide thing). I felt like even my husband must think I am such a crazy loser...then...

In my heart a voice/presence communicated, "You are loved, your life is precious and I will take care of you." I got the feeling that it was a father figure who spoke to me. But it wasn't even a voice I could hear, I just felt the words. I knew it was not my Dad, and I had no other explanation, except that it was God.

At the time, I didn't believe in God, (my philosophy was man created God, not the other way around). I had not even considered praying to a God, or asking for divine help. But there was no way I could dismiss this feeling in my heart (not in my brain). It had happened. If it had not happened to me, I would never have believed it. I fell asleep, feeling like I was sleeping in someone's hand.

I got up the next morning and was so amazed. I thanked "God"—I didn't know what else to call this presence, and promised to bring all my children into the church and have them baptized. Bob has always been a Catholic, but because of my unbelief, we had never had our children baptized. I told Bob about this and he said, okay, we can bring them into the Catholic Church. At that point I did not care what church, I was just so thankful for the presence in my life, I felt I needed to repay "God" for his love for me. That was the beginning of my journey into the Catholic faith and my baptism in 1992. For 9 months I learned about God in religious education and so did our children, then we were baptized at Easter in 1992.

When you wrote the quote about God speaking to the heart, I understood fully. As an unbeliever, someone not even considering the option of God, God came into my heart and spoke to me. When I told my religious education teacher about this experience, he said I was very fortunate to have had such an experience—rather like Paul on the road to Damascus. For some people, like me and Paul, it takes a rather profound miracle for us to believe. We are called by God, even when we are not considering Him as an option!

So, there's the story of the beginning of my faith. I truly feel I have been called, and I definitely did not deserve it, but I am a willing follower, as I know what is true in my life: God has touched me.

That's my story I was saving for the veranda. As is always the case in my life, my agenda and God's agenda rarely coincide, He has his way of having me do things according to his timing, not mine. We'll have to come up with other subjects for our veranda—not something too difficult for you and me, as we always have plenty to talk about!
Love, Sal

Subj: destinations are the same, the roads are different
Date: 10/2/00 10:17:49 PM Central Daylight Time
From: debbiesb13@aol.com
To: sarahjf50@hotmail.com

Dear Sal,

Your story is quite incredible. As you have said, the timing of our veranda stories is not as we had planned as I was going to wait until later in the week to share mine with you. But here goes…

I started attending an Episcopal church and school when I was 3. I was told growing up it was a compromise between my father's Catholic and mother's Methodist faiths. In fact, it was because it was only a block from where we lived. I went to school there through the first grade and loved it! Then we moved. My mother shunned all churches in the new neighborhood. I felt so left out all those years with no church. All my friends went to church, but we didn't go - no discussion. When I got to high school, my mother would let me go with my best friend to her church some on Wednesday nights and to day camps. I was so excited to be learning something about God again, but it didn't feel the same as the Episcopal church.

When I went to college I will tell you right out, I lived every mother's nightmare. I had never been without someone watching me every minute, and took full advantage of my freedoms. Despite this, most Sundays I would walk up the hill to the Episcopal church and "confess my sins devoutly kneeling." I do not say that with any disrespect. I was always repentant, but could not keep to my good intentions for long.

When I moved back to Houston, working days, law school at night, I went around to all kinds of churches — all denominations, in my neighborhood and out. Trying to find the place for me. Instead what I found was the fear of God, one night as I drifted over the double yellow line on a winding road in the hills somewhere outside of Austin with headlights coming in my direction. I can only tell you that I do not know why God chose to save me at that moment, but He did. I do not know why our cars did not collide except for the simple fact that God said it was not our time. My life changed from that moment on. I had not yet found my church so to speak, but there was no question about having found God.

Tom and I were married in the Episcopal church that my aunt belonged to as neither of us had our own church. Tom had spent many years in the Baptist church, and he did not like the ritual of the Episcopal church. Ironically, I think it is that very thing I like most about it. I love the way it smells when you go in, sort of that lingering incense, old wood kind of smell; I love big stained glass windows that tell the story of Jesus; I love holding a prayer book, even when I know the words by heart, and feeling like I am praying with all the people who have held it before me; I love the rhythm of the prayers, their responses and their familiarity; I love the priests' flowing robes; I love a booming pipe organ that you can feel the bass notes in your chest; I love turning to my neighbor and saying, "Peace be with you!"

When Austin was a year or two old we had both boys baptized, and I was confirmed, at St. Marks's in Beaumont. The whole time we lived there and in Florida, the boys and I would go to church. Towards the end in Florida, the church had been without a rector for over a year and visiting priests were getting pretty meaningless. I began to feel the church of "our family" was a better place for us to be on Sundays. So we quit going.

When we moved here, the boys fought hard not to go back to church. I felt like they had reached an age where if they had to be forced it wasn't the right thing. So here we are.

It was important to me to tell you that I had not been going to church since we moved back to Texas because I didn't want you to think I had misled you in any way about my faith or beliefs. And although we had not specifically discussed it, I assumed you were Catholic, and I know their rule requires good attendance at church. I firmly believe that a person's closeness to God comes from what is in their heart and the dialog they maintain with God. I am trusting that in the friendship we have developed you know I would in no way mean that to be offensive to the Catholic doctrine, only a difference of opinion. Also I know without a doubt this experience has brought me closer to God than I have ever been before. For me personally, as opposed to my family, attending church is something I miss.

So there you have it … the veranda story that couldn't wait for the veranda. And in God's time frame not ours. You are no doubt right, as usual, there will never be a lack of things for us to talk about, but also probably nothing we could ever talk about that would bring us closer than these two e-mails tonight.
Good night and Blessings to my Friend, Deb

Subj: Read second please
Date: 10/3/00 8:21:07 AM Central Daylight Time
From: debbiesb13@aol.com
To: sarahjf50@hotmail.com

Morning Sal!

I had such a hard time going to sleep last night (yes, even with the drugs). I kept thinking about your story. I kept being haunted by the vision of sleeping in God's hand and why that seemed so significant to me. Then, I realized it was the Sunday school song! "He's Got the Whole World in His Hands"!!! "He's got you and me sister…" That was it! Then I could finally go to sleep.

It's only a few minutes after 8 and I'm already back from my walk. I found it difficult to stay focused in my prayers this morning - finding my dialog sometimes to be with God and at other times back to an e-mail with you. I wondered if we were having some kind of spiritual conference call. I was distracted by what ever it was that made that particular passage from *Mitford* stand out to me. It was such an overwhelming sensation at the time of NEEDING to share it with you. I didn't know why, but I had to do it right then, even if you didn't read it for two days.

Travis made fun of me to Tom that night at dinner. He said I was acting like a child begging for five minutes to send an e-mail. I denied it, but it was true. I felt like I was 12 years old and had to tell my very best friend a most important secret and it had to be right that minute. Now I know why.

As usual, you were succinct and to the point, and I have to ramble on taking a night and day to get my thoughts out.

And another beautiful day has begun…

Love, Deb

Southern Christians

Subj: *Me too*
Date: *10/3/00 9:33:42 AM Central Daylight Time*
From: *sarahjf50@hotmail.com*
To: *debbiesb13@aol.com*

Dear Deb,

I have to smile at your description of you having to sit down and do the e-mail to me, and your family thinking it funny. The same thing happened to me last night when I read your Mitford *quote!*

Your story is lovely and I learned so much about you! It sounds like God has always been a force within you and you have tried, over and over again to find the place where He speaks to you. Please don't ever apologize for the difference in our church going habits or any other aspect of our faiths that differs. God is our only judge when it comes to our faith and it is a very personal thing as to how we celebrate it with Him. You and I both know that going to church every Sunday is no insurance of a good walk with Christ.

On a secular note, WOW!!! You went to law school! Did you get a degree? I am so impressed! Do you ever have thoughts of going back into the law field?

I only finished two years of college and then began our family, and have always wanted to have a good career other than my family some day. We'll see!

I have read a lot of Balcony People. *Wow! Speaks right to us, does it not! Not only are we affirmers (and we weren't even trying to be) but we also have a lot of the experiences discussed in the book! Yes, we may have to change one thing, however. We may have to become the "Veranda People." Those are balcony people with southern grace!*

Will write more later. Am excited about your progress here with the medication, walking and on to therapy on Thursday. Again, please do not think I would ever encourage or discourage your going to church. I do not mean to preach, but to share. I'm sort of new at this thing, as I have not shared my faith like this with many people.

Have a great day, Deb, you deserve it!
Love, Sal

Subj: to my partner on the veranda
Date: 10/3/00 5:35:19 PM Central Daylight Time
From: debbiesb13@aol.com
To: sarahjf50@hotmail.com

Hi Sal!

Here's what I did today — my volunteer time in the college room and then 1½ hours waiting in a bookstore full of restless children to get Eric Carle's autograph on books for Tristan and Zachary. (Yes, the medicines DO work!)

And I love the thought of "veranda people." How perfect! Did you get your southern charm from your years in Texas or have you lived other places in the South as well.

Don't think you ever need to apologize for "preaching." First, I have never taken anything you say in that way. I have always considered our discussions of faith a sharing of ideas. That is probably the very reason I can discuss them with you. Second, I do in fact shy away vigorously from people who are "converters" (for lack of a better word). When I first met Nancy, the hospice chaplain, I was sooo reluctant to talk with her. I thought she was going to try to change me in some way. She must have sensed that, as the first time we met she said she believes in "conversation not conversion," and put me at ease.

On the secular note … law school was my mother's dream. My dream was to be a debate coach at a small college.

I've had a few different jobs, and frankly find my current life doing volunteer work way more rewarding than any of the paying jobs I've held (except for maybe being director of the MDO program at Trinity when we were in Beaumont). I have friends who feel incomplete if they aren't working. I feel complete in and of myself (OK the last few weeks excluded). I had a very good friend/mentor in college who basically told me I had wasted my life after a few years of staying home with my kids. People who think that way are the sad ones.

So in all that philosophizing (is that even a word?) be proud of what you have accomplished and do not EVER think of yourself as having done less than your best for making your family your career. In my opinion the three worst things that have happened in our society — 1. too many kids with no one at home for them; 2. no prayer in school; and 3. too many guns! So there you have it, like it or not, the Debbie Harwell philosophy of life. Must go.
Love, Deb

Subj: I love your letters
Date: 10/4/00 10:11:38 AM Central Daylight Time
From: sarahjf50@hotmail.com
To: debbiesb13@aol.com

Good Morning Deb!
     You know, what did I do before I had your letters?

Your academic life and work life sound like you could do any thing you WANTED to do, as you have many talents. Have you ever considered going back and getting a teaching certificate after the boys are in college. What plans do you have now? (Maybe just being at peace is enough of a plan right now, yes?)

Do I consider myself southern? Well, at this point I do appreciate the southern grace of the women. I am very comfortable with the manners and hospitality. I think it's an affirmation to our feminine side. But I have lived too many places to try to put one label on myself, as I am a part of every place I've been. When I was two we lived in Alabama. We had a maid called Beatrice, giant African-American woman, who took care of me. My earliest memory was when I was two, sitting at the kitchen table and Beatrice was telling me to eat my grits—which I still have for breakfast to this very day. When I was four we moved to Washington, DC, as my dad worked in the Pentagon—there for four years. So, in the 1950's, I spent a few years of my youth in the south, then returned in 1985 to Beaumont, TX.

Getting back to you, today is a big day as you have your therapist meeting today! Hope you have a good first session, setting the basis for your continued recovery. The medication seems to be working (yeah!) but the therapy will help you to develop strengths and protections against hurtful situations in the future, which could once again sap your emotional reservoir.

Must go, taking Mom shopping today, running errands! Pray for rain for us, and I'll pray for cooler temperatures for you!

Joke for the day: you know you're getting old when you stoop down to pick up something and stop to think, "What else can I do while I'm down here?"
Love, Sal

Subj: love yours more
Date: 10/4/00 6:06:59 PM Central Daylight Time
From: debbiesb13@aol.com
To: sarahjf50@hotmail.com

Hi there, Sal!

Well, I don't know what you did before, but I think I probably yawned a lot... You always give me something to smile about.

Went back to the psychiatrist today (therapist tomorrow). She told me to double the anti-depressant starting tonight and to taper off the anti-anxiety medicine. Even though lately I often felt I no longer needed this med, when she told me to taper off, I felt almost panicky: I HAD to have it. She also said I'm anemic and have to go for blood work.

G.R.I.T.S. Girls Raised in the South! I'm glad you like the southern women thing. I love the southern culture (not the rebel flag, KKK kind) the magnolia, grits and fried chicken with gravy kind. I do, however, also have a great appreciation for my dad's Slovenian heritage as well.

Have given more thought to what you said about wanting a career, and can see where you would want to do that having not yet had that opportunity.

You had asked me about returning to school, and, yes, I have thought about it, but my goals have changed now. You are right just being at peace is far more appealing.

Have thought of something else I'd like to do. Sit down, OK. I thought we could write a book together. Hadn't decided if it should be fiction or some kind of self help-how to deal with families-or build relationships kind of thing, but I think it would be fun. You could do all the great catch phrases and humor and I could make it be long. Maybe it would be in e-mail format. So what do you think, Sal?

Well, I need to go. Hey, that old joke — doesn't everyone do that already?
Love, Deb

Bookworms in Recovery

Subj: *music to my ears*
Date: *10/4/00 9:41:56 PM Central Daylight Time*
From: *sarahjf50@hotmail.com*
To: *debbiesb13@aol.com*

You would be a great writer—excuse me—you ARE a great writer because you write like you're talking...The thoughts really flow. And you're pretty funny, too...Who knows? We may have to write this book. We could call it:

FE-MAILS!

It could be a self-help, interior decorating, legal advice book with thoughts on parenting, favorite foods and what to wear to company conferences! If Martha Stewart and Maya Angelou can do it, why can't we?

On your drugs—you'll be surprised, especially with your anti-depressant kicking in, that going down to one pill or maybe even no pill for anxiety will not be a big deal. Right now it just feels like getting out of the boat and walking on water. You'll sink! But NO YOU WON'T. The increased effectiveness of the anti-depressant will take the place of the other pill. It will be your life preserver. It seems miraculous but these drugs work and you will not need the anti-anxiety pill.

It's just to smooth things over until the anti-depressant works. Rather like putting the car air conditioner on max-full blast when you get into the car, but as you cool down, you only need the regular air to keep you comfortable. It's a chemical thing, Deb. (Don't you get tired of hearing me say that?)

What kind of car do you drive? I drive an Explorer that I adore. I can fit 20 bags of bark mulch in that car, but it also has leather interior and a 6-cd player, so I'm so comfortable while getting dirty.

So now, who's the motor mouth? (pardon the pun) Okay, Night-night, Deb!
Love, Sally

Subj: *Good mornin'!*
Date: *10/5/00 8:36:00 AM Central Daylight Time*
From: *sarahjf50@hotmail.com*
To: *debbiesb13@aol.com*

Are you awake yet? Did your increase in meds make you more sleepy or was there no change? It really shouldn't make much difference to take a larger dose. Starting you on a lesser dose to begin with gets your body used to the med gradually, so you shouldn't really notice big changes, as you are adjusting slowly and surely.

I am so glad you have finally got your appointment today with the therapist. This is another step in the right direction and this will probably be the most positive feeling so far. She sounds like a good candidate for your therapist needs.

Won't keep you, as I know you need to get going. So do I...many little errands today. Have a peaceful, positive day!
Love, Sal

Subj: FE-MAILS!!!! So perfect!!!!!!!!
Date: 10/5/00 8:58:54 AM Central Daylight Time
From: debbiesb13@aol.com
To: sarahjf50@hotmail.com

Good Morning!

See! I would have never thought of that title in a million years. So we are really writing a book?! Yes, yes, yes, yes, yes! How exciting! Now that is something to look forward to.

This is a "cool down" email. Just got back from my walk. I was slow (should wear one of those orange triangles for slow moving vehicles). You may not believe this, but it was your encouragement about the medicine/chemical thing that did it. So, no, I DON'T get tired of hearing it. I was feeling so anxious when I went to bed last night. I was worried about whether or not to take the medicine and if I could do without it this morning. You put my mind at ease. (It was sort of like being tucked into bed). My hands are still a little shaky.

So you drive an Explorer. I had been speculating for some time that you probably had a Suburban or Expedition so I wasn't too far off. It seemed to fit the graceful, appreciative of luxury side of your personality while allowing for the practical working in the yard side. I have a midnight blue Olds Sillohette (I know that's spelled wrong). It's the newer body style not the old one that looked like a space shuttle without wings.
TTFN! Ta, ta, for now, Deb

Subj: *bookworms*
Date: *10/5/00 3:21:42 PM Central Daylight Time*
From: *sarahjf50@hotmail.com*
To: *debbiesb13@aol.com*

I think we should do the book thing. Start thinking of just what would be a good format: how about 500 pages of bitching?

Or maybe just a how-to-book on reading books as a form of therapy! We could call it: Bookworms in Recovery!

But, am anxious to hear about you! Will check back later and see how things went, when my sense of humor returns (living with teenagers is at times a joyless experience).

GO GIRL on your walk! Yes, it is in your mind, all the power. You will win, and are right now.

Must go, time to run errands. Pray for my son, Romeo.
Love, Sal

Subj: at a loss for words?
Date: 10/5/00 4:25:17 PM Central Daylight Time
From: debbiesb13@aol.com
To: sarahjf50@hotmail.com

Hi My Friend!

Can understand your frustration. It is so hard to watch our kids make mistakes, and they are so stubborn, they do not listen. You know you're in my prayers, as is Oct. 30th.

The therapy thing was good. I was mostly relaxed and did not need the anti-anxiety medicine. (Still from your encouragement). Can't say that there were any great revelations, but Mary Jo did offer some viewpoints from which I had not looked. Today was goals for therapy and establishing where I am. When I go back next week we'll start on where to go from here. She did say I probably should wait a little longer before going back to see my mom.

Will say though, that afterwards I was so tired. Why is that so draining? I wasn't crying or anything, just talking. Came home and layed (or is it laid or is it lied— see how screwed up I am! — cna't even sort out the English language!) down and finished reading *Mitford 3* and still feel tired. What happened to all that energy from this morning?

Have been forgetting to tell you all week that we bought 5 rose bushes on the weekend and they are all blooming. So pretty!

Will be praying for you some peace of mind as you have prayed for mine.
Love, Deb

Subj: moving forward
Date: 10/05/00 9:17:46 PM Central Daylight Time
From: sarahjf50@hotmail.com
To: debbiesb13@aol.com

Therapy sounds good, plus she already knows how to protect you from hurtful situations at this point in your life. Good. Glad to hear the anti-depressant is filling in where the anti-anxiety drug took off. You can, for the time being, have that bottle around, and you may have times when you need to take one—that's okay. You will find that you no longer need them on a daily basis to control anxiety. I kept my anti-anxiety meds around for a year, and there were a couple of times, in very stressful situations, where I took half a pill and it helped. But you'll see as time goes

87

on that your safety net during this journey is your anti-depressant and therapy. Guess you already see that!

It is very draining to go to therapist. It's confronting the beast, so to speak. But the therapist knows how to do it, so trust her to take you safely through this journey. It really helps that she knew your parents!

Must go, am beat and need to rest—have a good night's rest, I'll see you in the morning!

Love, Sal

Peaks and Valleys

Subj: TGIF?!
Date: 10/6/00 2:57:12 PM Central Daylight Time
From: debbiesb13@aol.com
To: sarahjf50@hotmail.com

Hey Sal!

Hope you are feeling TGIF. At any rate, I hope your load has lightened.

Got a hair cut which always comes with a free spiritual lesson. The lady that has cut both Tom's and my hair for the last two years is neat. She's about 5'2" with heels on, very flamboyant, African American woman with very blonde hair, and a strong devotion to her faith. I always get a spiritual lesson of the day, and she is an authority on being positive in the face of adversity. She's 46, lost a daughter and is raising her grandson who's in 6th grade; lost her sister to medical malpractice a few months ago, and is now sharing responsibility for her niece as well. Tomorrow she wants me to come by and pick up a book on depression and how to resolve it. Will let you know how it is.

Have given a lot of thought to a question Mary Jo asked me yesterday about whether or not it hurts me to watch my mother's physical decline. I said yes and no— it is hard to see her suffering, but she is 88 and has led a remarkably healthy life, having never been in the hospital till she was 86. The more I thought about it today, the more I felt like a real ingrate, but I don't feel sorry for her. Is this domestic schizophrenia? I felt so guilty. I called her today just to say I love you. She was glad I called and we stuck to safe subjects and kept it brief. Mary Jo said the mother-daughter relationship is by far the most complex.

Well, my friend, I hope you have a peaceful, quiet Friday night.

Love, Deb

Subj: got your pictures!
Date: 10/6/00 4:22:05 PM Central Daylight Time
From: debbiesb13@aol.com
To: sarahjf50@hotmail.com

Sally,

Thanks so much for the card and the pictures!! They are terrific! Zachary is such a doll! I can see a bit of you in all your kids, but in the wedding one Anthony looks exactly like you. Is that right? What a beautiful family you have! We are truly blessed are we not? Challenged sometimes maybe, but blessed.

Love the picture of you on your trusty steed Apple.

Love, Deb

Subj:　*Peaks and Valleys*
Date:　*10/7/00 1:35:59 PM Central Daylight Time*
From:　*sarahjf50@hotmail.com*
To:　*debbiesb13@aol.com*

Hi Deb,

　We're really having to work through some stuff with Anthony...it's very difficult but necessary. A prayer would be a wonderful gift from you about now!

　As for reading a book on depression, let me issue a caution: ask your therapist first. I know when I was in therapy my therapist told me to not read any depression/anxiety self help books, as it tends to increase one's preoccupation with the illness, and get in the way of the therapy. Rather like consulting two therapists at the same time. Maybe your therapist feels differently, but since she is in charge of your recovery program, I would get her opinion.

　Interesting question about your mom...I see you have normal responses, however, as you are looking at her realistically (she's 88). Here comes the domestic pschizo: guilt about not being more compassionate. For protection we sometimes try to distance ourselves from "caustic people," but that is not always possible. The reality is we can't change them so are we stuck?

　NO. WHAT WE MUST DO IS CHANGE OURSELVES—BECOME STRONG IN BROKEN PLACES. Part of that is happening in our e-mails. Part of that is happening in anti-depressant therapy, and part of it will happen in your cognitive therapy.

　You do have the power to change yourself, so these hurtful situations will not overpower you. You are taking the right steps. Good for you! Your future is bright!

　Many people would rather wallow in blame, anger, depression, self-pity, and self-abasement. You have chosen not to. You want to become strong and in control of your own happiness, rather than let someone else determine your happiness. Again, good for you!

　Must go, have to take some roses to my mom—my roses are doing so well, I have told them they are truly winners under very adverse conditions—maybe like you and me?
Love, Sal

Subj:　*Too much resemblance*
Date:　*10/7/00 1:42:39 PM Central Daylight Time*
From:　*sarahjf50@hotmail.com*
To:　*debbiesb13@aol.com*

　Glad you liked the pictures. Yes, I see a lot of myself in Anthony both physically and emotionally—that's probably the most distressing realization: your child has the same personality faults you do...hopefully I can use my history and knowledge of my failures to help him make better decisions.

But realistically? He'll make his own mistakes, anyway. Like Bill Cosby said, essentially, you pick them up, dust them off, and put them back in the race.

Gina and I went shopping yesterday, looking at pink baby things, and cribs, etc. It was fun, and something I needed after a difficult morning with Anthony. God may shut a window, but always opens a door.
Love, Sal

Subj: Peaks and valleys are right!
Date: 10/8/00 10:34:13 AM Central Daylight Time
From: debbiesb13@aol.com
To: sarahjf50@hotmail.com

Good Morning!

Hope the weekend is being more restful and relaxing for you than the week had been and that some of the rough edges have smoothed.

It is scary sometimes what of ourselves we see in our children! Sometimes don't you wonder why we can't just pass on the good things?

Do appreciate your caution on reading books about depression.

It is true that I find myself thinking too much about how I feel. Today, for example, is crappy! Back to the anxiety type feeling, but I'll leave it at that.

Knew you would understand about the mother guilt thing. Yes, it is we who must change, because they never will this late in the game.

Had fun with Tracey and Tristan yesterday. She brought her goddaughter. You're going to have so much fun with those little granddaughters!! I have a new "grandmother" name. I'm now "Grandma D." But wait it gets better — Tristan gave Tom a new name too. He is now "Grandpa Hotel!" At 3 years old, it seems perfectly logical to name someone for where they work.

Well, the dryer is buzzing, so I'll go for now. Have a great day.
Love, Deb

Subj: Children
Date: 10/8/00 11:36:50 AM Central Daylight Time
From: sarahjf50@hotmail.com
To: debbiesb13@aol.com

Good Sunday morning!

Sounds like you're in the valley right now! It happens and your job is to remember that you're not cured yet, and you will occasionally have these days where you don't feel so good. I know it's disappointing, after going through a few good days, you thought you would not go down there again. The good news is your episodes of anxiety are decreasing and will continue to decrease and become a rare occurrence. Try not to be too hard on yourself, do some things that are comforting. Ruefully admit that feeling crappy is part of your beast right now. It's not like you're backsliding or getting worse, it's just the remnants of months of strain on the brain.

There is one thing you can do to help yourself: do look at how much activity you have been having. Is there a chance that you've been taking on too much, since you've begun to feel better? Your down time may be brought on somewhat by exhaustion. Look at yourself as a case study, rather objectively, and examine your levels of activity and see if there is a pattern or correlation between "too much fun" and a subsequent down time. If so, you will know that even though you're having a great day, take it easy, don't do too much. You're dealing with a chemical imbalance that takes some time to adjust and you need to respect that process. Rather a balancing act.

Aren't grandchildren adorable? I look at young couples and think how much fun and activity (it was exhausting but not draining) we had as young parents.

As you mentioned "passing on the good things" to our kids has been important to me. Alas, I was not perfect: My own daughters bring up things from time to time, from the past that I did that really disturbed them. Their favorite was the time when I had had it with all of them—the squabbling, the messes, etc.—and Bob was way too busy at work to deal with the four kids, so I walked out of the house, told Tisa, who was 16, that I was leaving and to tell Dad to handle them. I drove to the park, sat in the back of my van and cried for a couple of hours, then finally went home. Scared the kids to death. Bob took it all in stride, we talked, worked things out, but the kids never forgot.

So yes, I, too, as a mother, am guilty of inflicting lifelong pain on my children. The salvation is that we, as a family, can talk about it, and I can validate their feelings. Someday they may understand where I was coming from, but that is not a realistic expectation. They will probably always feel I was temporarily insane. OH WELL!

Must go, lots to do today. Read a little Mitford, *if you need some solace, and remember everyone has dark days, and if we didn't, we wouldn't so treasure the good days.*
Love, Sal

Subj: speaking softly
Date: 10/9/00 11:46:08 AM Central Daylight Time
From: debbiesb13@aol.com
To: sarahjf50@hotmail.com

Hi Sally!
    Want to thank you for speaking softly and leading me gently along the path to recovery rather than saying, "Listen dummy, you're doing it wrong!" I will admit — I am impatient; force myself to do things to prove I can; and was completely worn out by Friday night, but kept going anyway, and it caught up with me yesterday. It is so hard at times to wait for the time frame laid out by God and the

medicines. But I am renewing my vow today to take things as they come, go back to breathing, which was sliding, and as you said, "respect the process."

As for your experience with your own children — I think they will every one understand someday why you walked out of the house. I can't think of anyone I know with teens who would not. And one day their kids will drive them to that point and a little light will go on and they'll say, "So, THIS is how we made Mom feel!"

I tend to be more of a yeller when I've had all I can take. The kids get this sort of volcanic eruption then I go for a walk or get out a book for whatever time it takes me to calm down. The interesting part is they don't seem to hold a grudge, whereas if they do the same to me, I stew on it for hours. (Not as bad as my mom though, she gave a three-day silent treatment.) Travis has, however, reminded me of one occasion where he thought my language went too far. I don't really remember it, but wouldn't deny it either.

I think it is reasonable to expect our kids to go through that right-of-passage time where they think their parents are just the worst. It is the fact that, hopefully, we do resume dialog on the other side that determines what happens afterwards.

You are now in my kitchen. My sink looks out to a corner of four windows with a ledge where I have little knick-knacks. I had created this sort of friendship corner with a picture from the last meeting of ladies at the wineless-wine-bar and a couple of others, so now you and Apple are there too.

There is no school here today. It is drizzly and cold. The plan is for a quiet relaxing day so I can follow your suggestions (which are GREATLY appreciated) and take it easy. I hope all is well with you.

Love, Deb

My Skin is Growing Longer

Subj: *monday musings*
Date: *10/9/00 1:22:11 PM Central Daylight Time*
From: *sarahjf50@hotmail.com*
To: *debbiesb13@aol.com*

Loved your newsy e-mail.

Okay, I have had some rough times with parenting, and it's wearing me out...not sleeping. Going to go not only to a therapist, but also the school's counselor to get some ideas on how to handle a difficult situation with our son.

Still want to co-author a book? How about this title: "My skin is growing longer, and my body's getting shorter."

I just had this awful realization when I was putting on my lipstick. My ear lobes are growing. Pretty soon I will probably have to lift them up to turn my head...also, have you ever leaned over and then looked at your face in the mirror? It is so scary: I look like Orson Welles in The Hunchback of Notre Dame. My skin totally falls forward, creating cheeks and jowls a bulldog would be proud of. Makes you think twice about being "on top" if you know what I mean.

Then there's my thigh skin. For years I thought it was just sagging because I was bending over to look at it, and that if I straightened up, it would all pull back up away from my knees. I now realize I was in denial about thigh skin. It begins a relentless march towards the ankles. That's why garters were invented...not to hold up stockings, but to hold up the thigh skin so you could see your knees. We just told the men it was for stockings so they would still find us attractive.

Then there are my TOTALLY over-extended, lax to the max, stomach muscles due to giving birth to four children, three of which were over 8 pounds, one was 10 pounds. My doctor shook his head and said no amount of exercising would get rid of the deflated balloon that used to be my tummy. Better to hide it or get surgery. So far hiding has worked...Only problem is when I sleep on my side it rests by itself on the bed, and I have to be careful not to roll over on it.

Then there's my double chin, which becomes a weather vane in a stiff breeze. I could get a job on a ship as an indicator of the change in wind position and velocity. When my chin starts slapping the side of my cheek, I would forecast a severe storm front approaching...and talk about insubordination: when I turn my head to look at something, my chin refuses to come, it just hangs there pouching.

I could go on and on, what with nails splitting, facial hair, leg cramps, reading glasses, memory loss. And this is all in one chapter. So, let me know your thoughts on skin growing...what has been your experience...let's write about it. This is good therapy.

I am so honored to be up on your windowsill, as you look at that picture of me and Apple, smile and think of loose skin. Must go, time to run errands.
Love, Sal

Subj: you could do stand-up
Date: 10/9/00 4:49:58 PM Central Daylight Time
From: debbiesb13@aol.com
To: sarahjf50@hotmail.com

Where would I be without getting a laugh from you today?! You could do a whole stand-up comedy routine on skin, Sally. I was laughing out loud.

Oh yes, I remember the doctor saying not only about the stomach, but the pelvic floor muscles as well, "Ha, Ha, Ha! Honey, those muscles will NEVER be the same!" Some sort of cruel joke don't you think. As for thinking twice about being on top, for some of us it is the only way to form an actual cleavage. On the bottom, your boobs just sort of fan out like jell-o on a plate, further victims of gravity.

On parenting: the best we can do is try to teach our kids to make smart choices, to be a good example for them, and to pick them up when they fall. No matter what, they will still make some mistakes. We can only pray together they won't be too major. And if they are, then we love them anyway, unconditionally, because they are still ours.

Well, there I was on my soapbox again. I can't think of lose skin with that picture in the kitchen. You will have to send one with the leaning forward in the mirror look, and even then I'm skeptical. Must go pick up Austin.
Sleep tight. Love, Deb

Subj: *Jell-o Boobs*
Date: *10/10/00 9:00:35 AM Central Daylight Time*
From: *sarahjf50@hotmail.com*
To: *debbiesb13@aol.com*

Good morning!

My stomach and I arose this morning and are trying to get into the day here! I have jell-o boobs! Also referred to as cherry tomatoes. Only part of me that doesn't sag, as there isn't enough to go anywhere…but they do dissolve into nothing when I am on my back.

God must have been in a good mood when he put me together. He thought, "Here's little Sarah Jane, can't make her too ugly or too pretty, because she has work to do for me, and I don't want her to let her concern for her appearance get in the way" (he forgot about the sagging skin, obviously). "If I made her pretty, she would be vain, if I made her homely, she would never come out of her house…so I'll give her this mediocre body and good sense of humor. Then I will bless her with the Holy Spirit to encourage her to use her earthly temple as a beacon of light for others to find me. Therein will lie her true beauty."

Yes, Deb, I will acknowledge I have that inner spirit, but I don't nurture it enough, and I pray for the guidance to do His work as a lighthouse.

My dog wants me to play with her...so I'm typing with one hand, playing tug-of-war with the other.

You are right about the children, even though they may make major mistakes, we still love them unconditionally...it's a blessing from God to love at that level.

Seeing a therapist this morning to discuss my parenting concerns. Want to get her professional advice. Also, when I start losing sleep on a regular basis, and losing my appetite, that sends up warning signals to me that I need to pay attention to this issue and make sure I'm on the right track. She may just tell me to keep plodding along...which is fine, as long as she thinks I'm plodding on the right path. Will see!

Have a good day, dear friend! Will check in with you later and see how the day is for you!
Love, Sal

Subj: why are we in these hand baskets?
Date: 10/10/00 2:05:21 PM Central Daylight Time
From: debbiesb13@aol.com
To: sarahjf50@hotmail.com

Hi Sal!

Hope you found your time at the therapist helpful. It concerns me for you to be losing sleep and your appetite...as in it sounds a little too familiar. I know you are strong and know what to do. But, you aren't getting in this hand basket with me are you? I am praying, not, but want to know how you're feeling about things.

I was in Walgreen's at the check out and started laughing about thigh skin. The lady says, "What are you laughing about?" Now how do you tell someone you are thinking of an e-mail your best friend wrote to you about thigh skin?! She would have thought I was loony for sure (OK, I am, but that's not the point).

And about that temple, I don't know where you're getting all this stuff. The Sally I met is a tall slender woman who carries herself gracefully. And unless you have done something major to yourself since those wedding pictures were taken you are still that same person. I couldn't believe the other day on the phone you thought of yourself as Rubenesque.

That is me — perfectly Rubenesque. Short, large butt, microscopic boobs, round tummy. I will not take responsibility for the butt, as it is the same one found on ALL the women on my mother's side of the family — large and square. My philosophy on this is two-fold. First, I was born in the wrong century, just about 400 years late, a mere timing error between me and beauty. Second, it could be altered in some way, but why? It wouldn't be real then would it? (And actually, I'm not sure you can shave off pelvic bones.) Think of bodies as you might a vintage car — one that has been refurbished brings a fairly good price and is nice to look at, but one that is well taken care of and has all it's original parts — now that's a prize. (Do

96

not misconstrue that into thinking I think of myself as a prize — hardly! The point is we are what we are, and even a Corvair is now a classic car.)

Going to lay down and read a little *Mitford* (I do still get tired). Looking forward to hearing from you later about your day.

Love, Deb

Subj: life is still okay!
Date: 10/10/00 5:40:09 PM Central Daylight Time
From: sarahjf50@hotmail.com
To: debbiesb13@aol.com

Deb,

Don't worry, I am okay, but this year's many family crises are taking their toll on me.

I told my counselor all that has gone on in the past few months and asked her opinion on many subjects, including going back on my anti-depressant, even though I am not at that depressed a level, other than not sleeping. She reacted much like you have reacted to all my sob stories: she said I have had too many major issues this year, which were out of my control to prevent, and she thinks I am strong. She asked me how I have managed to stay on top of all this. I said, "God." It's that simple. I told her I am walking very close with God on a daily basis, and know He will see me through this.

I just wasn't sure if I should include drug therapy in my program. Her answer was an unconditional yes. She said (just like I have told you) that the drug will help my physical issues, of the neurotransmitters having to deal with too many stressors, which tends to make them shut down (overload reaction). I will take an anti-depressant just like before, and will taper off after 6 months. If my family continues to have constant crises, then I will simply be moving to the south of France. I am not at a bad place, emotionally, don't need anti-anxiety meds, etc, but I have learned to be very aware of these warning signs and get professional advice to maintain a healthy mind and body.

Let's face it, this has been a difficult year for me...but I, rather like Pollyana nursing a boo-boo, think I'm handling it well despite everything.
Must go for now.
Love, Sal

Subj: maintaining sanity
Date: 10/10/00 7:43:12 PM Central Daylight Time
From: debbiesb13@aol.com
To: sarahjf50@hotmail.com

Hi My Friend!

I felt much better after reading your e-mail tonight. (I think it's important for at least one of us to maintain a modicum of sanity at all times). Just kidding. I really am concerned that you're feeling OK. I think going back on your anti-depressant sounds like a good idea. I'm not sure I would ever care to go off them, if it meant going through another period even remotely like this. On the other hand, I greatly admire that you can and have been successful doing that, putting your faith in God. I have certainly put mine in Him to help me through this, but would not yet be ready to wing it on prayer alone so to speak.

Your parenting challenges really ring a bell here too. It is so hard when they are seeking their independence, but not quite yet ready to fly alone.

I got pictures back today of us tubing on the river last summer. I'm sending you one of neck skin. Sending this picture is a true statement of trust!

Well, that's about it for now I guess.

Love, Deb

Subj: how's it going?
Date: 10/11/00 10:25:38 AM Central Daylight Time
From: debbiesb13@aol.com
To: sarahjf50@hotmail.com

Hi Sal!

Thinking about you and hoping you are finding some solutions. I think issues with our kids are really the most demanding of us emotionally.

So did the doctor go OK? Do you go through that sleepy period again?

I really liked the therapy session today. I actually felt good afterwards. Mary Jo gave me a tough question to think about over the next week. I'm not sure I'll ever know the answer, but will give it much thought. You were so right about the direction of a Christian therapist and the way the values etc. are incorporated into your life, outlook and discussion. You have given me such great guidance — where would I be without you? Probably in the rubber room at that stupid hospital.

Well, I'm going for now. More later.

Love, Deb

Subj: just rambling
Date: 10/11/00 2:49:05 PM Central Daylight Time
From: debbiesb13@aol.com
To: sarahjf50@hotmail.com

Hi There,

Talked to Nancy, the hospice chaplain today. She had an interesting observation. She said people who have basically positive outlooks on life (Pollyanas) have a harder time recognizing when they are in a valley. I thought that was an extremely interesting thought. Also thought it was interesting she used that term valley which you had used just the other day.

Hear (pun intended) is something I forgot to tell you. Can't believe when you were talking about ear lobes and skin I didn't remember it. I had plastic surgery when I was 17. On my ears: they stuck out like Howdy Doody - very literally! I hated it and was so self-conscious about pulling my hair back. I went to school with lots of kids who got nose jobs, so I thought plastic surgery was very cool. Begged my mom, and she said OK. I would like to say it was stupid and that I'm now above all that. Not true, I'm still there.

Still hoping and praying that you had a good day today and have found some resolution to the conflicts that are daunting you. You know I'm here for you either way.

Love, Deb

Subj: *I am so slow!*
Date: *10/12/00 10:44:45 AM Central Daylight Time*
From: *sarahjf50@hotmail.com*
To: *debbiesb13@aol.com*

Good Morning!

Do you wear reading glasses? I do but I am always leaving them someplace... found a pair on the back seat of the car yesterday. When I have my contacts in (so I can see far away) I cannot read close up. When my contacts are out, I can't see far away, but I can read close up...when I wear my regular—near sighted—glasses, I can see far away, but have to take them off to read anything. So, I now have three pairs of reading glasses—somewhere—I honestly cannot tell you where even one pair is right now.

Hope you still can find time to ponder on the tough question your therapist posed for you. Sounds interesting! But don't feel you have to tell me what the question is.

The therapist may have already told you that your sessions are private, and sometimes it is better not to share some subjects with other people, as the therapist wants you to work through this on your own, without outside input. She is in the job of getting into your true feelings, and sometimes that's difficult if you are talking (and listening) to your family/friends about your therapy sessions.

As for my life, am on a lower dose of anti-depressant than usual, and hopefully it will be adequate, as I always felt tired on the larger dose. Drank a lot of coffee!

Interesting about the chaplain's view on positive "Pollyana" people and valleys. I agree! I think we (you, me, all positive people) do not like valleys, and try to ignore them, try to run across them as fast as we can, not looking back, not paying attention to the mud until we're stuck in it. Then we go, "Where did this mud come from?" And our friends and family say, "Silly!!! You've been in the valley, what did you expect?" Well, we expected not to get our feet dirty! The only problem is sometimes the mud is deeper and wider than we expected, and no amount of positive outlook can prevent us from wading through.

Right now, for example, our feet are muddy. We hate it, we are disappointed and embarrassed we have to have dirty feet. As the mud falls off, as we cleanse ourselves of the dirt, we are learning about those mud holes, and how to avoid them in the future. Part of that is learning about the valley, taking our time and paying attention to where we are going in the valley. And you know one beautiful thing I have learned about walking through the valley? Sometimes, when it has been too much for me, God has lifted me onto his shoes and walked me across the mud...

Must go! Time to get on with this day...I need to rake and mow.

You are sounding like you're feeling a little better, is this true? Do you feel a little less foggy?

Take care, have a great day!

Love, Sal

IV

Purple Hearts

*

On the Battlefield

Post Traumatic Stress

It Feels Right (...or Is That Wrong?)

The Drug Wars

Two Are Better Than One

A Time To Die

Autumn Star: A Poem

Skeletons in the Closet

*

On the Battlefield

Subj: anyone who can build a gate from chopsticks is NOT slow
Date: 10/12/00 1:07:22 PM Central Daylight Time
From: debbiesb13@aol.com
To: sarahjf50@hotmail.com

Hi Sally!

Hope it's as beautiful a day there as here. Just came home from shopping and took your e-mail outside to read and have lunch on the deck. Maybe there is something to be said for this mental relaxation after all!

Yes, I wear reading glasses and have since turning 40. I also have a slight distance correction for one eye, so now I wear the progressive lenses. The eye doctor tried to get me to do a contact in each, one for distance and one for reading, but that was too complex for my pea brain. Glasses will be fine thank you.

Sal, about the therapist question: You should know by now I have very few if any secrets from you — things we may not have gotten to, yes, but not much of anything I would not trust to tell you. I thought about telling you the question, but was not sure you would want to know as it deals with the day my dad died. I'm never really sure how much of that to discuss with you as I am sure it brings back things from your recent loss of your own father that you may not want to discuss. So you can tell me if you want to or not. If you don't want to know skip the rest of this paragraph, I guess. On the day my dad died my mother wouldn't sit with him, hold his hand, or offer him any comfort (in fact she had not done so through most of his illness), and the question was how did I feel? I couldn't answer that. I could tell Mary Jo everything I thought and did, but not how I felt. I don't even know really if I can go back and ever recapture what I might have felt. So that's the question.

About my therapy: Mary Jo did not say anything about the wisdom of talking to or not talking to my friends or family about my therapy. You and I have already determined that sharing our thoughts is helping.

Really liked your being in the mud analogy. How very true.

You asked how I'm feeling. Well, last night was the first night off the anti-anxiety drug, and this morning was a little rough. Although I can still function fairly well. I'm just going along trying to pretend I'm normal. Like mother like daughter — denial!

Today my aunt who died in December would have been 90. This is amusing, her husband of over thirty years went to his grave thinking she was 10 years younger than she was. All my mother's sisters have such a hang up on age! Once he saw her passport and said, "Look sweetie, they made a mistake on your birthdate." Men are soooo naive. When I was a child she lived next door to us and would take me downtown to Woolworth's and let me pick out something for a quarter. I would take forever looking over all the fake jewelry as if it were the greatest treasure. Did you ever do that? Where were you then, Washington? Isn't it funny how we remember certain things from our childhood? Like you with Beatrice and the grits.

OK, must go. Promised Travis he could use the computer at 1:00. I really want my own laptop. Some day.

Love, Deb

Subj: *Oh My Gosh!!!*
Date: *10/12/00 6:28:54 PM Central Daylight Time*
From: *sarahjf50@hotmail.com*
To: *debbiesb13@aol.com*

Dear Pal Deb,
   What is it with the parallels in our lives! Listen to this: you know the story you just e-mailed me about being in Woolworth's, and, in the same paragraph, you asked me about where I was when I was about that age, in Washington? This is one of my most vivid childhood memories: Yes, not only was I in Washington at age 5 or 6, but also I went to Woolworth's with my parents. They left me in the little girls' department, as I loved clothes, even then. I wandered over to the pet department, attracted by the parakeets. Then I got disoriented and could not find my parents. I walked out to the street looking for our car, but could not find it and started crying (This was in the 1950's—a gentler time). Two elderly ladies took me back into the store and had my parents paged. Happy ending.
   Isn't it interesting how we can have a memorable experience in the same named department store, and you just sort of ask me if I was in Washington about that age. How did you know, Deb?
   Look for the e-mail to follow.
Love, Sal

Subj: *therapeutic*
Date: *10/12/00 7:03:21 PM Central Daylight Time*
From: *sarahjf50@hotmail.com*
To: *debbiesb13@aol.com*

Dear Deb,
   Thanks for the stuff about how you feel about sharing things with me. I think a great friendship transcends these kinds of limits, but some rare times, it's important to respect another's privacy, no questions asked, just know you're safe with me, no matter what you decided to, or not to, divulge.
   The story about your father's death is very tender and sad to me. I am not sure what was going through your mind at the time, but it sounds like you were focused on your relationship and experience with your father, and anything else that was happening at the time was secondary, even the way your mom was

handling/not handling it. You knew what you needed to do, and hang everybody else.

It rather reminds me of the mentality that a soldier must adopt when he is on the battlefield: he must keep going, not stop to grieve over a wounded or dead comrade, because if he does, he may put his own life, and the cause he is fighting for, in jeopardy. He is there, defending a larger cause than his own emotions. He must override those, so he can achieve the goal of keeping the platoon moving forward, and capturing the hill.

I think your goal (your cause) was to have a special experience with your father, right to the end, and anything else just paled in comparison. Were you mad at your mom? Ask yourself, did you even care enough about anything else at the time—other than your father dying—to have emotion about it? Sometimes God gives us the saving grace of no emotion so we can move on and do what is most important. I guess it's also called numbness, but it is a bridge we take when we do not have the capacity to deal with a lot of issues at once.

Now that time has passed, you are a safe distance to look back on that and think about it, and see if you have any feelings to acknowledge. God has given you the blessing of distance from the event, so you can look into it and learn from it, without being so close to it, it swallows you up. Learn from your journey back there, that is all that is asked.

On your drugs and your shaking. Maybe I can help. When you suffer from anxiety, the shaking hands and pounding heart would not be a constant symptom. They would occur in "attacks" that would subside after a few minutes. What you are describing sounds like a mega dose of caffeine—nothing to do with going crazy or anxiety. Sounds like reaction to a drug you are taking—what all are you taking? Let's look them up on the internet, and check out drug interaction and stuff.

Also, how much caffeine do you consume during the day? Even a couple of cups of regular tea may be too much given the medications you are taking. I would approach it from the point of view of drug reaction, Deb, as it doesn't sound like anxiety. At any rate, let's get to the bottom of this right now, as it is getting in the way of your feeling better. drkoop.com is the web site you can go to for drug info. Let me know if you want me to help you with this.

Will let you go—two long e-mails in one day will get in the way of your life! Tom and the boys will start hiding the computer…

Love, sleep well, and do you have a name for your guardian angel? Mine is named Elizabeth and she's always working overtime, as I am a hazardous site! Your pal Sal

Post Traumatic Stress

Subj: Sally, I have a problem
Date: 10/12/00 7:31:02 PM Central Daylight Time
From: debbiesb13@aol.com
To: sarahjf50@hotmail.com

     Need your help my friend. The doctor's office called after 5:00 in response to my call on Monday about the trembling hands etc. They said cut back both drugs. I said OK but the more I thought about it the more anxiety ridden I became. The nurse said something about trying other drugs etc. I CANNOT DEAL WITH THIS! So now what do I do? Take the medicine for anxiety anyway before I become a basket case and call them in the morning or what?
Your desperate lost soul friend, Deb.

Subj: I'm here
Date: 10/12/00 7:35:43 PM Central Daylight Time
From: sarahjf50@hotmail.com
To: debbiesb13@aol.com

Dear Deb,
    I would call you but I don't have your phone number! E-mail it to me.
    In answer to your question, take the anti-anxiety med, be calm, until you can get this straightened out with the doctor. It should not make you jittery...
    Give me a list of your drugs and I will look them up in drkoop.
Love, Sal—will call you right away if you want me to—just e-mail your number.

Subj: thank you so much
Date: 10/13/00 8:27:55 AM Central Daylight Time
From: debbiesb13@aol.com
To: sarahjf50@hotmail.com

Good Morning my Friend!
    You missed your calling as a counselor/therapist. Cannot thank you enough for talking me through that rough spot, no make that very deep hole in the mud, possibly quick sand, last night. The advice and calming influence helped more than you know, or maybe that's it, you do know! As for the difference this morning - I slept till 5:30, my hands are still shaky, but not as bad, and instead of a pounding heart it is more like a racing one.
    On a more serious note, you are doing it too. I couldn't quite go there last night. I wanted to, but couldn't. When you wrote about the analogy of the soldier. It

is almost exactly what Mary Jo had said to me on Wednesday. She said what I was experiencing was similar to a post-traumatic stress syndrome that a soldier might experience in combat. (What you said sent a chill right through me when I read it).

My dad's death was imminent and I was focused on so many details: being there for him first and foremost, being there for myself; trying to help my mom cope so that she would not regret her actions. The day before he died she had a major bladder infection and would not get out of bed, refused her meds, hit and spit at the nurses. On top of everything, it seemed she would have to be hospitalized until the director of nursing insisted on antibiotic shots for her. Tom and I are convinced my dad held on one extra day for her to get through that. Then I had to make all the necessary arrangements for his funeral, and at the same time, shift my primary focus to comforting my mother in her loss.

God has given me the distance from the event, and yes I can look back without being so swallowed up by it; but I still can't say how it felt. Other than maybe very painful. And yes I was mad at my mother. I was mad because that one day I needed her to be strong and be MY mother, not the other way around, but she wouldn't do it. However, I'm softening in these last few weeks to see, that maybe she COULDN'T do it for me then, anymore than I can go to her now. It is just so complex or maybe it's so simple I can't see it. Nevertheless, I think it is incredible that your analogy would be so similar.

As for a name for my guardian angel — I never thought about having one. A name, not a guardian angel. I know I have one as he or she (had never really thought about gender either) has DEFINITELY been by my side on many occasions. Where did you get Elizabeth? Maybe mine should be Sarah Jane.

Will write back later after I talk to or go to the doctor. Have a great day!
Love, Deb

Subj: TGIF!
Date: 10/13/00 3:41:38 PM Central Daylight Time
From: sarahjf50@hotmail.com
To: debbiesb13@aol.com

Well, well, we just keep on connecting don't we? A lot of it is because I have been where you are, and have had the hindsight to see some of these patterns in myself.

I do think that we should look at depression as a good sign (yes, that's right: a GOOD sign). It is our body signaling that the danger is over, it is now time to heal, to catch up, to take inventory, to have some down time to recoup the strength. What therapy will help you with is identifying the stressors while they're happening so rather than holding it all in and coping, coping, coping, you can learn to have releases while the issues are popping, popping, popping. That way you won't get the depression after the fact, that sends you into the mud puddle.

Also, I got your pictures, thanks so much!! Your mom looks pretty good for 88! Also, I have to take issue with your neck skin: your shoulder was pushed up and it made your skin fold! The only part of that picture that was a little unpleasant was the man's hairy leg in front of you!

Here's a question maybe you can answer for me. Why, when men's legs are so incredibly hairy, and women just have fuzz, why do women shave their peach fuzz but men don't shave theirs? If anyone should shave their body hairs, it should be men, for heaven's sake...and then there's the whole issue of underarm hair. If a man sees a woman with underarm hair it is so gross, and she's probably rather "manly"...but with men, it's accepted to have hairy pits, and they sure don't try to hide them (much to our dismay). I'm sorry, it's still a man's world when it comes to hair...

Then there's the opposite issue of facial hair. They can shave and it's okay, or they can grow a beard. But let a middle aged woman get a few hormonal (perfectly natural) chin hairs and she becomes a hag...What is going on Deb? Why are women always removing hair from their bodies, while most men just coast hairily along, complaining that they have to shave every day, like that's a big cosmetic deal.

AND let's not even go into why we do the whole make-up thing and they don't. The sad end to this dissertation is that I will continue to pluck, shave, and wax anyway, because I would be afraid I would start looking like a man...

HEY!!!...maybe, that's it! We're trying to be as far from men as possible, by denuding our whole bodies!! What do you think, are we shaving to attract them or shaving to make a statement of separation of the sexes?

I am glad you are talking about your mom and dad...probably you have an occasional "Aha," as Father Tim says. A moment of understanding about yourself. It sounds like it was a very, very difficult time...I can't imagine what was running through your head, during all this, except that you just had to do the right thing...post traumatic stress, sounds close! You were a good soldier...I may have to give you a red heart for love and compassion in the line of duty. Now it's time to heal, tired friend!

Elizabeth just came to me, as I was walking through Wal-Mart one day. It sounded right for my angel.

Here's a piece of scripture I am trying to memorize, thought you might like to read it: Philippians 4:4-9. It actually is two paragraphs so I'll memorize one at a time, as my brain would probably bleed if I tried to put too many words in there at once...But the message Paul is giving speaks to my heart, and I wanted to share it with you.

Must dash. A bientot, mon chere amie!

Sal

Subj: Yes! we have so much to be thankful for
Date: 10/13/00 5:41:56 PM Central Daylight Time
From: debbiesb13@aol.com
To: sarahjf50@hotmail.com

Dear Sal,

Well, much has happened today and there is so much in your e-mail to reply to!

I like this doctor (the psychiatrist) more and more. She has my behavior nailed. Without my even saying, she told me exactly everything that happened last night (with the exception of our phone call of course). So here's the deal. I'm switching to different anti-anxiety and anti-depressant meds. And yes, the drugs do have a cumulative effect, so I don't go back to square one, and still get credit for the two weeks on the current drug so to speak. So that's good to know, yes?

Read your bit of scripture. Isn't it amazing how God has become such an important part of our communication and friendship — coming at us from so many different realms in our daily lives, and truly giving us peace.

I can agree with you now that, yes, depression can be a good sign. I wouldn't have thought so initially. But it is sort of an awakening to a better way of doing things next time so to speak. Going around the mud puddle maybe?

One other thing from the doctor: She said to me, "Do I have to come with you and hold your hand?" I said, "No, I have a friend who's doing that." She said, "I thought you looked like a hand holding woman." Now what does that mean? At first I thought it was funny. Then I thought maybe she was saying I'm weak. But why would a psychiatrist say that?

Well, that's about it for now. Peace be with you!!!!!
Love, Deb

Subj: Hair, etc.
Date: 10/14/00 11:14:32 AM Central Daylight Time
From: debbiesb13@aol.com
To: sarahjf50@hotmail.com

Hi Sally!

There are a lot of things to think about on the subject of hair. For example, last night my friend refused to consider using our hot tub because she had not shaved her legs. Why would that be? It doesn't contaminate the water. No men were going to be present. So what is it about women that they will not be seen even with each other wearing stubble? I could not understand, but got no discussion on the matter.

Then there is the leg shaving curse that we have at our house. Shaving my legs for the purpose of romance is a guarantee that absolutely no romance will occur. Something will happen if even at the last minute to waylay what ever plans are made. The phone rings, the dog wants out, a child needs to ask a question, someone comes to the door, a dead possum explodes in the attic, and by then someone has gone to sleep (usually me) and the moment has passed.

So, why do we remove all this body hair and they don't? Think you're right we don't want to look like them. Or most us of don't anyway. Maybe it's the statement that attracts them. But what about us? How are we attracted to them? It must go beyond hair. Did you know licorice is supposed to be the #1 aroma for attracting the opposite sex? So what does that mean? We are supposed to be tucking little pieces of licorice in our bras if we want to be attractive? What if you only like the red kind? What does that attract?

Here is my thought on makeup. Mascara is a must (even in the depths of depression). Without it I have bunny rabbit eyes. If you ever see me, even sick, without mascara you know something is seriously wrong.

I thought maybe you got Elizabeth from your interest in queens. It's a nice name. So what queen was it you were supposed to be? Or was that just something you said in passing?

Hoping you are having a great and peaceful weekend, enjoying the outdoors and your family.

Love, Deb

Subj: *holding hands*
Date: *10/15/00 11:04:25 AM Central Daylight Time*
From: *sarahjf50@hotmail.com*
To: *debbiesb13@aol.com*

Are you a hand holder? I certainly hope so. We all have times when holding our hand is needed. The question is, do we have the strength and honesty to admit it and ask for that hand? Then there are those times when we need to hold someone else's hand to help them. One of the most wonderful actions we can perform in life. Being a mother develops strong hands, don't you think? My husband and I hold hands when we're walking places. I always have hold of little Zachary's hand when we're out in the big world. I hold my own hands when I pray.

So, in answer to your question why would a psychiatrist ask you if you were a hand holder and if she was indicating you were weak, I would think she was acknowledging that you needed her attention a little more than usual on Friday, you were a little more anxious, and you needed a helping hand. As for weak, yes, you are weak right now and yes, any help that goes toward making you stronger is welcome!

You are weak in that you are emotionally exhausted. Your strength of character and ability to cope under extremely difficult situations is still there. In other words, I think she was just commenting on your temporary need for extra help. She knows what you've been through and how you have survived, so I don't think there's any doubt about your ability to endure!

Nice sunny day today, kids coming for dinner. Good day to take the football to the park. Will hope that you have had a lovely day yourself!
Love, Sal

Subj: blessings on Sunday
Date: 10/15/00 4:29:14 PM Central Daylight Time
From: debbiesb13@aol.com
To: sarahjf50@hotmail.com

Hi there my friend!
It is so nice to hear your voice of happiness and reason. You can always find the forest and I can't seem to even focus on the tree? Why didn't I look at the hand holder question like that. Of course I love to hold Tom's hand anytime, and Tristan's and all four kids when they were little, and all those little ones at Trinity, and I held my dad's hand so many times. And, yes, there have been times mine was the one being held, and sometimes I was the holder. Someday there will be this part of my brain that can actually process information and find perspective. Instead of this feeling I'm always racing down hill on one ski bumping into all the trees. Hopefully I will have this resolved before one of them takes me out.
Enough wallowing. I hope you're having a lovely day with your family eating some tremendous comfort food enjoying this beautiful weather.
Tom and I are going to sit outside, play Scrabble, and cook some hamburgers in a while. Austin has friends over and Travis has gone to the Pearl Jam concert (the new greatest day of his life.)
Sorry Sal, the new meds make me a little sad and too tired to even think. This too shall pass. Will try again tomorrow.
Love, Deb

It Feels Right: or Is That Wrong?

Subj: on the right path
Date: 10/16/00 2:53:56 PM Central Daylight Time
From: sarahjf50@hotmail.com
To: debbiesb13@aol.com

Dear Sad Deb,
        I loved the poem you just sent. How odd the prayer I just sent to you basically says the same thing. Wait on the Lord.
        The weather today is lovely, breezy, lots of clouds floating by! I have just been doing little house things. Will take Anthony after school to get his truck.
        For dinner yesterday, to feed the starving pregnant hordes, we had chicken parmesan, garlic pasta, zucchini and salad. The girls were a little cranky...each for her own reason, other than being pregnant.
        Wait...let's interrupt this program for an announcement: I keep forgetting to tell you that you should be receiving a little package for Tristan in the mail.
        Back to our regularly scheduled paragraph: Zachary has memorized the words to his book about the Lady and the Alligator Purse. He knows all the words and will recite them as you turn the pages. It's so cute. His rendition of the title is, "Ladee wif duh owigatoh puss." Thank heavens for little boys (and girls!)
        Oh, my laundry is buzzing, time to fold! Take care dear Deb! Go ahead and feel sad, it's a release and a relief, maybe!
Love, Sal

Subj: good morning!
Date: 10/17/00 7:46:18 AM Central Daylight Time
From: debbiesb13@aol.com
To: sarahjf50@hotmail.com

Good morning1
        This is a mentally visually challenged hello tro start your day. In other words, meds are on the upswing and I forgot my glasses.
        Thanks for being understanding about being sad. Most people try to give you a lot of rah-rah stuff instead of just respecting the moment.
        Just thought I would wish you a bright and cheerful day before starting out to save the world from injustice (translation, save the poor little town of Humble from having an addle brained woman sit on a jury)
        How are you feeling? Less stressed? Wishing you a beautiful, happy day.
Love, Deb

Subj: *I'm okay*
Date: *10/17/00 7:06:26 PM Central Daylight Time*
From: *sarahjf50@hotmail.com*
To: *debbiesb13@aol.com*

Dear Deb,

I have many answers to your questions, but I have run out of time today to answer them! Ended up running errands with my mom, then Gina popped in earlier than usual, now Bob's on his way home from work.

At the moment I am plugging along, surviving well. I can only attribute any of my good habits, as far as coping skills, to my increased faith in God, and perceiving a better perspective of family issues, based on scripture.

Another tool, which I have learned the hard way: Understand that feelings are based on beliefs. We believe something to be so, and we react to that with feelings. Sometimes our feelings about people are based on beliefs we have created from trying to guess what they are thinking or what motivates them. Our guesses (hence our beliefs) could be wrong, which means our feelings are wrong. The moral of this story: don't trust your feelings if they're based on judgment made without all the facts.

This has happened to me many times with people. I make up my own rendition of why they did something, and I get upset, only to find out later, they had a legitimate reason for their behavior, and had I taken the time to talk to them, I would have avoided a lot of bad, unnecessary feelings. Communication is the only way to honestly try to deal with people—I have learned the hard way, not to make up my own version of the situation.

Take care, dear friend, you are sounding better all the time. Feeling better, tiny bit by bit?
Love Sal

Subj: That's Good
Date: 10/18/00 11:16:22 AM Central Daylight Time
From: debbiesb13@aol.com
To: sarahjf50@hotmail.com

Dear Amiga Mia,

I'm going to have to refresh my Spanish. You wouldn't believe this now, but I took Spanish for 6 years and was actually reasonably fluent at one time. Now I can count to ten. I'm glad you're OK.

More connections: Went to the doctor this morning. I had the *Rise and Shine* book with me as it fits in my purse easily and is pleasant reading while waiting. I opened to the spot where I left off and there is the opening verse Phil. 4:8. There you were wishing me a good morning with a prayer from your heart. How did YOU know, Sal?

I'm doing OK on these meds except it is not that "normal" feeling. My mood vacillates, and one of these drugs makes my equilibrium a bit off. (Probably not the best thing for someone who is already clumsy.)

Thanks for the advice on not letting my feelings take control when the facts are missing. You know Sally, there was a time I was a sane, intelligent, patient, individual who could see these things. I will be so glad when that person comes back to live within me.

Today I got a fortune cookie that said, "You are patient." That's a laugh! Proving there is absolutely nothing to the theory the fortune cookie pointing at you holds the message intended for you.

I need to go back and read the prayers on patience, maybe memorize them. Hang them from the mirror in the bathroom, perhaps some *Mission Impossible* type glasses I could wear and read them at the same time.

Are you still going to see the therapist for a while or was that just a one time consultation?

Will send this now, and write more later.

Hasta Luego, Deb

Subj: *Yo hablo espanol tambien!*
Date: *10/19/00 9:14:06 AM Central Daylight Time*
From: *sarahjf50@hotmail.com*
To: *debbiesb13@aol.com*

Another thing we have in common: I took four years of Spanish, two of French, thinking I was going to travel the world someday...Now I, like you, have forgotten most of what I learned. However, I think if we took a refresher course, combined with the fact we would actually pay attention this time (I was always thinking about my social life), we could catch up, if needed.

You know, Deb, God is doing things to you like he does to me: your story about Philippians 4:8. Those kinds of things happen to me often. That's when I know I'm going down the right track, he's giving me signposts. Yesterday I started memorizing Phil. 4:6-7. It is the cornerstone of my prayer life.

Your mood vacillating with your new meds could be a good thing: not quite so insulated as before. Maybe a little more like real life, even though it's unpleasant, at times. This would be a good time to practice looking at your feelings, realizing they are only feelings, not always to be relied upon, and become more objective about the way they may control your life. And analyze the belief that provokes that feeling. How reliable is that belief?

Last winter I prayed for God to send me a friend when we had moved to north Texas. I am always amazed at how he answers our prayers, as he sent me a friend who is a real kindred spirit, and with whom I have so many connections—and I don't have to go anywhere to talk to her, she's here every day, only an e-mail away.

Vaya con Dios, Sal

Subj: Alliance Francais (sp?)
Date: 10/19/00 10:35:33 AM Central Daylight Time
From: debbiesb13@aol.com
To: sarahjf50@hotmail.com

Morning Sal!
     We're going to have to start keeping some kind of tally on similarities. I also took French after I came back from Europe thinking I'd go back. Here's what I learned—do not date a mama's boy from your class with a big German shepherd as it will take a large chuck of flesh from your butt which will itch for years and leave an odd bulge in your bathing suit. Can also count to ten in French. Here's what I got from my days of fluent Spanish—a marriage proposal from a bus boy on a cruise ship who wanted to be an American resident. Who knows what would happen if I tried some other languages!
     My mood swings were out of control this morning, but I am feeling good now. I woke up all trembling, nauseous and crying. It took about two hours for the anti-anxiety med to kick in and get things right. I have difficulties, I guess, separating the feelings from the physical symptoms.
     Sal, I had prayed for a friend as well when we went to that conference in Florida as I felt so overwhelmed not knowing a soul in the company. The friend God gave me in you is beyond my expectations!
     Vaya con Dios tambien mi amiga.
Love, Deb

The Drug Wars

Subj: So what's cooking?
Date: 10/20/00 4:13:47 PM Central Daylight Time
From: debbiesb13@aol.com
To: sarahjf50@hotmail.com

Hi Sal!

Well, I'm feeling better today, but seem to be running into things. Nothing major has been injured so far. We have a fairly quiet weekend planned. I think Tom and I have the house to ourselves tonight. Thought I'd fix him a nice little dinner, hit the hot tub, and maybe a game of Scrabble.

Will pray you have a glorious family weekend with Andrea home. Enjoy yourself my friend.

Love, Deb

Subj: scheduling surgery
Date: 10/22/00 10:17:56 AM Central Daylight Time
From: debbiesb13@aol.com
To: sarahjf50@hotmail.com

Good Morning Sal!

Hope you have had a wonderful weekend. It has been a quiet weekend around here, which is good since I am so up and down with these medicines. Yesterday I evidently hit my rearview mirror on the side of the garage and didn't even know it till later. I am calling tomorrow to sign up for a lobotomy. Enough is enough. Hope you have a happy day. Blessings to you.

Love, Deb

Subj: to everything there is a season…
Date: 10/23/00 9:21:41 AM Central Daylight Time
From: sarahjf50@hotmail.com
To: debbiesb13@aol.com

Good Monday morning!

Had to sit down and read your e-mails, catch up on how you're doing and write a little. Priorities, right?

Our weekend was very full and fun. We had great dinners and great fun. Our daughter Andrea is doing okay! I know she enjoyed seeing her brother and sisters again and she absolutely adores Bob, so she spent a lot of time with him. I wish her a happy life, hoping her dreams will come true. With her being 1000 miles away, it is hard to do anything to help her out. I always tell her that our door is open and, she can always come home where she is loved and supported.

I know you remember (because I keep talking about it) that as of my birthday, next Monday, there will be no more stress and strife as this year has been so full of poopy things. Well, apparently we're going out of this year with a bang: as Bob received a phone call from his dad last night and his mother is very ill. She was on chemo for liver cancer, but her cancer had metastasized, and now they have taken her off chemo, and said it's no use. She is suffering from dozens of problems, and she's so miserable. She is pleading with Bob's dad to take her home from the hospital, but she is in such bad condition he can't take care of her at home, the hospice is full, and he doesn't like the look of the convalescent homes he's seen so far. The doctor would not tell him how long he felt she had to live, but she has so many different illnesses that we are all amazed she's held on this long.

Bob will have to fly out there sometime in the next couple of weeks. Please say a prayer for her to have some peace in her suffering. I am praying for an opening at the hospice, as she deserves some quality in the life she has left.

So, you seem to be bumping into things? Be careful, maybe we should get you a helmet, or padded suit! You sound like you are maintaining a sense of humor about all this. We need to remember to laugh and keep our lives in perspective: think of Bob's mom: life could be a lot worse. We have so much to look forward to, we're only middle-aged and God is still working on us. Thank you, Lord, for being at our side, and for giving us a sense of humor! Will be interested to hear what your doctor has to say about your medication. You are getting good at observing yourself and your reactions. Does it help to detach yourself from your mood and look at it like it's a symptom of your condition? Are you remembering to note that these moods are not a true reflection of the inner Debbie?

I have another piece of scripture for you: Psalm 40:1-4. It's another defining piece of scripture, mirroring my thoughts. Must go for now, have a lot to accomplish today, and will write you later.
Love, your pal Sal

Subj: you're doing it again
Date: 10/23/00 12:25:13 PM Central Daylight Time
From: debbiesb13@aol.com
To: sarahjf50@hotmail.com

Hi Sal!

Wow! I read your Psalm, which spoke to me loud and clear today as I am a bit in the mire and clay. I did get the *15 Minutes* book and read the first five chapters last night. I found the part about telling a friend you are praying for them to be interesting, as we have been doing that for some time. Something I have not done (meaning the telling) with anyone else and have found quite fulfilling about our friendship.

117

I am really sorry to hear about Bob's mom. What a difficult time for all of you. You know I will have all of you in my prayers but especially her to ease her suffering and find some respite with hospice. Will also be praying for Bob's dad that he is not overwhelmed by the pain of her suffering as well. Do they not have hospice services there that come to the home? The one we use does everything from nursing to bathing, etc, in the patient's own home. Maybe she just requires too much care.

I am waiting to hear back from the doctor today on my meds. So back to not eating, not sleeping, and zero motivation. I know it could be so much worse, but it has become very wearing.

I wish I had something fun and witty to tell you instead of that, but alas the mood seems to be in charge of the inner Debbie.

Hope you have a productive day.

Love, Deb

Subj: *two steps forward, one step back*
Date: *10/23/00 10:04:16 PM Central Daylight Time*
From: *sarahjf50@hotmail.com*
To: *debbiesb13@aol.com*

Dear Deb,

It does not sound like you are doing too well! You are not sleeping and have lost your appetite...not good. You must stress with the doctor that if you can't sleep, you can't heal. You have got to rest at night. Also loss of appetite is not good. Okay, sounds like it's time for another drug change: is it the anti-anxiety drug that's making you hyper? YOU NEED YOUR SLEEP—Is the anti-depressant supposed to help you to sleep?

Sorry for all the questions, but your doctor needs to find the right combination for you...know you're getting tired of all this. Keep plugging along, because even though the anti-anxiety drug may be making you too nervous, the anti-depressant is doing its job of building up in your brain. If the anti-anxiety drug is making you nervous, are you at a point where you could comfortably stop taking it and just hang out with the anti-depressant?

I have to go, Bob just found a puddle courtesy of our little dog. He's livid...will write more tomorrow.

Love, Sal

Subj: Happy Anniversary
Date: 10/24/00 9:48:22 AM Central Daylight Time
From: debbiesb13@ol.com
To: sarahjf50@hotmail.com

Dear Sal,

Happy Anniversary! 30 Years - What an accomplishment in today's world! Hope you and Bob have a wonderful day today and really celebrate on your trip this weekend.

That was really all I came up here to say, but then your e-mail is here so I guess I'll answer it even though my intent was to just be cheerful.

Here's the truth - I feel like shit - almost back to the beginning just not panicky. Trying to sleep with these two drugs together is like drifting off and having someone yank on your chain and say, "Oh, no you don't." This all started building up on Thursday until now I just want to roll up in a ball and cry (something I had not felt like in a month at least). I don't think anything has built up in my brain but dead cells.

So that is my sad story that I did not intend to tell you today, but you are kind in asking. I really appreciate that!

I think the hardest part is that tomorrow is our anniversary and I know Tom's hoping to have something remotely resembling a happy occasion. He will be understanding no matter how I feel, but it really hurts me to know I may be letting him down.

That's enough negativity. Think I'll just go have a good cry. Still hope you have a wonderful day.

Love, Your highly screwed up friend, Deb

Subj: Re: Happy Anniversary
Date: 10/24/00 5:17:05 PM Central Daylight Time
From: sarahjf50@hotmail.com
To: debbiesb13@aol.com

Dear Deb,

When I was suffering from depression it took me 6 weeks to feel better. So don't be too hard on yourself if you are still having bad days. It really sounds like you are suffering from the effects of still too "hyper" an anti-depressant. Not getting enough sleep is hard on anyone, let alone someone who suffers from anxiety/depression. Hopefully you will get some satisfaction tomorrow at the doctor's appointment. Just remember the anti-depressant is still working on a cumulative level. But you need some kind of anti-depressant that helps you to sleep.

I'm so sorry you are not feeling well! Just remember I wandered the earth like that for months and months and now I'm here to tell you not only can you get through this, but you will be strong in your knowledge of how to conquer it. In the meantime, if you feel like curling up in a ball, go ahead, if you want to cry, go ahead. When you see your therapist, ask her for pointers on how to handle your bad days. She can help.

About 15 Minutes *by Barnes: I noticed you said you read five chapters. I did that the first time I began reading it a few years ago and did not get much out of it.*

This time I did it a little differently. See if this sounds like something you would like to try: First I read the forward to get her ideas on how to read the book. Her main point was skip around the book. So, every day I thumb through the book until I hit upon a subject that speaks to my heart for that day. Then I write the date at the top of the page near the little square boxes. Then I read the scripture, read her words, do her suggested exercises, and read the additional scripture. If I like the scripture, I write it down in the chapter as a reference.

When I am done with that, I write in my prayer journal. All that takes me 1/2 to a whole hour, depending on the subject. I only do one chapter per day, that way I really am able to absorb more of the point of the chapter. Also, my prayer journal takes time as I go back and read my requests and mark down answers I have received.

Try reading the chapter titled, "Becoming New, Becoming Strong" on page 256. This chapter was the beginning of my new prayer life as it really showed me how to conduct my scripture/prayer time. Then try doing like I did above with one chapter/day, and see if that works for you.

I have to go, but will write more later.

Love, Sal

Subj: I'm listening
Date: 10/24/00 6:03:21 PM Central Daylight Time
From: debbiesb13@aol.com
To: sarahjf50@hotmail.com

Dear Sal,

Thanks for the words of encouragement, advice, and solace. You're too kind. I hope you're doing something fun with Bob tonight and not concerning yourself with your goofy friend. Not that I don't appreciate it, but your special day is more important.

Just got off the phone with the doctor. She told me to take the original anti-depressant she prescribed tonight so I can sleep. I see her tomorrow.

Tom will be home any minute so I need to go for now. Will take your advice on the Barnes book in the next day or two.

Love and Happy Anniversary, Deb

Two Are Better Than One

Subj: friends
Date: 10/25/00 9:55:29 AM Central Daylight Time
From: sarahjf50@hotmail.com
To: debbiesb13@aol.com

Dear Deb,

Glad to hear about your med adjustment and know you will have a good visit with your doctor today!

You did not spoil my time with Bob: he was at work late, and I gave him a hard time about coming home late on our anniversary. His thought was since we are going away for the weekend to celebrate, it was not a big evening. And he's right! I am looking forward to being with him all weekend in the Ozarks!

Wanted you to start out the day with this:

> *Two are better than one, because they have a good reward for their labor. For if they fall, one will lift up his companion. But woe to him who is alone when he falls, For he has no one to help him up. —Ecclesiastes 4:9*

God has given us each other, you are never alone, Deb, you have lots of angels (human and other) around you to lift you up…I'm holding your hand.
Love, Sal

Subj: thanks for being there
Date: 10/25/00 1:17:23 PM Central Daylight Time
From: debbiesb13@aol.com
To: sarahjf50@hotmail.com

Dear Sal,

Thanks for being there, for holding my hand, for lifting me up! Thanks too for anything else that I, being brain-dead, may have left out, as there is bound to be something!

It is amazing what just one night of uninterrupted sleep can do! And not feeling sick either, I could actually eat lunch today (which is good as the scale read only 118 this morning - even I thought I was looking too thin with the exception of that upper thigh fat that just wobbles there no matter what you weigh). So you can tell I feel better, yes?

The appointment was good. I am going back on the original tetracyclic anti-depressant she prescribed. She thinks my current problems are withdrawal from the anti-anxiety medicine and the anxiety itself. So pray for me that is true, and it works.

The most recent anti-depressant made me SICK, SAD AND SLEEPLESS!!

She also wants me to consult with a hematologist. There is an unexplained discrepancy in my blood work.

Bob talked to Tom on his way home last night, as we were getting ready to go out for our big anniversary dinner — a hamburger at Skeeter's. I'm not complaining, it was all I could stand to eat then. Hope you at least had a little anniversary toast — wine or brandy or something. I know your weekend will be fabulous! And well worth the wait of a few extra days. You certainly deserve a break from the last year, and to celebrate thirty years of marriage.

Guess I will go for now. Oh one more thing, I got my first bloom from Mr. Lincoln! It's beautiful and smells so lovely! The others have had beautiful blooms, but are not nearly as fragrant. Enjoy your afternoon.

Love your getting it together with a hand up friend, Deb

Subj: part of the healing process
Date: 10/25/00 4:06:15 PM Central Daylight Time
From: debbiesb13@aol.com
To: sarahjf50@hotmail.com

Hi Sal!

Thought you'd want to know Mary Jo said not only is it OK to talk to you about issues etc. but that you and the thoughts we share are part of the healing process. She had asked me to put down the things that were important to me physically, mentally, spiritually, and emotionally. I explained to her a little bit about how our friendship had begun and evolved and she thought it was quite remarkable, and definitely a positive influence. So professional confirmation of what we already knew.

She thinks also it is time for me to go and see my mother. I think I'm ready. I'm really starting to miss her in fact. We also talked about my separating her issues from my personal beliefs and feelings. Hopefully that will not be tested yet, but if so, then so be it.

I always feel like when I go through one of these medicinal crises I lose sight of your life. You put so much effort into helping me that I miss out on what's going on with you. Most importantly how are you doing and didn't you go to the therapist on Tuesday? Do you feel like your anti-depressant is already working? Also need updates on the young and pregnant, young and NOT pregnant, and the not young. Is that too many questions for one installment? At least my memory doesn't totally short circuit!

I liked the scripture you sent to me today.

With regard to scripture, I have come to rely so heavily on the prayers through which I find comfort in the prayer book, I really don't know a lot, but you are inspiring me to learn.

Well, it's about time for dinner to be ready. My appetite is returning. Have a good evening my friend. Hope you are sleeping well now.
Love, Deb

Subj: Friends are the best!
Date: 10/26/00 8:52:41 PM Central Daylight Time
From: sarahjf50@hotmail.com
To: debbiesb13@aol.com

Hi there! You sound better!!! Glad to hear your therapist is working well with you and that she thinks we are good for each other—we think so too! Good luck in seeing your mom, little doses at a time, and you now have the back up of your therapist to work out the kinks. It will be a good journey.

As for me and therapy, did see Julie, my therapist, and she says I'm moving along just fine, being very realistic about everything, even my depression, and she feels that I just need to keep on doing what I'm doing and she will be there if I need her. I do not really feel better yet, but I am tolerating it, and not letting it get in my way. Rather like having a cold that slows you down. I do find such joy in my scripture study and my relationship with God, and I am using this down time to really develop my faith—something that is more difficult when things are going smoothly—funny thing. Joyful, even when depressed: it's possible!

In two weeks, we will be having two baby showers, one on Saturday, one on Sunday. One for Gina, one for Tisa. Lots of pink! They are both getting tired, and cumbersome, and cranky, and have rosy cheeks! I just smile and tell them when they look at that baby girl's face, they will know it was a minor price to pay for the gift of that beautiful little girl.

Have a peaceful, relaxing weekend with your boyfriend, and enjoy the spa!
Love, Sal

Subj: enjoy!
Date: 10/26/00 9:20:13 PM Central Daylight Time
From: debbiesb13@aol.com
To: sarahjf50@hotmail.com

Hi Sal!

Today has been a busy one for me catching up on errands, etc. that got left behind on those days when I wasn't feeling well. So far the anti-depressant seems to be controlling the anxiety.

Well, I started this e-mail over two hours ago, and am just now getting back to it. What is it about being 17 years old that you think the whole house, no, make that the whole world, is there to serve you and you alone? That no one else's needs or interests could possibly be equal to yours let alone be more important!

Teenager frustration! But then I guess in a few months I'll be moaning that he's leaving to go to college. OK, I know, it could be much worse.

Just got your e-mail. I'm sorry you aren't feeling better yet, and hope that it will not stop you from enjoying your weekend. I don't think it is odd at all that you find it easier to develop your faith when things are down as opposed to going smoothly. It's because that is when we need it the most. Like rest or anything else, we only "treat" or "heal" ourselves when we get almost to the point of desperation sometimes.

This morning when I was walking (for the first time in about a week,) I felt really at peace and in touch with God, actually being able to pray without letting myself be distracted and going off on one of my many mental digressions. It was a really nice feeling. Have a great weekend!

Love, Deb

Subj: have fun?
Date: 10/29/00 7:24:37 PM Central Standard Time
From: debbiesb13@aol.com
To: sarahjf50@hotmail.com

Hi Sal!

Tom and I got to go out to celebrate our anniversary on Saturday. We went to the Veranda and had a wonderful dinner and enjoyed the atmosphere and each other's company. It is safe to say my appetite is back as I have been eating like Templeton the rat (in *Charlotte's Web*). Better be careful before the pounds really start to materialize.

The visit with my mom went well. I was pretty nervous in the morning, but managed to go and relax during our visit without resorting to additional drugs, which made me feel victorious. After our initial hello—missed you—how are the boys stuff, she was basically noncommunicative. Personally, the silence is fine with me; it's safe.

I got to see the quilt Sandra finished making while I was away. Not sure if I told you about that. Sandra took care of my parents from the day they moved in, and she had a heart attack the day before my dad died. While she was home recovering from heart surgery she started on this quilt I asked her to make out of my dad's flannel shirts. I got the idea from something I read in a magazine years ago. It's lap size and just such a happy remembrance of him. My mom loves it.

This is probably terrible to say, but one of the best parts of the day was seeing some of the people both staff and residents who I have come to consider my friends. In some ways it was difficult to give up seeing them in order to avoid seeing my mom. My plan for now is to go when I feel like it, no set days or schedules, just pop in when the mood strikes.

Have more to chat about, but must go for now. Will give you a call tomorrow — now why would that be? Have a good evening and welcome home.

Love, Deb

Subj: HAPPY BIRTHDAY
Date: 10/30/00 7:21:46 AM Central Standard Time
From: debbiesb13@aol.com
To: sarahjf50@hotmail.com

Good Morning Sal!

Before heading out to walk, thought I would send you a little birthday prayer from the Book of Common Prayer to start the day:

Watch over Sally, Lord, as her days increase; bless and guide her wherever she may be. Strengthen her when she stands; comfort her when discouraged or sorrowful; raise her up if she falls; and in her may the peace which passes all understanding abide all the days of her life; through Jesus Christ our Lord. Amen.

This is your day - enjoy it to the fullest!
Love, Deb

A Time to Die

Subj: Boo!!!!
Date: 10/31/00 9:40:13 AM Central Standard Time
From: sarahjf50@hotmail.com
To: debbiesb13@aol.com

Happy Halloween!!!
Thank you so much for the birthday prayer! It is lovely and I know my life is better because you are praying for me.

Talked to Bob last night, his mother's death is imminent. It is amazing that she has endured this long, it is a tribute to the woman's spirit. She is off all life support. Sadly, I am expecting the next phone call from him to be news of her death.

You know, Deb, I said this past year of family strife was over as of my birthday, and there would be a cease-fire on the traumatic news front. Well, it did begin on my birthday! The first good news we've had about Bob's mom in a long time: she was admitted to the hospice on my birthday. Bob said the hospice and staff were great and she is in the best place for her now.

News of her death, and an end to her suffering, and her family's suffering, will not be traumatic. It will be a profoundly sad moment, however, we will all feel she has been released from her pain.

Your prayer walk the other day sounded like a very satisfying time for you. Perhaps your communication with God will become a walk every day! I know I have been so positive about my scripture study with Emilie Barnes, but you will find your own way to daily prayer time, that fits into your life and personality. I love that you and I, while being kindred spirits, can still be different in so many ways.

Please keep Bob and his mom in your prayers today. I know his heart is breaking.
Love, Sal

Subj: Happy Halloween
Date: 10/31/00 4:17:22 PM Central Standard Time
From: debbiesb13@aol.com
To: sarahjf50@hotmail.com

Dear Sal,
    Was so glad to hear Bob's mom was able to get into the hospice and find some comfort for herself and all of your family as well. Thank God for that one positive note. You are all in my prayers for I know as Bob's heart is breaking, yours is breaking for him as well. You know I'm here if you need a prayer or to share your sadness.

Finished reading the fifth *Mitford* book today. I found the final chapters to be as profoundly moving as the man in the attic chapter in the first book. Yes, I cried. What a truly wonderful story! Want to thank you again, Sal, for bringing these books into my life at the time I needed them most.

Think I will go carve our pumpkin. We don't get a whole lot of trick-or-treaters, but it's still fun to see all the little ones and think back when our own were trick or treating not all that long ago. Keeping you and Bob in my thoughts and prayers.

Love, Deb

Subj: *All Saints Day*
Date: *11/1/00 10:15:57 AM Central Standard Time*
From: *sarahjf50@hotmail.com*
To: *debbiesb13@aol.com*

Good Morning!

I haven't got a lot of news, mainly been doing the mundane and praying for Bob's mom and family. I talked to Bob last night, and he did not expect her to live through the night. He had stayed up with her the whole night on Monday...he still does not want us to come out, he does not want me to have to go through the dying bit again, when he feels it is so much like the experience with my father. I am trying to convince him that I just want to be by his side, but he wants me to stay at home with Anthony. I am comforted by the fact he does have his father, brother and sister and aunt there.

Will just keep the home fires burning...I would find it of note if she were to die today, on All Saints Day, as it is the day in the Catholic Church in which we honor the dead, especially in our families. Bob's aunt, an ardent catholic, sent a priest to Marilyn's bedside to issue her the last rights, and anointing, even though she did not believe in God. I am hoping that having her surrounded by prayers and holy rites will help her to slip into heaven, under God's almighty mercy.

You once asked me about English queens, or something...I am an ardent admirer of Elizabeth I. I have read many books about her and feel she was an awesome old girl! She and Abigail Adams are my favorite famous women. As far as saints go, St Therese of Lisieux, and St Elizabeth Ann Seton (started Catholic schools for children in USA) are my favorites.

Hope you have a blessed day, and will keep your father in my prayers on this All Saints Day when we honor our beloved dead.
Love, Sally

Subj: you've got a friend
Date: 11/1/00 11:27:56 AM Central Standard Time
From: debbiesb13@aol.com
To: sarahjf50@hotmail.com

Good morning!

    I know being away from Bob at a time you know he needs you and you want to comfort him is very hard. I guess it is the soldier thing again — I am not sure why at times like this the men we love will not let us help them. I have you all in my prayers today.

    I hope you are right about the granting of last rites by the priest — I pray it will help pave the way for Bob's mom. In fact I am counting on it as it was something I had done for my father even though he had left the Catholic Church when he married. He had been offered and received communion while in the hospital for the first time in years and had visited with Mike (Mary Jo's husband) about being ready to go home to God (a fact I was unaware of until Mike shared the story during his eulogy at the funeral — offering a surprisingly happy moment at an otherwise sad time). We have last rites in the Episcopal Church as well. Thank you so much for thinking of him on this day. To be honest, even though I knew today is All Saints Day, I cannot remember having known the significance of it; another call to prayer today for your father as well as mine and others we have lost.

    After my walk this morning I sat down with my glass of water as usual thinking if I had really offered any new prayers this morning which I might want to record as I was casually flipping through the Barnes book thinking if I wanted to read a chapter. The word "Afraid" caught my eye so I went back to find it. Sally, there were the four things Mary Jo had me discussing last week that I told you about. It's on page 227. I decided this was a sign as I go back today for more on this topic. And get this — the reading from Isaiah is about God holding your hand. Truly amazing! I may give more serious consideration to making this part of my habit immediately after walking.

    Speaking of weight — I have put on four pounds since returning to eating. You are right — it's not fair! Sure it MUST be water! And terribly we had three whole bags of candy left over from last night. Why couldn't I have been smart and bought things I hate! Did I ever tell you my mother brainwashed me as a child by telling me I didn't like chocolate. All those years of abstinence wasted before I knew the truth!

    Well, guess I will get on with the errands for the day. Therapist later and back to the resale shop tomorrow. I'm really looking forward to that!

    Will be here you know, if you need a friend and keeping you in my prayers.
Love, Deb

Subj: morning prayer
Date: 11/2/00 7:29:41 AM Central Standard Time
From: debbiesb13@aol.com
To: sarahjf50@hotmail.com

Dear Sal,

    I don't know what the day or night has brought for your family, but wanted you to know before I leave today that I am still thinking of you and praying for you all.

    May God comfort you today in your vigil. Find comfort also in your recitation of the 23rd psalm and knowing our God has compassion beyond all others.

Blessings my friend,
Love, Deb

Subj: a lamp
Date: 11/2/00 9:57:24 AM Central Standard Time
From: sarahjf50@hotmail.com
To: debbiesb13@aol.com

Good morning,

    The sky is so blue this morning! It does inspire me to get a lot accomplished today. The scripture, which I found that best describes my prayer/scripture time each day is this:

    Your word is a lamp unto my feet and a light to my path—Psalm 119:105.

    Talked to Bob yesterday, he seemed at peace as he has had time to adjust to his mother dying, and he said the hospice is a very calm place. She, as far as I know, is still with us. I am not surprised, if you knew this woman you would be impressed with her ability to always be involved in all family events—she hated to be left out of anything. I am sure that somewhere in her mind she is aware that everyone is together around her and she does not want to be the first one to leave.

    How did your therapy session go yesterday? I imagine your therapist was very glad to see that finally your medication is kicking in and you have found the right med combination. You are now freer to explore in your therapy sessions the issues that cause your pain.

    I understand your experience of flipping through Barnes and finding a chapter that speaks to you. On a subject which I read today: I think when the Bible speaks of dying to self, it many times means giving up the emotions that nurture self interest, feeling sorry for ourselves, blaming other people, and focusing more on a bigger plan/picture which means focusing on God's plan for me.

    "But we have this treasure in earthen vessels, that the excellence of the power may be of God and not of us"—2 Corinthians 4:7
and as for discerning what inside of me is from God?:

"For God has not given us the spirit of fear, but of power and of love and of sound mind."—2 Timothy 1:7

So, dear Deb, food for thought? Must be on my way with this day, will write later and tell you about the baby shower we're having for Gina.
Love, Sal

Subj: I'm here for you
Date: 11/2/00 6:24:51 PM Central Standard Time
From: debbiesb13@aol.com
To: sarahjf50@hotmail.com

Dearest Sal –

Tom just came home and told me Bob's mother passed away this morning. Our hearts and prayers go out to all of you.

I know, Sal that you are all relieved her misery has come to an end even though her passing is a tremendous loss.

I was not sure of your plans — if you are still staying home, or planning to join Bob now, but if you need a friend to share your sorrow with, to pray with you, or to help you in any way you know I am here for you by either e-mail or phone. I will hold your hand as you have held mine. You are not alone — God is with you, I am with you, as are all the other friends and family who hold you dear.

I would give anything now to have a beautiful piece of scripture to offer you and Bob in comfort, but feel completely inadequate in this regard in comparison to your own scripture study. Just know you all have my prayers.
Love, Deb

Subj: Family News
Date: 11/2/2000 10:05:27 PM Central Standard Time
From: sarahjf50@hotmail.com
To: friends of the family

Today we lost Bob's mother, Marilyn Fugazi who went to her rest surrounded by her family.

She will be remembered as a devoted wife, a loving mother, a wonderful grandmother, and an adoring great-grandmother.

We thank you all for your prayers and support during her illness. Please direct any gestures of sympathy to a local hospice or the American Cancer Society.

Join us in cherishing her memory and celebrating her life.
The Fugazi Family

Autumn Star

Subj: *Mourning Star*
From: *sarahjf50@hotmail.com*
To: *friends and family*

The following is a poem that I wrote in honor of Bob's mother, Marilyn. I'd like to share it with all of you.

Autumn Star

On the early hours of this November morn,
As the dew glistens on the eighteenth tee,
A new golden star is gracefully born,
In the heavens: a beautiful sight to see.

Our Marilyn, who was loved by all,
Threw us an everlasting kiss goodbye,
And ascended beyond the celestial wall,
To her own world of dreams in the sky.

There's a front porch and grandchildren to kiss and greet
And a never ending list of family to care for,
It's a Hawaiian lanai with breezes soft and sweet,
Vodka tonics, hors d'oeuvres, and snorkeling galore.

It's a world where golf trophies abound and glisten,
On the mantel, next to her worn golf glove.
It's a home where teenagers actually listen,
To her good advice on life and love!

And then there's the fish that got away...
She's waist deep in the Klamath, reeling in slow,
Heidi's barking, and Raymond is having his say,
Agnes is peeling carrots, her face all aglow.

Do not tarry long, on sadness or sorry,
Marilyn has earned her place as an autumn star.
We celebrate her life, we honor her memory
She will always be with us, never ever very far.

Marilyn Fugazi
At Peace November 2, 2000
—SJF: I will always treasure her light in my life.

Skeletons in the Closet

Subj: a new day dawns
Date: 11/3/00 10:36:42 AM Central Standard Time
From: debbiesb13@aol.com
To: sarahjf50@hotmail.com

Good morning Sal,

Hope this new day finds you at peace, and that you find comfort in another day of beautiful blue skies. Yesterday and today are very gray here.

It was good to talk to you last night. I always find our e-mail so satisfying, but there are times as in expressing sympathy to you at the loss of Bob's mom when a more personal sharing of thoughts is needed. Our phone call was a comfort to me, hope it was to you as well.

Thought so much during the evening of how difficult the lack of a funeral service for your dad must have been for you, and now, how difficult the lack of a funeral for Marilyn will be for Bob. I can't imagine how it must add to the sorrow. My heart goes out to you. Know it will ease Bob's pain to be home tonight.

In answering your e-mail from yesterday — I really like the piece of scripture regarding the lamp. God is our guiding light. I always find the Psalms to be the most beautiful part of the Bible. Though I know very little from memory, they always seem to speak to the heart. The quote from 2nd Timothy is one I have come across very recently. I remember thinking at the time that in my story to you about my faith life, that perhaps it was not the fear of God I had found, but in fact, the love of God in his protection. A better direction, yes?

You asked about the therapist. On a positive note, Mary Jo said I seem to be getting more sparkle in my eyes. She said I will know how to better recognize my "red flags" (your exact words) so that I do not let myself go this far in the future without the appropriate help.

I told her I was beginning to feel more like my normal self. She said, "You will never be like you were." At first that was unsettling, but think this means that I will learn from this experience and it will change me in a positive way that will make me more understanding of myself and others.

We have begun to delve into some issues about my mother. I could see myself moving towards an acceptance and understanding I have not had before, and even a forgiveness, but I will table this entire discussion for a later time.

Tell me what intrigues you about Elizabeth I. Wasn't she one of Henry VIII's kids? Assuming you like Abigail Adams because she was a woman fighting for women so to speak — is that right?

I officially declared it fall in my house even though the weather is not cooperating. I put away the Garden Cucumber candle in the kitchen and got out the new Spiced Apple one. It is really my favorite. It makes the house smell like baking.

Went on Wednesday to do early voting so that Travis would leave me alone about voting for his candidate. At least he won't be old enough to vote himself till January. We have argued quite extensively on the ethicalness of vote swapping. Sometimes he reminds me too much of me at his age — having a cause and thinking you can change the world. Then sometime in your twenties, real life sets in.

So how are your pregnant girls coming along? You must be working on the shower plans now — they're next week, right?

Early in the summer there was a magazine article, something about how e-mail for women is taking the place of the coffee klatches (sp?) of the 50's. Cannot speak to that directly, but know it just makes each day feel good even when it's bad!

Have a blessed day and a comforting evening.

Love, Deb

Subj: bring it on!
Date: 11/3/00 3:40:11 PM Central Standard Time
From: sarahjf50@hotmail.com
To: debbiesb13@aol.com

Dear Deb,

Pertaining to the e-mail on your mom: bring it on! This is a journey you need to take. I am along for the long haul.

One thing that helps when we are going through trying times is to have some balance—a little of this, a little of that. It definitely keeps me from obsessing on some part of my life (or someone else's) that needs to be fixed (or not). So, let's throw a little of your feelings about Mom into the mix. Little by little you will step onward through this cactus patch, and I'll be there, with the Bactine and cotton balls, to dab your scratches and give you a tiny kick in the butt to move forward again—I know you will do the same for me!

Bob called, saying goodbye to his dad at the airport. Will be glad to have him home. Know it's difficult to leave his dad right now. We'll keep in close touch with him.

You asked about the weather. It is a rainy day. I love rainy days, especially when I can curl up in my window seat and read, and watch the rain through the oak tree...

Tisa is due Dec. 3. Gina is due Jan.3. They're both having a little trouble with shortness of breath—baby's dancing on their lungs. So, both have to have buddies with them when shopping, etc. Two baby showers next weekend. Gina's will be here, with Tisa as hostess.

Elizabeth I was the daughter of Henry VIII and Ann Boleyn. Henry chopped off Ann's head when she wouldn't produce a son...joke was on him as his daughter turned out to be one of the best monarchs England has ever seen. Elizabeth fully understood and appreciated her role as a woman ruler—she refused to marry and make any man King, she had a love but did not let it get in the way of

133

her ability to rule the country. She inherited a kingdom, which had been bankrupted by her irresponsible father, and turned it into one of the wealthiest in the world. She also inherited the problem of protestant vs. catholic, which could have become an enormous civil war, instead, she proposed religious tolerance—she slipped out of being accused of ordering the execution of her cousin (and a more legal heir to the English throne than Elizabeth) Mary, Queen of Scots (a Catholic). Most likely she just turned her back on any plots, hoping secretly that someone would succeed in killing Mary. Elizabeth was awesome.

Someday, while chatting on the veranda, we can discuss Abigail Adams—a true renaissance woman.

Your therapist is right—you will never be the same—you will be stronger, wiser and more humble. It's too bad we have to pay such a price to achieve such admirable traits…but the big issue is, can we retain these traits when everything is going great and we don't need a lot of help? Yes, through the balance of daily prayer/meditation with scripture.

Aren't teenagers a joy! (yeah, right!) They have to behave in a contrary fashion to sever the umbilical cord—I just wish it could be done with laser surgery instead of a dull razor…

Thank you for all your friendly words of support.

Hasta La Vista, Baby, as Arnold S. likes to say. I'll be back,—also Arnold's line. Wow, he is really incredible…and what I mean by that is that he is a republican married to a Kennedy. Love it.

Love, Sal

Subj: a long story re: mother
Date: 11/3/00 5:58:14 PM Central Standard Time
From: debbiesb13@aol.com
To: sarahjf50@hotmail.com

Dear Sal,

Have been thinking recently that my mom's childhood probably played a role in her inability at times to relate to my dad and me.

From things she told me over the years, I gather that her father was fairly abusive emotionally and physically. My mother often spoke of how he beat them with a razor strop for even the slightest misbehaving. He was a fanatic at the dinner table and made them chew every bite of food 32 times. He also did things like buying my grandmother expensive jewelry when there was no money to buy winter coats for his 11 children.

My mother has always spoken of her father as if he were the most wonderful man possible, despite his temper and misplaced priorities. Something that just seems ludicrous to me.

So when I related these facts to Mary Jo on Wednesday she suggested the possibility that my mother's deep-seated pattern of denial could be a pattern established years ago as her way of coping to protect herself from emotional pain. "If I don't admit it is so, then it will not be so."

This morning I was thinking about this and began to wonder how this may have affected her relationship with my dad. Maybe it is why she couldn't be openly affectionate with him. Maybe it is why she could not comfort him in his final days and now feels guilty for that. What a sad thing for her!!!!! It has made me see her reactions in a new light and feel a sympathy for her I didn't feel before.

I feel on the verge of some sort of forgiveness but am not sure forgiveness for what. I don't know yet if I can come to terms with the fact that she turned her back on her husband of 55 years when he was dying. It is that internal conflict between the good daughter wanting to reach out and hug my elderly, ailing mother to make her pain go away; and the wounded daughter, who finds it hard to be compassionate for this woman who seemed incapable of compassion when her dying husband (and grieving daughter) needed it. Domestic (daughter) schizophrenia on a major scale.

I find this conflict a bit overwhelming. I know the former route of forgiveness is the one I want to be on; it's the getting there, changing my long held emotional reflexes that requires God's help.

Would love to hear your thoughts on this when you have time.
Love, Deb

Subj: new toys/old toys
Date: 11/5/00 5:22:45 PM Central Standard Time
From: debbiesb13@aol.com
To: sarahjf50@hotmail.com

Hi Sal!

Who needs *Encarta*?!!! I know right where to go with all my history questions! Had no idea Elizabeth was so with-it.

Know you are having a busy weekend. Have been thinking of you often and keeping you all in my prayers. Hope that you have had the time to offer Bob some comfort and that the support of friends and family have helped to ease his pain. I'm sure it will be tough for him for quite some time even if he doesn't always show it being the good soldier he is.

In referencing "sympathy" I found something I quite liked in regard to the situation with my mom. It is from 1Peter 3:8-9:

> "To sum up, all of you be harmonious, sympathetic, brotherly, kindhearted and humble in spirit; not returning evil for evil or insult for insult, but giving a blessing instead; for you were called for the very purpose that you might inherit a blessing."

This caught my eye as "trading insult for insult" is probably what I have found myself doing with my mom way too often over the years and do not find it a very pleasant trait.

We got a new computer on Saturday night. I am not quite sure how this happened even though I was there (sounds like, "How did I get pregnant?"). We started out to H&H for trumpet accessories and to LOOK at a furniture store. The next thing I knew we had bought a new computer.

Really just wanted to say "hi" and share the piece from 1st Peter with you. It's about time to start making some dinner.

Wishing you peace — Love, Deb

Subj: *Re: a very long story re mother*
Date: *11/6/00 9:43:26 AM Central Standard Time*
From: *sarahjf50@hotmail.com*
To: *debbiesb13@aol.com*

Dear Deb,

It's Monday morning and I just read your e-mail about your mom. I wanted to wait until it was quiet around here, because I knew you were writing what was on your heart and I wanted to really listen.

Your mother has been through a lot of pain. It's the kind of pain that stays with you forever, unless you work with God to heal.

Fact: You, Debbie, will never know the true story of what happened.

Fact: Trying to make sense of this situation is impossible.

Fact: You are POWERLESS to change her.

Fact: You cannot go back in time, only forward.

Fact: Even if you did discuss this with your mom you would only get her point of view—which is just her opinion—not the truth.

Probably the most important message I can give you is that we, as individuals, are cautioned not to judge. Everyone sees the world through a different window. What causes them to rest at that window is their past experiences in life. They are a total of their experiences and most of us do not truly know what effects life has had on our fellow man.

You are trying to excuse your mother from all the pain she has caused you and the pain you saw inflicted on your dad. The excuse you have formed is that she was abused and lived in pain, thus she abused others. You are probably right. But your job is not to figure out why anybody else does things—because you probably won't know the real truth until you see God. You are trying to forgive her because you think she was also a victim.

Think about this: maybe you should just forgive her because you (and I) have no business condemning anyone, because we are all sinners. Jesus died so your mom's sins could be forgiven by God—not by us!

I am in the same boat as you, Deb, but recently I have been having a change of heart—through the grace of God. Through reading scripture I am beginning to see a new picture and it's very liberating.

136

It starts with this piece of scripture—can't think where it is—that says,"
before you pluck the cinder from your neighbor's eye, pull the log out of your own."
And here's the other—with reference—

"...seek those things which are above...Set your mind on things above, not
on things of the earth." Colossians 3:1-2.

In other words, your job is not to figure out what motivates others, or try to
fix them. Your job is to fix yourself—God wants you to work on you, not anybody
else. You can point the way for others, and God wants you to, as long as it's
through His direction. But you cannot walk their walk. And, only God can change
them.

Let's face it, we have enough trouble walking our own walk! No where in
scripture does it say walk somebody's else's walk.

Deb, let's help each other. We can achieve "the peace that surpasseth all
understanding."

We've all felt this way: we want to confront the people that have hurt us
and want them to say they're sorry for hurting us—we want them to admit they were
wrong. Instead of nurturing our little feelings and licking our wounds, we should
strengthen ourselves and walk away from the pain.

Here's my final scripture:

"In God I have put my trust; I will not be afraid. What can MAN do to
me?" Psalm56:11

Will close for now—you may never tell me anything more about yourself,
as I have responded in such a long winded way! I am trying to say, Deb, with all
these words is let God work on healing you—He will, He promises that as long as
we trust in Him.
God Bless You, Sal

Subj: going forward
Date: 11/7/00 9:17:12 AM Central Standard Time
From: debbiesb13@aol.com
To: sarahjf50@hotmail.com

Dear Sal,

As usual you are full of thought provoking ideas and an eye opening
approach.

In general let me say, I can see where devoting yourself to scripture study
has served you well in a way that my devotion to prayer alone has left a bit of a
void.

I remember you telling me months ago this experience with depression
would make my faith stronger, and there is no question that has been true. I will
probably always remember that exact moment I thanked God for this experience
because it had brought me closer to Him, and found myself stopping dead in my
tracks at the realization of what I had just said. It was not until that moment of

137

realization that I began to explore some of your suggestions regarding scripture study.

Your statement that my mom should be forgiven just because it's not for me to condemn anyone was very powerful, to the point, and yet so simply true. It is God who is to do the forgiving, and it's not our place to judge. Ironically, judgmental is one of the things I have always thought myself not to be in comparison to my mother, when in fact I have probably been judging her all along.

Also such a simple truth — I am powerless to change her. I don't think I fully accepted my inability to change her and that I must change myself until starting the therapy. The mental side of me knew it, but the emotional side could not lay it to rest.

I realize on the mental side you are right, that only God can change the people who hurt us. Only He can give them comfort through their own prayer, not me. (Which isn't to say I can't pray for them, only that I am in fact powerless on my own to make their change.)

Putting the unhappiness of others behind us while we work on strengthening ourselves would be a good thing. I cannot promise I will do scripture study the same way you do, but I know it is something that will enrich my relationship with God. That is not to say that some of those old feelings won't creep back in ever, but that I know I have the tools to shut them out and will work on sharpening them. A step in the right direction.

Blessings and Love, Deb

V

One Lump or Two?

*

Tea and Roses

Commenting on Life

Foul Weather Friends

Thanksgiving: Mixed Blessings

Red Hot Mamma-grams

The Young and the Nestless

Intermission (or Remission?)

*

Tea and Roses

Subj: *tea for two*
Date: *11/7/2000 5:31:53 PM Central Standard Time*
From: *sarahjf50@hotmail.com*
To: *debbiesb13@aol.com*

Dear Deb,

    If you were here right now, we would be sitting in front of the fire, sipping hot, spiced tea and maybe chatting about our favorite holiday memories. In fact, we probably need to bring our conversations in from "the veranda" to the "fireside" every November! Along with changing our location, thus we would change our beverage! Let's get creative!

    Let me tell you how amazed I am that I am quoting scripture to you. This is a relatively new thing for me. But since I have been doing scripture devotionals and prayer journal, I am learning to incorporate so many of the passages into my daily experiences. I certainly am no saint when it comes to actually living by these scripture passages. For me, they are a beacon of light, an arrow pointing the way to turn in a given situation. I can only hope to remember them at the appropriate times. I notice as I continue with the devotional, I am getting better at recalling certain verses.

    And, while we're at it, let's talk about doing different styles of scripture study. ABSOLUTELY, we should both continue to do our own walk with God, and that relationship is very personal and will be very individualized. What may work for you, may not be the right path for me and vice versa.

    Took Mom and Zachary to Babies-R-Us today and bought two strollers for gifts for my two expanding daughters. When I had to leave him and go home, he pulled a little chair up to his window and watched me drive off. I saw this little face in the window and he was waving at me. I tell you Deb, he's adorable.

    Tisa has dropped, her stomach is heading towards her knees. The doctor said anytime, as the baby's head is in position, but she's really not due for three more weeks. We'll see!

    Well, time to make chili! Take care, dear friend, and don't forget to come in out of the cold, and sit by our fire!
Love Sal

Subj: love spiced tea!
Date: 11/7/00 7:37 PM Central Standard Time
From: debbiesb13@aol.com
To: sarahjf50@hotmail.com

Hi Sal!

Yes let's have spiced tea - I love it! Monday is the boys' wrestling night. Tom and I often go to la Madeleine sit by the fireplace, have dinner, share a Napoleon and I always have spiced tea. When I saw the weather was so much colder there today I thought maybe you'd be wrapped up in something warm reading in your window seat with a cup of hot chocolate. Yes, we will have to come in off the veranda for a while at least.

My mom is trying to do the guilt thing with me about visiting more often now that I am "well." Sometimes she sounds so pitiful when I call, it's hard not to go, and of course now there is that added little "ease her pain" voice in the back of my mind. (Not sure if that part will ever completely leave my mind, even with the realization that it is out of my hands and in God's instead.) But I am sticking to my not more than two or three times a week pledge. Think her dementia may actually be getting worse as twice she has called later in the day, forgetting I had been there.

I can just see little Zachary's face watching you through the window. I'm so glad you sent those pictures!

Well, guess I'll go check out a few election results with Travis. It's kind of fun actually having these political discussions with him. Keep warm.
Love, Deb

Subj: happy trails
Date: 11/8/2000 9:27:12 PM Central Standard Time
From: debbiesb13@aol.com
To: sarahjf50@hotmail.com

Hi there!

Hope you had a good day and didn't freeze. Saw your wind chill was in the 20's today - yikes!!!!! You better be by the fireside maybe with the spiced tea and a brandy. It was cold here today but not that bad. Just enough to get you going on the fall/holiday kind of mentality.

Last night on the phone my mom told me she was sad because my dad was gone. I told her that was completely normal and that is was OK to be sad. She seemed so surprised that it was OK. Isn't it funny how we can overlook how just something that simple can be a comfort. I've given up on telling her he's in heaven, it just makes her mad.

Well, time for me to go to bed, the drugs are starting to kick in. Hope you have a good evening. Have you got your house all decorated in pink for the shower yet?
Sleep tight – Deb

Subj: Friday Chat
Date: 11/10/2000 11:58:14 AM Central Standard Time
From: debbiesb13@aol.com
To: sarahjf50@hotmail.com

Hi Sal!

Hope all is well with you and you are feeling TGIF! Know this is going to be a busy weekend for you to say the least.

I'm here waiting for the heaters to be serviced. It is no doubt some law that you are not to receive your service until the final hour promised so that you will be so glad they came, you don't care what is wrong or how much it costs.

Cannot be certain, but think yesterday was a test for me. When I arrived at my mom's she was dressed in my dad's clothes! (She won't let me take them out of the closet.) At first there was this fleeting thought, "Why is she doing this to me?" But I quickly realized she doesn't pick out her own clothes. As it turns out, a new hospice aide had come to bathe her and had put them on her to keep her warm. The CNA's that take care of my mom were equally surprised — well, maybe not equally. It was a bit unsettling, but not overwhelming.

I know I'm not supposed to be critical of others, but I couldn't help thinking, "Why would someone put the clothes of a 6'2" man on a 4'10" woman — especially the pants!!!!" Poor thing, though, she didn't even realize she had them on, and was quite happy to change into her own clothes, as she has always insisted on wearing a dress.

On a very positive note for her — I did see her doctor yesterday and she is going to try her on an anti-depressant to improve not only her mood, but her appetite, sleeplessness, and pain level as well. Please keep her in your prayers for this to offer her some comfort.

Hope you have a great weekend and that you get to enjoy the showers without it being too hectic!
Love, Deb

Subj: Rose
Date: 11/13/2000 10:15:41 AM Central Standard Time
From: sarahjf50@hotmail.com
To: debbiesb13@aol.com

Good Monday Morning!

I'm sitting here, cozied up in my bathrobe, sipping a welcome cup of hot coffee, gazing outside at the blue sky—it's 33 degrees outside and breezy. I can just imagine this polar wind sweeping down over the great plains, across those farms, and rolling fields, leaving its frosted kiss. I love cold weather and so does Bob...so do our children, actually. We all rejoice and call each other when the temperature gets *below 40. And if we're graced enough to see some snow, it's a holiday! Bob and I were both raised in homes that saw white Christmases every year. When we were in college in Sacramento, it was so depressing to not see white during the holidays, but both of us were lucky to go home for Christmas to snow (he to Lake Tahoe, me to Ohio). We have this ingrown need to have the holidays be chilly, and at least frosty...something we have never been able to count on since we've been married, as we've always lived in spots where it rarely freezes.*

Enough about the weather! Want to talk about your e-mails. I am rereading the first Mitford *book—I read it when my dad was dying and I knew I did not really pay a lot of attention to the words—and I was wondering if you ever saw (when reading* Mitford*) a little of your mother in Rose...what struck me in the comparison was your story about seeing her dressed in your father's clothes. It reminded me of Rose and her funny outfits and her cantankerous, insulting ways. You remind me of Billy, her husband, (gender aside) as you are coming to a place where you are learning to deal with a totally difficult, permanent situation, which seems to have no end. When seeing your mother (in drag), it must have been rather shocking, funny, endearing, maddening, frustrating, sad, and lastly you just had to shake your head and say, "Oh well...!" You are finding ways to survive this storm in your life by accepting her ways, good and bad, and skirting (no pun intended) any confrontation. You are just like Billy in that he uses his sense of humor to soften the tragedy of his life. And later on, he becomes more spiritual...*

New meds! You may see a difference in your mom. Why don't the professionals give out the anti-depressants earlier to seniors who are suffering? Do they not see that their elderly patient's unhappiness, whether a chemical or emotional cause, is very real and these seniors are helpless, as are children, to help themselves?

Thank heavens for good therapists. There is such a stigma attached to seeing a therapist. I have to be careful to whom I tell that I have seen a therapist—as a lot of people think it is an avenue which only the mentally ill and weak travel down. As a therapist once told me, the people that really need to be in therapy will never go. Most people in therapy are there to learn how to deal with the people who SHOULD be in therapy. Mary Jo is really working with you on this mom thing and that's so valuable to have her input, to steer you in a direction you could not go on your own.

Okay, this is becoming one of my longer dissertations...so you might want to take a break and read the rest later!

My weekend of showers...it was very sweet. That's the adjective to describe my very pregnant daughters and their friends and the gifts that were shared. It was also so sweet to see my two daughters stick close to one another and help each other at each shower. Gina at nineteen is beginning to show her vulnerability for her condition and her fears about childbirth, etc. Tisa is beginning to show her frustration for her own condition slowing her down and she just wants to have that little girl in her arms. One mom at one of the showers told the story, in detail of a woman who lost her baby in the seventh month, including the funeral, etc. Gina was mortified and it worried her. I will tell her, when we are alone tonight, that these stories always pop up when a woman is pregnant, and she needs to remember 98% of pregnancies are ended in healthy children...

    Gina's shower was hosted by Tisa in our home. When I prepare for entertaining I always get out my silver...when I say "my silver" most of it I have inherited from my mother and my mother-in-law. They know I love to entertain and have been very generous in passing down the silver to me. I have silver serving pieces over 100 years old. My silver tells a story about my women ancestors and it's valuable to me because I never knew them. My grandmothers both died when I was a little girl. So when I use my heirloom silver it is like having these lady relatives present! I also put out Gina's baby book and two cards from her great-great aunt and her great grandmother welcoming her into the world nineteen years ago.

    Before you are so star-struck by the opulence of the silver: I still had dog hair hanging on the side of my sofa, and the cat walked on one of the buffets...beauty and the beast?

    So what's up for this week? Christmas shopping and going to the doctor with Tisa, and she will give me a tour of the hospital, where I have been told I must be present for her labor...we have an elaborate plan covering every contingency: middle of night, c-section, where to keep Zachary, it's so complicated that I finally told her to just tell me where to be and I will be there.

    So, dear friend, hope you're not cross-eyed by now, I will let you rest and get on with your life! God continues to bless your walk out of the darkness into his light. It is so awesome when we start to look at the world through God's window, how people and events are transformed into something more lovely, something more understandable.

    Dear Lord, thank you for your vision, instead of my earthly sight.
Amen, Sal

Subj: A Rose by any other name…
Date: 11/13/2000 1:00:29 PM Central Standard Time
From: debbiesb13@aol.com
To: sarahjf50@hotmail.com

Hi Sal!

    Glad to get your long e-mail, which is a beautiful cool winter breeze in an otherwise dull day. I am home today while both our heaters are being replaced. Sometimes we are too close!!!! I'm taking a break from—you may even guess—polishing my silver! Although mine is not heirloom, I love using it. Setting a beautiful table was something my mother taught me that I really enjoy.

    I love hearing about how you have managed to put together the silver pieces from your different family members. What a special treasure!!!! The showers sound like they were wonderful! I'm sure Tisa and Gina both feel so blessed.

    Have you had snow since you've lived in Dallas?

You sounded last week and today like you are feeling better—is that right? I hope so, with the upcoming births and holidays there is so much to celebrate. Not that you wouldn't feel blessed and joyful at heart anyway.

You are right about the therapy being such a big help. I probably have told a couple of people that I should not have told that I was going. Oh well, cest la vie, que sera sera, etc. Have found it interesting to see who my real friends are and aren't. Very much an eye opening experience.

Gardening question: what should I do with the roses when there is a frost or freeze?

About Rose…that's an interesting thought and not one that occurred to me. But yes, that's exactly how she looked and how I felt! I have to laugh at it, as I learned to do with so many things my dad would do (like trying to drive his bed) or the sadness would sweep me away. Mary Jo is definitely helping me on that front— to find the strength to separate what I can and cannot control (which is most things) and to work through it with God's grace.

Want to finalize my menu for Thanksgiving and make a shopping list. Assume you are cooking for Thanksgiving as well (unless of course Tisa's having the baby then). Oh Sal, you must be so excited!!!!! What a blessing! I haven't even met your girls, but feel like I know them from our e-mails and I'm excited for you and them as well!!!

Time for lunch and back to work. Wishing you every blessing my friend.

Love, Deb

Subj: *A Rose is a rose, is a rose.*
Date: *11/13/2000 3:33:03 PM Central Standard Time*
From: *sarahjf50@hotmail.com*
To: *debbiesb13@aol.com*

Hi twice in one day!

Read your e-mail, and at the risk of being labled as an e-mail junkie, will respond to rose question but then respond later to rest of your note.

It will freeze here tonight but don't know about you, so wanted to get this info to you:

Don't worry, the roses are tougher than we are. They will survive any freeze. Any buds on stems will die when it freezes, but the plant is fine. Just let it go, you may even get a few more blooms in between cold snaps. Your potted rose just needs heavy mulch and some protection around the pot so the roots don't freeze— this shouldn't be a problem in Houston, as it never freezes long enough to work through to the roots. They really don't go dormant in Houston until January. I remember having mild winters there and getting blooms all the way through to Feb. 14.

Important: You will cut back your bushes on Valentine's Day.

Have to add that pruning my roses took on more meaning when I was brought to my knees with my first depression. I learned the value of dormancy, pruning drastically (and painfully) then regaining strength and coming back stronger and healthier for the experience.
Love, Sal, the rose lover

Commenting on Life

Subj: A Season of Thanks
Date: 11/14/2000 9:00:25 AM Central Standard Time
From: sarahjf50@hotmail.com
To: debbiesb13@aol.com

Dear Deb,

Aren't we having a great fall with a lot of cool, rainy days and crisp cold sunny ones? After our summer in hell, it has been such a welcome change. Another thing to thank God for today.

Was thinking about you when I arose this morning to a very chilly home. Were you without heat yesterday while they fixed your heaters? I think our units are about ready for rehauling…They heat and cool well, but they are making interesting vibrations…

Yes, it snowed here last winter! It was so pretty—but really closed down the cities. They were probably laughing at us in Buffalo, New York, as we barely had 2-3 inches on the ground, but everyone stayed home. Anthony was thrilled to be out of school, I ran out and took pictures.

Confession time: My journaling and my scripture study took a giant dive last week what with all the preparations for showers and shopping chores. I am going to jump back into it this morning—I promise.

I am feeling better, as I knew I eventually would. It is nice to get back to sleeping at night and life is not so overwhelming anymore. Am slowly creeping out of my protective sleeping bag and stretching. One day, one problem at a time. I find that my moments of happiness come when I look into Zachary's eyes, or have good talks with my daughters & son or when I read scripture…also it is nice to spend playtime with Bob.

Oops, time to get going on my day! Many projects planned—let's see how many I can achieve. One completed task would be good, don't you think?

Have a lovely, thankful, seasonal November day,
Your pal Sal

Subj: have a cup of something warm
Date: 11/14/2000 5:25:48PM Central Standard Time
From: debbiesb13@aol.com
To: sarahjf50@hotmail.com

Dear Sal,

Yes, these cool days are a welcome respite from the summer that seemed it would never end! You are so right about how things shut down here when snow and ice hit. People in the northern states probably think we're all idiots here.

I'm really happy that you are feeling better. You are strong, Sal!

How did you end up in California for college when you lived in Ohio?

Went to see my mom today and thought a little more about the Rose comparison. Actually her cantankerous behavior could well fit, as my mom can be quite rude. Once we were having lunch in Chili's and she told this little two year old girl at the table next to us to "shut-up!" I was so embarrassed!!!! I told her if the girl had been her grandchild she would have thought the child's behavior was cute. Her comment, the obvious, "But she's not."

Have a quote to share with you that I read today. The person quoted is Charles H. Spurgeon. "Many might have failed beneath the bitterness of their trial had they not found a friend."

That is us—there to help each other through the trials, on good days and bad days, following God's light.

Love, Deb

Subj: *what a pal!!*
Date: *11/15/2000 8:56:08 AM Central Standard Time*
From: *sarahjf50@hotmail.com*
To: *debbiesb13@aol.com*

Good morning,

I always sit down with a cup of coffee or tea to read your notes on life.

A long, long time ago when I was in high school I was accepted at a university in California, which fit in well with my father's plan to retire in northern California. So, they sent me light years away from my dear friends, most of whom were going to school in Ohio.

What a culture shock. In 1967 California was in the middle of the hippie movement. Ohio was still in the Ivy League. Anyway, it didn't take me long to fit right in—forgot I was there to get an education...but I did have a lot of fun (not my proudest memories). These were the days of Janis Joplin at our women's gym, Jimmy Hendrix and my friends back stage and at his hotel room, walking around Haight-Ashbury, having friends put in jail for demonstrating in Berkeley, LSD passed around at the rock concerts, girls getting pregnant, getting abortions, party party party, fraternities were for nerds, sororities were for someone from another planet...in the midst of all this I met my future husband. I find now, that it was only by the grace of God (I'm sure he was looking down on me shaking his head) that I made it through all the turmoil of the sixties and into a stable, loving relationship with Bob.

By the time my parents moved to Sacramento, which was at the end of my sophomore year, I was a different person. My poor parents were in a totally alien environment, Ohio and the Air Force base were a little different from California in 1969. Not only was the culture alien for them, but I was an alien. And they looked at Bob like he was something from the pits of hell...I look back on it now, from the "been there" perspective of a parental survivor of four teenage children of my own, and I have great sympathy for my folks!

Enough of my past. Sounds like you have "put on the armor of God" when it comes to your mom. Of course, as with anytime we are striving to change, we will find chinks in the armor—places of vulnerability. But it sounds like you are approaching her on a more objective level, and fortified with God and Mary Jo. Let's hear it for teamwork! How much we both have learned through our pain!

I know you have quite a busy day planned, so will go for now. You sound so much better! You are really being so responsible and focused on your recovery.

The mistake a lot of people make, and one that I made, is that once a person begins feeling better, they think they can continue on their own and leave all those memories of the past depression in the past. They stop therapy, they jump back into life, feeling normal and invigorated. But they haven't given themselves enough time to practice the new (and tedious) emotional exercises that will make them strong. They do not pay attention to the yellow flags in the issues in their lives. Yellow flags that remind us to practice what we've learned, deal with the problem when it's an ant hill, instead of ignoring it until it's a mountain. And if it's a mountain overnight, out of our control, we go to God, put on his armor, ask for guidance. Life becomes a little simpler, a little more manageable when God is the determining force in our lives.

Have a great day, friend.
Your pal Sal

Subj: best part of the day
Date: 11/15/2000 7:48:02 PM Central Standard Time
From: debbiesb13@aol.com
To: sarahjf50@hotmail.com

Hi there my friend!

I really enjoyed hearing about your college life!!!!!! It must have been really exciting to be in the center of the cultural revolution! You were there living all the things the rest of us were watching from afar and emulating. Although Ft. Worth was certainly not California, it wasn't Ivy League either. The college years were just about the most fun years of my life — as you said, not my proudest memories, but still VERY fun. I can see where it would have been culture shock for your parents!!!!

My parents sold their record shop in 1959. Several people have said it's too bad they didn't keep it given how music took off during those years. My parents would have NEVER made it through the drug culture music and would have gone bankrupt trying to live off Frank Sinatra and Elvis Presley. As the mom of teens I can say on the plus side, my experiences would make them hard pressed to put much over on me, having been there and done that, so to speak.

Did you meet Jimi Hendrix?

Saw Mary Jo today and as I have come to expect, it always seems to tie in directly to something you have said. You spoke about how we have learned through our pain. Mary Jo said that we can use our pain or let the pain use us. You and I are obviously choosing to use the pain by learning from it. She used the analogy of God bringing us through the pain and then wrapping us in it, but it has transformed to something like a blanket, protecting us in the future. I thought that was a really great analogy! We talked also again about using this experience to know how to avoid future problems (yellow flags).

I appreciate you saying I have done a good job working through this with the help of God and Mary Jo. Tom has been a great support as well, but you left out a major element of my coming out of the fog. As a voice of experience, you were a big part of God's way of helping me—a beacon of light at a very dark time in my life.

Have a good evening, Sal, and a great Thursday. I'm off to the resale tomorrow. Will look forward to a day of "rest" on Friday. This has been a busy week!

Love, Deb

Foul Weather Friends

Subj: you'll want wine, not coffee
Date: 11/16/2000 7:29:20 PM Central Standard Time
From: debbiesb13@aol.com
To: sarahjf50@hotmail.com

Hi Sal!

E-mail disclaimer: I'm in a really bitchy mood and am writing to you in an effort to improve it. It's 5:30, Travis beat me to signing on to AOL, my back hurts, and my body has been trying for two days to no avail to start a period for the first time in almost two months. So now you know anything I say should not be used against me by additional reasons of insanity besides the usual ones! (You realize this is just temporary insanity I hope!)

The resale shop drug on forever today. Guess the nasty weather kept everyone away. So how was your day?

OK, it has been over a week now and we have not yet discussed the presidential election. I for one feel the need to "vent" on this matter (maybe it's PMS). Isn't it absolutely stupid that in this day and age of technology that we have such a screwed up mess?!!!!! I cannot believe that the future of our government hangs in the balance on whether or not a few people can follow an arrow and punch through a card, or some other well meaning soul deciding what you meant when you "dimpled" your ballot. I have got to stop watching the news as it just adds to the insanity!

What are you having for Thanksgiving? What kind of dressing do you make? We have cornbread. My mom made the absolute best!

When you were growing up did you have a lot of people around for the holidays? Our get-togethers were really large (sometimes 30 or more), and then dwindled as my generation married and had their own families. Being part of a stepfamily, it's even more complex to insure everyone is able to get together.

Here's another question I had, which one of your grandmothers were you named for? Was she called Sally as well?

I've calmed down a little bit and seem to have run out of things to say (yes, that does happen sometimes).

Hasta manana.

Love, Deb

Subj: cyber blues
Date: 11/17/2000 9:20:53 AM Central Standard Time
From: sarahjf50@hotmail.com
To: debbiesb13@aol.com

Hello Deb!

I am having so much trouble with my e-mail transmissions. Keeps cutting me off with "sorry, internal error." Anyway, "the mail must go on!" So I will attempt to get this out to you.

I was very interested in your session with your therapist. She sounds like she is really working well with you. That is so important! I, too, like the analogy of the blanket. Rather reminds me of the similar comparisons of a cross to bear, which I am learning is an honorable thing, not a burden.

You know Deb, I am thankful that I have a daily connection with the tiny Christian community of Deb and Sal. Some days I feel you and I are candles in the darkness of the world.

Jimi Hendrix: My girlfriend and dormmate, Janis, went to Jimi Hendrix' hotel room after his concert. A few people were there. They all got stoned together. Jimi took a movie camera (too soon for video cams) and recorded a show on TV. He was apparently very friendly with many girls, but we won't go there! He wanted to sleep with one of Janis's friends but she refused. Janis has always given her a bad time about not sleeping with an incredibly famous rock star...

Will go for now, and try to send this to you.
Love, Nana Sarah

Subj: lunch break
Date: 11/17/2000 12:49:22PM CST
From: debbiesb13@aol.com
To: sarahjf50@hotmail.com

Hi Sal!

Wouldn't it be fun if we could have lunch together? Maybe one day...probably an instant message lunch if we're ever on the same provider.

Thought your discussion of a cross to bear very interesting. I have often thought about God not giving us more than we can bear. There were times when I wondered when enough would be enough and thought surely that point had been reached only to find that the load grew ever larger. Now I can look back and see that when that happened there was a reason — maybe there were multiple reasons, but at least I got part of the lesson. It brought me closer to God as you said it would. And it gave us this connection you called our candle in the darkness.

I love our discussions on all our various female issues — even thigh skin and jell-o boobs. I was reminded of thigh skin yesterday as we were pricing stuff at the resale and there was a royal blue silk garter belt trimmed in black lace — you wouldn't believe some of the stuff people give away!!!!

Am looking forward to hearing news of your pregnant daughters. Does Zachary call you Nana Sarah? Cute!
Love, Deb

Subj: foul mood friends
Date: 11/17/2000 1:13:32 PM Central Standard Time
From: sarahjf50@hotmail.com
To: debbiesb13@aol.com

Dear PMS Deb,

PMS is so-o-o irritating. I feel, on the day before I start my horrendous monthly flow, like every event is like someone is running their fingernails down a chalkboard...I grit my teeth and snarl under my breath. Then my period begins and I am cleared of all hateful thoughts. Rather like pushing the delete button.

Personally, I thought you could have used a few more swear words...we should go back and reread our correspondences on those eventful black days! It is probably rather grim!

I was named after my great-grandmother Sarah Jane, who was born in 1856 (which is how old I feel on the first day of my period). They called her Sally too. I have pictures of her and if this is any indication of what's in store for me, it's time to see the plastic surgeon!

I too make cornbread stuffing and it's delicious! Make it with a combo of cornbread and dressing cubes. Secret ingredient: butter. How do you make yours?

Our family holidays when I was a child were always just our family of four. We moved every 3-4 years, being in the Air Force. But Mom and Dad always made the holidays fun. Mom is such a good cook and we always had lovely holiday meals. Now with our own family, Bob and I have always made a point to have Christmas at our home—door's always open to any relatives who want to visit. For 30 years, with only one or two exceptions, I have made the holiday meals. We usually had grandparents show up for Halloween or Thanksgiving. This Christmas we will have Bob's dad and brother. I cook turkey, both Thanksgiving and Christmas as the family loves turkey and the smell of it roasting and the great leftovers!

Latest on Tisa: Baby Lyndsey won't be coming until after Thanksgiving, as it seems now. Latest on Gina: she keeps buying all these adorable clothes and hats for her little girl. That baby will be a fashion plate.

I am going to be present, by request, for both the girls' labors, and Bob can't figure out why they want me there, when he and I did it all by ourselves. I told him it's a security blanket for both of them: Tisa, because she had a terrible labor with Zachary which ended up in emergency c-section. Gina, because she's only 19 and scared.

Will close this with a wonderful, warm wish for you to have a lovely, chilly November weekend, curled up by the fire, feeling the peace and promise of life.
Love, Sal

154

Subj: coffee break
Date: 11/17/2000 2:51:48 PM Central Standard Time
From: sarahjf50@hotmail.com
To: debbiesb13@aol.com

Good Afternoon,
I am so bad...I finally got my e-mail sort of functioning and am able to slowly retrieve stuff and send stuff. So, the Friday house cleaning has suffered greatly, but somehow I am not worried enough to get up off my ample derriere and do something about it.
Zachary calls me plain Nana, but depending on the grandchild, if there are other Nana's in the family, I will be Nana Sarah. It is a joy.
Okay, will go for now. All this talk about mess reminds me that I am surrounded by mess...Have a great weekend!
Love, Sal

Subj: It's working!
Date: 11/17/2000 3:17:26 PM Central Standard Time
From: debbiesb13@aol.com
To: sarahjf50@hotmail.com

Happy Friday!
Have been out in the cold and rain and came home to find your first two e-mails and here comes another while I'm reading!!!! We are both talkative today!
OK explain this — my PMS symptoms are gone, but still no period. Yes, PMS is as you described, leaving a VERY short fuse. Did you ever decide to take the hormones? I take it you are still having the mega periods and therefore the answer was no. Why can't the ramifications of our choices be more clear cut and less scary? I send you my sympathy on the horrible periods, but should probably send a box of chocolates instead. I crave it when I'm PMS-ing, which could explain how I have breezed through an entire package of holiday Chips Ahoy with the white and dark chocolate chips!
Saw you're having snow?!! How fun for you! We are having our second day of gray miserable rain, and are on tap for a cold wet day tomorrow — 40's, rain, and high winds. This would be great for the fireplace and a game of Scrabble. Austin has a basketball game tomorrow night, which Tracey and Tristan are coming to watch and then we are heading to Chuck E. Cheese. Sometimes I think getting to do all those kid things again is one of the best parts of grandkids, but then there's holding hands, and wet kisses, and sticky hugs that are pretty special too!
Meant to say this earlier — in my brief errand stops today people seemed to be quite in the holiday spirit — holding doors, smiling, being courteous, etc. Do not know if it is the cold weather or the coming of the holiday season, but it did leave a nice warm feeling to come home with. Have a warm, cozy, weekend.
Love, Deb

Subj: sunday blessings
Date: 11/19/2000 4:15:47 PM Central Standard Time
From: debbiesb13@aol.com
To: sarahjf50@hotmail.com

Hi Sal!

Tristan loved his "Grand Hotel" book you sent!!! He had a lot of fun opening all the little windows and had Tom and I both reading it to him while he was here. We all laughed at the owner being "Thomas." Thanks for such a great gift for him as we had never seen any hotel books! He is still calling Tom Grandpa Hotel, by the way.

I am in between cooking assignments. I have been making cornbread for dressing, chopping celery, etc. (Could not resist having a piece of cornbread hot out of the oven with a glass of buttermilk — yikes! I am turning into my mother!) When my mom made her holiday meals the kitchen looked like something out of a cartoon with pots piled a mile high and things everywhere and she would be maniacal. I on the other hand try to have my entire meal (except the turkey, mashed potatoes, and gravy) be things I can make ahead so that the day is less stressful and less messy.

So I am still on this quest to duplicate my mother's dressing. I get very frustrated trying to make things like this when the person carried the recipe around in her head. I want the instructions to be right and I just follow them.

Is Anthony out of school this week? This is our first time for the boys to have the entire Thanksgiving week off. I am really quite looking forward to it. Sleeping a little later and just being generally leisurely about life (and cooking).

Guess my break is over and it's time to go back to the kitchen. Am looking forward to taking a walk after dinner as we are starting to have at least a few trees with the leaves turning. I love walking when the leaves are falling, like little kisses from the angels above. The perfect setting to give thanks to God for this wonderful life: our world, our families, our friends, candles in the darkness.
Love, Deb

Thanksgiving: Mixed Blessings

Subj: *A prayer*
Date: *11/20/00 8:45:05 AM Central Standard Time*
From: *sarahjf50@hotmail.com*
To: *debbiesb13@aol.com*

Hello and welcome to Thanksgiving week!

I have read your Sunday note and have a lot of answers to your questions and things to share with you, but will save that for a later e-mail.

For now, let me start out this week appropriately, on a thankful note:

Lord, thank you for the incredible gift of my new and dearest friend, Deb. Thank you for the many difficult times you placed not only in my life but also in her life, so that we might be humbled and seek solace not only in your loving embrace, but also in one another. Thank you for making your presence so obvious in our friendship, that we may learn how to bring You out of our hearts and into our daily tasks as daughters, wives and mothers. And lastly, Lord, thank you for your Word, which has been a guide for me and Deb, in our tiny, remote, Christian community we call "candles in the darkness."

Amen

Love, Sal

Subj: what a beautiful gift!
Date: 11/20/2000 10:46:21 AM Central Standard Time
From: debbiesb13@aol.com
To: sarahjf50@hotmail.com

Dear Sal,

Thanks so much for the beautiful prayer to start my week! The very moment you were writing and sending it, I was stepping into the greenbelt which is, you know, when I begin my morning prayer. And I was paying special attention to giving thanks, mirroring your prayer in many ways.

My day is a little house cleaning, making some breakfast breads, and the hematologist this afternoon.
Love, Deb

Subj: they shoot horses
Date: 11/21/2000 10:24:39 AM Central Standard Time
From: debbiesb13@aol.com
To: sarahjf50@hotmail.com

Hi my friend—

Hope you had a good day overall. How is Tisa feeling as her due date draws ever nearer? Are you working on your Thanksgiving meal yet? Sure you must be.

Yesterday did not go exactly as I had expected. Went to the hematologist who is also an oncologist. After talking and doing an exam, he ordered blood work and then said I needed to have an immediate needle biopsy on a LUMP IN MY RIGHT BREAST. They are to call me later about an appointment time. Guess I will go.

It's just a strange feeling. I don't feel scared, just tired. Tired of doctors, tired of finding a new question every time I seek an answer. Here's what I know: Last August, I sought medical help for the pinched nerve in my back; I was diagnosed with severe anxiety and depression, B12 and folic acid anemia, and a concern for a lump in my breast. To top it all off, nobody has done a damn thing for my back that is more bothersome with each passing day.

Please accept my apologies for this wallowing in self-pity or terminal PMS. And at the same time, thanks for being a friend who will give me this indulgence. Know that things could really be much worse. Thinking of your beautiful gift of the prayer yesterday, (which I reread many times last night to lift my spirits) I know how infinitely blessed I am, truly. Blessed to have my family, and you for a friend, and blessed in knowing that through prayer this too shall pass.

Waiting for Tom to call last night, I found comfort reading through my favorite prayers in the prayer book. And walking this morning I have told God I surrender. Surrender whatever He thinks I have not yet given; waiting to find out what lesson I am to learn now.

You sounded so happy yesterday!! It's a good thing I have a wonderful friend like you who is praying for me, as I seem to need it.
Love, Deb

Subj: Thanksgiving wishes
Date: 11/22/2000 1:56:21 PM Central Standard Time
From: debbiesb13@aol.com
To: sarahjf50@hotmail.com

Dear Sal — wanted to take a moment to wish you and yours a happy Thanksgiving.

I got a very early start this morning. The sun had just come over the horizon and the clouds were that combination of orange on the bottom and purple on top that occurs only so briefly at sunrise or sunset. They looked almost like snow-covered, mountain tops reflected in a vast lake. I was struck by their beauty, and at the same time, what a short time they would be looking just that color. That in a moment it would be gone as the sun rose ever higher in the sky.

It reminded me that we must not forget in our thankfulness to not only be thankful for the grand things in our lives, but to be thankful for the moments as well. For it is the moments we share with our kids, our husbands, our parents, our friends; an e-mail; a sunrise; each simple moment that God gives us that makes life beautiful. Wishing you beautiful moments and God's every blessing.
Love, Deb

Subj: Candles in the Darkness
Date: 11/25/2000 8:20:51 AM Central Standard Time
From: sarahjf50@hotmail.com
To: debbiesb13@aol.com

Oh Deb,

It's Saturday morning, after a busy Thanksgiving week, and I just sat down for the first time since Monday to catch up on our communication. I am sorry I waited so long to check my e-mails. I seem to have such a serious problem with time management...that's my "Holiday Blues" issue.

Now I feel so terrible.

I read your Tuesday e-mail about the doctor, the lump in your breast, and the burdens that keep being heaped upon your tired spirit. I am asking God right now why you have been chosen by Him to be tested and strengthened time after time.

Now, let me descend from the clouds for a moment, and succumb to my earthly, human self: shit, shit and double shit!!!! What next??? You must have just rolled your eyes and wanted to lie down and make every medical professional go away. This is too much...the next thing is what???? You have just been going along, doing the healthy things for you, climbing back into the driver's seat of your life,

159

and WHAT HAPPENS? Someone throws you out of the car and decides to drag you along behind!! BREAST CANCER??

Now, let me ascend again into a place where there is a possibility of healing, and even a place of joy. It is the grace of God; ask His guidance, do His will, and He will do the rest.

Please don't get mad and think to yourself, "Sally doesn't understand, this is not that easy." I am sure that I cannot understand the depth of your pain, and anxiety right now, and how fragile your recovery has been. Am I oversimplifying a bad situation? I hope so. You need simple answers right now.

I am sending you today the book Joy for the Journey, *which is a book of God's promises. It has taught me the most, along with Emilie Barnes, on how to use God's word to guide my heart. It will help.*

Will go for now. I'm here, always, and have thought about you so many times in the past few days, and hoped that your Thanksgiving was good and warm.
Love, Sal

Subj: Re: Thanksgiving wishes
Date: 11/25/2000 8:53:32 AM Central Standard Time
From: sarahjf50@hotmail.com
To: debbiesb13@aol.com

Dear Deb,

Thank you for the lovely Thanksgiving wish. I could picture and share in the joy of the beauty of your moment with the heavens.

Your perspective is changing, yet, again. The experiences you have gone through this week have not pulled you down into a bottomless pit of anxiety. You have probably dipped your toes into that pit this week, but instead of jumping in and floundering, you walked away, looked at the sunrise and found joy. You have learned that no matter what comes forth on your horizon, you can still see God's beauty and draw strength from it.

Reread Philippians 4:8-9.

"whatever is true, whatever is honorable, whatever is just, whatever is pure, whatever is lovely, whatever is gracious, if there is any excellence, if there is anything worthy of praise, think about those things, then the peace of God will be with you."

Paul wrote many of his letters from dungeons, or while suffering with sickness, and he understood the power of the above passage. It was his gift to the Philippians, and then to us. Thank you, St. Paul.

Will write to you later about my pregnant hordes and how they are doing, plus turkey day, etc.—also about Christmas—which will be more meaningful to you this year, than ever before!
Love, Sal

Subj: friends - the eternal flame
Date: 11/25/2000 12:17:59 PM Central Standard Time
From: debbiesb13@aol.com
To: sarahjf50@hotmail.com

Dear Sal,

Please don't feel terrible about not having time to e-mail. Our friendship is way stronger than two or three days that pass between us without having the opportunity to sit down in front of a computer.

I have read both your morning e-mails. Thanks for your thoughts and prayers. Here is the scenario — new mammogram Monday, biopsy is on Wednesday, and I'll get the results of the blood work and biopsy next Monday. My prayers on this issue are just to make the best decisions and get the best care if any is needed. I will admit now that I am a little scared and that the possibilities have made me very pensive the last few days — not totally depressed or even anxious, just thoughtful. So maybe that is saying, "Whatever, Lord."

Our Thanksgiving was really nice. (My dressing, by the way, came out really good, as I experimented with adding butter till it tasted right — so thanks for that tip!!)

Yesterday my mom called and thanked me profusely "from the heart" for arranging the wheelchair lift van for her to be at our home for Thanksgiving. Tom and I stopped by later to visit her. She asked me about my dad being in the hospital. Of course, this meant I had to tell her once again that he had died. For the first time she cried — I think this was genuine dementia: not remembering. But then, she came back around to her usual denial phrases: "I don't want to hear about angels," "He wasn't suffering," "There are people that dig them up." (By "people" she means gravediggers from Oregon who exhume bodies and bring the dead to life.) I could put this aside as Mary Jo has taught me this is my mother's issue not mine.

Still want to hear about your holiday and "pregnant hordes." Tisa must really be ready!!!

I'll look forward to getting the *Joy* book. Should go for now and make Tom some ice tea for his yard work and think about finishing off the leftovers for our lunch.

Love, Deb

Red Hot Mamma-grams

Subj: *red hot mamas?*
Date: *11/25/2000 4:57:20 PM Central Standard Time*
From: *sarahjf50@hotmail.com*
To: *debbiesb13@aol.com*

Well, we do have an eternal flame! I think our NEXT book should be entitled "Red Hot Mamas"...People will think it is a book about two middle aged women exploring their plummeting hormones, which is sort of true, but in a Christian way!

Must go, time for mass, we go on Sat nights. Will pray for your continued health and well-being, dear friend!
Love, Sally

Subj: His Grace
Date: 11/26/2000 2:26:13 PM Central Standard Time
From: debbiesb13@aol.com
To: sarahjf50@hotmail.com

Dear Sal,

Have been thinking about yesterday's e-mails. I do not know why God tests us so. To strengthen our faith — sometimes — maybe he is showing us our faith is not as strong as we thought it was. Or maybe it is a certain direction our faith has not yet taken that He is searching for in us. I certainly have no idea.

My faith is not perfect. Maybe having doubt is part of the process. Nancy told me once that it was perfectly OK to get mad at God and to even question His decisions for us; it was, in fact, part of coming to Him.

I listen to an Alison Krauss CD a lot and have come to really appreciate the song "In the Palm of Your Hand." It says that if we trust in God and live our lives with that trust, His grace will see us through. Those are the words I am trying hard to live by even when my trust isn't perfect.

So… that was probably more philosophy than you were looking for on a Sunday afternoon.

Have my mammogram tomorrow. Maybe they can at least say if the lump has grown. I can't tell. It's sort of like seeing kids grow, you don't notice it so much when you're seeing them everyday. Not that I checked this thing every day, not even every month, truth be told, but periodically. Do you have any of these fibrocystic lumps? I have a lot and cannot tell them from this suspicious one.

Hope you are having a wonderful weekend. It is a beautiful day here and the trees have moved into shades of gold and red that are so gorgeous. Think I'll go get in the hot tub for a while and enjoy the outdoors!
Love, Deb

Subj: one positive step
Date: 11/27/2000 6:54:23 PM Central Standard Time
From: debbiesb13@aol.com
To: sarahjf50@hotmail.com

Hi Sal!
Hope you have had a good Monday. Don't know about you but I really wanted to rebel at the alarm going off this morning after a week of not even turning it on.
Went for the mammogram this afternoon. The technician said she didn't see anything on the film that jumped out as cause for concern. Even though she isn't the radiologist, I still felt relieved, and thanked God for this small reprieve.
Went to see my mom today. Periodically they do a "reminiscing" time for an activity. Today's was on going to Woolworth's! If I could have stayed for that I would have! You don't think that makes us old do you — the fact that we've already done the same "remember when" that the seniors are doing?
Sent you the package today with Zachary's book and the little things for Tisa and Gina. Hope Zachary shares your love of winter as the book is about Christmas snow.
Guess that's about it for now, my friend. Hope all is well with you. Have you started any Christmas shopping yet? Christmas … a whole topic with endless possibilities! Have a restful evening.
Love, Deb

Subj: Good!
Date: 11/28/2000 9:25:53 AM Central Standard Time
From: sarahjf50@hotmail.com
To: debbiesb13@aol.com

Dear Deb,
Glad to hear that the mammogram is looking rather negative! I have been praying for you! I hope you get all the results you need asap so you can move on in your life. Don't you find the most difficult part of a problem is not knowing exactly what's wrong, so it is hard to move forward to make things better. In order to use a map, you have to know where you are!
I have been zooming through the past few days, getting things done for Christmas, and I know this season is going to be very full.

My cats are wetting in the study again and up on Anthony's clothes. YUCK. I have to keep the cat box fresh or they won't use it. These are cats who have always gone outside. I hate cat boxes.

Okay, have to go, am off to run errands and have to paint a little table I'm making for Zachary. Am finishing it with chalk paint so he can not only use it to set up his wooden train set, but can also draw on it. It is just a square of plywood supported by some fabric covered boxes—it's going in the game room where I have made a little child's play area.

I am thinking about you, and praying that you will continue to have the positive results to your trials! Your Joy *book is on the way.*
Love, Sal

Subj: Zooming
Date: 11/28/2000 8:39:42 PM Central Standard Time
From: debbiesb13@aol.com
To: sarahjf50@hotmail.com

Dear Sal,

I can just imagine you zooming through your chores these days, being very focused on your goals. Christmas is such a busy time on its own, and you have the added attractions of pregnancies.

I got out the Christmas CD's today so I can start playing them and hoping they will get me more in the mood. What're your favorite carols? Mine are "Joy to the World," "Oh, Come all Ye Faithful," and "What Child is This" — not a carol, "Silver Bells" is my all time favorite; it reminds me of shopping downtown as a child. I also like the soundtrack to the Peanuts Christmas special.

Have you already put up your tree? Is it designer or eclectic? Our ornaments are varied — some we have bought in our travels, others were gifts, some from when I was a child, a few the boys made when they were little. It is a reflection of our years together even if it would never win any awards.

I will be glad when tomorrow is over so that there will be an answer and I can just move on where ever that may be. You are right that the lack of an answer is often the most difficult part of a problem.

Will go for now. Thanks for keeping me in your prayers.
Love, Deb

Subj: even more surprises
Date: 11/29/2000 3:02:53 PM Central Standard Time
From: debbiesb13@aol.com
To: sarahjf50@hotmail.com

Hi Sal-

Will warn you this is a completely self-absorbed, earthly-self e-mail.

The mammogram showed a new lump in the right breast 6mm in diameter that needed further assessment by ultrasound. The ultrasound showed 9 lumps— 9!!!! 6 are fluid filled (which is better?) and 3 solid, some very small. The radiologist did not want to poke a needle in each of these lumps as they are too numerous, and it would be painful. The doctor said we would discuss alternatives when I come to the office. Have already decided to have the radiologist's report faxed to my ob/gyn.

The radiologist said, "Don't worry." How can you find out you have nine lumps and not worry?! My poor little boob has been mashed, poked, squeezed, rubbed, frozen, and greased until it is worn out (but still not sagging—at least that's one thing to be thankful for).

Had talked to Mary Jo about this before I went but we didn't cover this scenario. This just totally blows me away. I want to think on this and pray, but my mind is totally numb. I can only think of my dad saying, "God, help me!"

Dear Sal, hope your day was happy and good.

Love, Deb

Subj: OK, new direction
Date: 11/29/2000 5:13:54 PM Central Standard Time
From: debbiesb13@aol.com
To: sarahjf50@hotmail.com

Dear Sal –

Did not want you worrying so much over the first e-mail as I have a little new information. I talked with my ob/gyn. He said, the fluid lumps are nothing to worry about, so at least I'm down to 3. He told me to go straight to a breast cancer specialist to determine what testing to do. I feel much better about this. My doctor was a very calming influence.

I'm going to send this now, but will write more later.

Love, Deb

Subj: learning
Date: 11/29/00 9:27:31 PM Central Standard Time
From: debbiesb13@aol.com
To: sarahjf50@hotmail.com

Dear Sal,

Have reread your favorite Philippians verses many times tonight, thinking about finding the good things in life. You are probably tired of hearing me talk about the outdoors, but we are having a true fall this year. I cannot remember such vibrant color here. I teased one of the gourmet lunch ladies who is from Pennsylvania because I saw her detour to walk through a pile of leaves in our yard. I

165

wish you could see the color!! Concentrating on these good things is the antithesis to my desperation of earlier today.

On a clinical note: Do you think the drugs make the mood swings more extreme?

Mary Jo mentioned today about a piece of scripture that talks about having open hands to God and he would then fill your cup. Are you familiar with this? Maybe it's in your *Joy* book. No surprise, I had not heard it before. She said sometimes we are so busy trying to be in control that we are holding on too tight and thus cannot open our hands to God. But when we let go, God helps us.

She gave me a book to read by a psychiatrist who survived the concentration camps. It's a study on how people who keep facing adversity manage to stay motivated to carry on. Perhaps it is also a subtle (or not so subtle) way of saying things could be much worse.

So how did your little table for Zachary turn out? What a cute idea!

Well, you probably have looked at your list of incoming mail from me today, and confirmed your suspicion (sp?) that I have totally lost it again. It's a learning curve. I am hoping your path on the other hand, is covered in snowflakes, to soften your way!!!

Love, Deb

Subj: *praise the Lord!*
Date: *11/30/2000 6:18:28 PM Central Standard Time*
From: *sarahjf50@hotmail.com*
To: *debbiesb13@aol.com*

Greetings!

Long story short: took Tisa to obgyn, she told Tisa to wait another week. Tisa burst into tears, she's so tired of being pregnant. Spent the day trying to get her to smile and telling her she's just healthy and her body insists on going the full 40 weeks—she didn't buy it. Anyway, I take her back on Tuesday. Her husband walked in tonight with a bouquet of flowers. What a prince!

Now, let's get to other health issues! My heavens, Deb!!! This is really too-o-o-o-o-o-o MUCH!!!!!! I'm so glad Mary Jo is there to walk you through this. Once again, you are about to learn how to be even stronger. Go ahead and have your mood swings, you deserve to scream if you want to.

Let me tell you what happened to me—you know, this is one of those "misery loves company" stories:

When I came out of my mega depression years ago, I was walking on wobbly emotions but I was doing well, progressing and learning so much. Then I started to notice my voice was rather shaky, it would tremble for no reason. It was the beginning of a four-month progression of testing which finally ended up with me getting the diagnosis of spasmodic dysphonia. It didn't bother me much at the time, but my speech therapist felt really sorry for me—I couldn't understand why—until six months later when I couldn't utter a word without my voice sounding strangled and cracking.

I thought to myself, "Okay, God, why did I go through the hell of depression and anxiety and come out of it not only stronger and closer to God, then to be struck down by my voice leaving me????"

The bad thing about Spas. Dysph. is that when you try to talk, nothing comes out at first, and when it does it sounds like someone has their hands around your throat. People began looking at me funny, asking me if I was okay (okay as in "are you about ready to have a nervous breakdown, or something?") Talking on the phone was worse, because you have to raise your voice a little and that makes it harder to speak...So, I was really in a pickle. But then I started the injections, and sometimes they worked, sometimes they didn't—Anyway, long story short, I have worked out a system of injections now that work for three months, then the fourth and fifth months are progressively shaky, but if I get an injection every 5 months, I can pretty much function. I just tell a lot of people in my fifth month that I have laryngitis.

So, Deb, once again, parallel universes...we both came out of the dark and were plunged into the frying pan. Sucks, doesn't it?

Well, keep me posted on your lumps, we will deal with them one by one. Like Mary Jo said, open your hands. I might add to that, and say, "Whatever, Lord." Anytime you want to cry or complain, or get mad, send it to me. I'll most likely agree with you.

I have been almost driving off the road enjoying the fall foliage up here! It is so beautiful...I am so glad you mentioned it. I have been just marveling over it!

I am hoping you received the Joy *book. You could use it right about now. And I will be waiting for you to let me know about your tests. Sounds like you, once again, took things into your own hands and redirected the process so you are getting better results.*

I will go for now, and remember, no illness can hurt our friendship.
Love, Sal

Subj: a flame warms the heart
Date: 11/30/2000 8:55:23 PM Central Standard Time
From: debbiesb13@aol.com
To: sarahjf50@hotmail.com

Dear Sal,

You must have known I needed some warm words this evening. Austin even asked when I picked him up this afternoon if I was sad. Yesterday I bought a little Woodstock with earmuffs to put on my dashboard to smile at me on the way to the hospital.

You are right about our parallel (sp?!) lives. Maybe we should just tell each other our complete life stories, so that we know what is in store that one of us has experienced and the other hasn't gotten to yet! Can only imagine how this voice problem must get so frustrating!

Breast update: The idiotic radiologist said to me with this huge smile, "You have a very active breast!" She seemed to think that was a comfort. I thought she was a moron.

Today I'm feeling especially sad. Last evening, when I finally looked at the mail, I had a letter telling me that the wife of a friend of mine had passed away before Thanksgiving. I met her only once when they were here this summer for a consultation at MD Anderson for breast cancer. She had been battling it for at least 6 or 7 years that I can remember. I called and spoke with him, my heart breaking for them both as he told me about the pain she endured the last couple of months.

Not only was I incredibly sad for them, but it was frightening as well. We have talked so often about the signs in our life. I thought, "What if this is a sign?" I think I can only maintain my sanity by refusing to accept it as one. I am having trouble with "whatever" on this issue.

I do realize not every lump is cancer, and not every cancer is terminal. Tom's sister had breast cancer 19 years ago with no further problems. My cousin Connie has survived two episodes of breast cancer as well. So, I'm not thinking of checking my will or anything. Just trying very hard to stay focused on my blessings.

I think I will try to start some Christmas shopping in the morning.

Did I tell you my mother has decided to move back to Ft. Worth? She's going to take the bus when I give her her money back. I said OK. She can be your neighbor! You better watch out!

Assume you will be taking your mom Christmas shopping. When you take her can you do your own shopping as well? Is she staying there for Christmas?
Love and blessings, Deb

Subj: *the home fires are burning*
Date: *12/1/2000 9:08:07 AM Central Standard Time*
From: *sarahjf50@hotmail.com*
To: *debbiesb13@aol.com*

Good Morning (shiver!)

It is a chilly, gray December morning here. Of course I am warm and snug inside but I love this weather. And when you are feeling a little cold and lonely, picture those beautiful fall leaves against the blue sky and think of the warmth of the colors. Then think of your kindred spirit up in north Texas who is feeling the seasonal loveliness right along with you.

Now we are going to trade the rustic warm and beautiful fall colors for the gold, silver, red and green of Christmas. Our savior's birthday. What a gift God gave us...

On Tuesday I went to the Cracker Barrel restaurant and bought one of their double rockers to put in my kitchen! I needed more seating as everyone crowds into the kitchen. Plus I like the fact the girls could sit and rock their little ones while we were preparing one of our family meals. Tell me about your kitchen.

Last evening I received your box and was touched by your thoughtfulness. My girls are asking me so many questions about you! I have told them we only met last June but we are kindred spirits. My girls understand kindred spirits because we all love Anne of Green Gables, *both the Disney movies and the books. The friendship of Anne and Diana is one of kindred spirits. At one point, when Tisa had decided on the name Lyndsey Anne, she told Gina to name her little girl Diana! Anyway, you are in their prayers as I have shared with them your difficult times. When you have the chance to visit us someday, I will have to arrange a time when we can all get together, as they would love to meet you.*

I loved your card to me! Did I tell you I have two calico cats? I love cards with calico cats.

Breast cancer. Let's attack this methodically:

When you get the biopsy results:

The huge majority of tumors are benign.

If the biopsy is positive:

When caught early, breast cancer is hugely curable.

That's the truth of breast cancer.

I know that doesn't get rid of the fact that this is a very earth shaking experience for you. Keep on venting to me in your e-mails: scream, yell, complain, whine, bitch and I will listen and understand you are scared and hurting.

While we (and I mean "we") are awaiting the results of the tests, we need to tell each other stories (Phil 4:6-10) and fill up your days with uplifting thoughts!

I'm going to tell you a story!

But first, let me comment on a couple of other things—Tell your mother that Fort Worth was leveled in the tornado last year and the home where she could have lived is now a shelter for the homeless...(in other words, there's no room at the inn!)

Yes, I have taken my mother Christmas shopping. And in the spirit of the season, I have to say, I had an endearing moment when I saw my Mom from behind, (after searching for her for 30 min. in Target) limping down an aisle on her bum ankle, pushing a cart: an elderly lady who has been through so much this year, and my heart not only went out to this dear woman, but also I was thankful that God has sent her here for me to take care of. It was a good moment.

The other answer to a question you asked, will my mom be here for Christmas. Yes, she will. I have bought her a new Christmas stocking, in winter white velvet. Beginning many, many years ago I was having trouble finding gifts for my parents, because they had everything. So I bought them personalized stockings: Nonny and Papa, and also for Bob's folks: Grandma and Grandpa. Every year I would fill the stockings with a bunch of little gifts, and I would wrap each one (even the little box of paperclips or rubber bands I got for my dad). This way they had dozens of little but fun gifts to open every Christmas morning. I thought this year, since both Mom and Bob's dad are alone, that it was time for new stockings for both of them, because the thought of using the matching stockings of the past years may be a little painful. So, on Christmas, both Mom and Bob (Bob's dad) will be together, at our home, opening the silly little gifts.

The next e-mail will be your STORY FOR THE DAY. So, when you have time, a quiet moment, grab a cup of tea (do you like Celestial Seasonings Nutcracker tea?) and put your feet up on the desk, and read a little story (this is a true story).

Love, Sally

Subj: deck the halls
Date: 12/1/2000 10:51:29 AM Central Standard Time
From: debbiesb13@aol.com
To: sarahjf50@hotmail.com

Hi again!

I've brought a few Christmas decorations down from the attic so I will reward myself with this break.

I know the rocker you mean!! They are wonderful and will definitely be a cozy perch for people in your kitchen! My kitchen is "early Cracker Barrel." The kitchen and breakfast room are like one big room. The wallpaper is big hunter green and white check with red apples. There's a shelf about a foot below the ceiling that goes around the room with all kinds of old bottles, antique kitchen items, and reproduction cookie tins. Prominently displayed is a sign that says, "Small busted women have big hearts."

You mentioned the stockings: My mom made our stockings years ago. My dad's is about 40" long and so cute even if showing age. Hers is the shape of an old button shoe. I can't see putting hers up alone and will not take his to further confuse her denial issues. Cannot decide yet if I will follow your example and get her a new one or just not have one in her room as it will still be one stocking all by itself. Maybe I will just put hers up here. Your little gifts idea is great!

I'm glad your girls enjoyed the gifts. Even though I feel like I know your daughters a little already from our e-mails, I would definitely love to meet them! I know they are one of the great blessings in your life.

No I haven't had the Nutcracker tea — what flavor is it?

Well, Sal, time to put out a few decorations around the house. It's pouring rain here now (your cold front coming this way) and the leaves coming off the trees are almost as numerous as raindrops! Like the idea of sharing the winter, a cup of tea, and a little Christmas cheer with my friend. Are you listening to Christmas music? Currently playing here – "Oh Come all Ye Faithful!"

Love and cheer, Deb

The Young and the Nestless

Subj: *Story time: George and Martha*
Date: *12/1/2000 1:29:44 PM Central Standard Time*
From: *sarahjf50@hotmail.com*
To: *debbiesb13@aol.com*

Yes, I am listening to a Christmas CD right now. My favorite tunes are "The Holly and the Ivy" and "The Christmas Song" (chestnuts roasting on an open fire...) I also like "Greensleeves."

Nutcracker tea tastes like Christmas! Cinnamon, cloves, apples—yum-yum!

Okay, this is a story about one of our animals! We have had quite a few different furred and feathered friends in our home. We still do...

The Young and the Nestless: Part 1

In the late 70's we lived in El Centro, California, (in the desert) Bob was GM at the Holiday Inn. We actually lived on property with our two little girls. It was great fun and so carefree, as we didn't pay any home bills, got to swim all the time, and the staff was like our second family. On Christmas morning we ordered breakfast sent up after we opened our gifts. It was a happy time, but nothing lasts forever.

I had been thinking about getting the family a bird, as it would be a reasonable pet to have on property. At the pet store I was entranced with the little zebra finches. The male is the size of a small canary, he has a dark gray coat, with a white breast. He has bright orange patches on either side of his beak and a black stripe along the top of his chest—rather dapper little guy. The female is beige and brown, very light and very camouflaged. The rather large finch cage at the pet store was peppered with little wicker nests, about the size of one's fist. In the nests sat males and females, all tending their little eggs. In talking to the clerk I learned that zebra finch couples are very prolific, and breed well in captivity.

So, I picked out a pair, and the clerk caught them, but in the flurry of flying feathers, and startled finches, I was not sure he had the right female for the male I had picked out. When I got the birds home, I put them in a tall rattan cage. I had named the male George and the female Martha. George sat on the top perch, Martha sat on the bottom of the cage. This went on for a day, they would never get near each other—very unlike the pairs in the pet store. So, I decided I did not have the right Martha and took her back to the pet store. Sure enough, there was the plump little TRUE Martha, sitting all by herself, rather forlorn, in a corner of the pet store finch cage. I made sure the clerk picked out the right Martha and I took her home. The minute I put her into the cage, she and George started chirping at one another and hopping around together. They had a rather touching reunion and from then on were side by side on the perches, snuggling together. I was amazed that they were so attached to one another!

One of the important pieces of equipment for a pair of finches is the tiny wicker nest. The male will find nesting materials and make a soft, fluffy lining for the nest. The next piece of necessary equipment was a box of tiny strings, which the expectant dad can pull from to make his nest for his mate. So, George, being a perfect husband (and home improvement specialist), began creating a lovely nest for Martha, and she was getting a little chubby. Every now and then George would pluck out one of Martha's feathers and weave it into the nest. I guess he was adding a little of her touch into this very time-consuming project. Every time I looked into the cage, here was meticulous George with something in his beak to add to the nest. Soon there would be no room for poor Martha in the nest!

The day came when I peered into the cage and saw tiny, plump Martha sitting nestled into her cozy nest. George was still adding to their wicker nest, and I had the thought that he was more of a fanatic about decorating his home than I am—and that's pretty bad...

One day there was an opportunity for me to peer into the nest and I saw two tiny white eggs the size of peanut M&M's, without the colors! I was not only excited but very concerned about prenatal care, and newborn finch care...I was about to become Nana to my finches—what a responsibility! George seemed to take everything into stride, chirping loudly, adding more junk into the nest, even switching off with Martha, sitting on the eggs so she could flit about the cage stretching and snacking.

It was a seemingly blissful scene...until, things started to look a little strange...

Okay, I'll break the story for now. Will send you the next installment tomorrow. This story would make a good children's story if it weren't for one rather twisted character...tune in tomorrow for another episode in "The Young and the Nestless!"
Love, Sal

Subj: WAIT TILL TOMORROW!!!!????
Date: 12/1/2000 1:52:09 PM Central Standard Time
From: debbiesb13@aol.com
To: sarahjf50@hotmail.com

Wait till tomorrow?! This is a beautiful story and I have to wait till tomorrow???!!!! Young and the Nestless — very good!

I have been making Travis wait for the computer to read your story, but since I have to wait till TOMORROW! to read the end, guess I will let him have it now. Will let you know somewhere between coming home, buying tree etc. how doctor's appointment goes......

or maybe I'll wait till TOMORROW!
Love, Deb

Subj: Thank you!
Date: 12/1/2000 5:22:43 PM Central Standard Time
From: debbiesb13@aol.com
To: sarahjf50@hotmail.com

Dear Sal,

Thank you so much for the *Joy* book! It's wonderful! I will make good use of it, learning more about our relationship with God.

Wouldn't want to keep you waiting till TOMORROW — the doctor said the anemia is so very borderline now that he feels it is of no concern.

He's VERY concerned about the lump on the mammogram and wants me to see a surgeon for a biopsy (probably not the needle one as there would be a risk of missing the spot). He said there were two options: check it now or 6 months from now. He said not to wait was better. I do agree with that, and told him I planned to follow up with the breast specialist.

So, no more news on that till end of next week

Went by to see my mom this morning, and was thinking on the way out how sweet your Target story is. I hope you continue to feel that union with your mom. My poor mother is so miserable, I just pray for God to give her some comfort, as she certainly isn't finding it with me.

Is Nutcracker tea the same as Celestial Seasonings apple cinnamon tea?

Must go for evening Christmas festivities and dinner.

Love, Deb

Subj: Et lux in tenebris lucet
Date: 12/3/2000 1:49:13 PM Central Standard Time
From: debbiesb13@aol.com
To: sarahjf50@hotmail.com

"'Et lux in tenebris lucet' — and the light shineth in the darkness"

You may remember that I am reading a book Mary Jo loaned me written by a psychiatrist who is a concentration camp survivor. It is *Man's Search for Meaning* by Viktor E. Frankl. I want to share a couple of paragraphs with you that I found to be profoundly moving. They are interesting in that they are the reflections of a person in the most dire of circumstances and yet, he finds that love provides him with the strength and will to survive. He does not address God's love directly, but I believe that is the love he found.

"In spite of all the enforced physical and mental primitiveness of the life in a concentration camp, it was possible for spiritual life to deepen. Sensitive people who were used to a rich intellectual life may have suffered much pain, but the damage to their inner selves was less. They were able to retreat from their terrible surroundings to a life of inner riches and spiritual freedom...A thought transfixed me: for the first time in my life I saw the truth...The truth—that love is the ultimate and the highest goal to which man can aspire. Then I grasped the meaning of the greatest secret that human poetry and human thought and belief have to impart: the salvation of man is through love and in love."

Before getting started, I wasn't sure why I was reading this book. But later decided the message Mary Jo wants me to see is that through the development of our spiritual sides, we can face and overcome any adversity no matter how large.

The next paragraph reminded me of our candles:

"I was struggling to find the reasons for my sufferings, my slow dying. In the last violent protest against the hopelessness of imminent death, I sensed my spirit piercing through enveloping doom. I felt it transcend that hopeless, meaningless world and from somewhere I heard a victorious "Yes" in answer to my question of an ultimate purpose. At that moment a light was lit in a distant farmhouse... 'Et lux tenebis lucet'—and the light shineth in the darkness."

Food for thought, yes? I am enjoying the *Joy* book. It's nurturing my spiritual side! Have already come across some of the pieces of scripture you have sent me, and inspiration to stay focused on the positive.

Hope you are having a nice Sunday staying warm by the fire. It's so much better when December actually feels like December!

Love, Deb

Subj: *Weekend*
Date: *12/4/2000 9:34:18 AM Central Standard Time*
From: *sarahjf50@hotmail.com*
To: *debbiesb13@aol.com*

Dear Deb,

I'm so glad you are enjoying the Joy *book. It is such a valuable tool to connect us to God through the words of scripture. And for people like me who have had no great training in reading the Bible, it offers me a way to use the Bible in a very personal way.*

As exciting as George and Martha may be, it pales in comparison to your continuing journey with your breast lumps. You definitely need to find out NOW what these lumps are—can you imagine waiting 6 months and going through this all again? Better to get on with it.

Sunday was Anthony's birthday and I was rushing around preparing for that—even braved the hordes at the mall to get him this special light he wanted for his room...We had a nice cold weather Irish feast: corned beef, parsley potatoes, carrots, Irish soda bread and my homemade macaroni & cheese which is Anthony's favorite food. The pregnant hordes were here, as was my mother and Anthony's girlfriend. Gina and Tisa are in another hormonal world at this point. All they can talk about is pregnancy and birthing. I remember doing the same thing, my brain was focused on giving birth. Anyway, we all had a good time. My mother loved sitting in a comfy chair, listening to Christmas music.

I gave the girls their presents from you and they begged to open them now, so I gave in—they were so thrilled with the darling (and I mean DARLING!) outfits and the little angels! My mother loved the angel! You are a part of our family now, and everyone wishes you were here to visit with us. We let Zachary open his gift from you. You don't know how thrilled he was to be able to open a gift before Christmas! He was entranced with the book—but the person that liked it the best was Tisa. So, thank you, you gave Zachary a very special gift.

So, all of a sudden it's Monday morning! I know you had trouble sleeping worrying about George and Martha—the sequel—so I will give you the next installment in the following e-mail—I thought maybe you would like to grab another cup of tea, before reading the drama that is about to unfold.

Before I close this one, however, I wanted to comment on the passage you sent me, which quoted from the concentration camp book. The passage spoke to me, I understood fully what the author was saying. Those two small paragraphs profoundly described to me the state of grace that appears when life seems at its lowest ebb. Of course, "the light shining in the darkness" makes me smile inwardly, as I think of our candles, and the signposts and affirmations that emerge as we journey together through our lives. Mary Jo, as you suggested, may very well be telling you that there is a place you can go, where no one or no thing can destroy your spirit. That place is God within you.

Must go—will close and come back in a little while to continue the George and Martha saga.

Love, Sal

Subj: The Young and the Nestless Part II
Date: 12/4/2000 12:03:49 PM Central Standard Time
From: sarahjf50@hotmail.com
To: debbiesb13@aol.com

Dear Deb,

Before we pick up with George and Martha, do you have your tea? Yes, Nutcracker is a lot like Apples and Cinnamon (which I love!). The other flavor I like is Constant Comment, do you?

The Young and the Nestless, Part II

When we last saw George and Martha, they were nesting. It was the classic birdie scene, that we have witnessed be it a Disney movie, or "Nature" on PBS: The mother nestles over her eggs, the husband flits about acting like he is doing very important stuff...most of the time, methinks, the male is doing the expected duties of hunting and foraging, but the rest of the time he is hanging out with his buddies, showing off his beautiful plumage, and entering into chirping contests, to see who has the biggest beak (or whatever...)

After a few days of watching and enjoying this perfect scene of domesticity, it became evident that Martha was becoming rather crowded in her nest...George would not stop adding to his abode: rather a feathered work-a-holic. But just about the time I decided to intervene by taking out the source of the nesting materials, the string box, the babies were hatched! I should say the "baby" was hatched! I could hear tiny peeping. Oh joy and rapture! A new little finch! I assumed the other baby finch would soon be born and we would have a full nest. "Full nest" was exactly George's goal, but not in the way we had projected.

He just kept on putting junk into the nest. One thing interior decorators such as George are good at doing, is replacing old with the new—sort of going for a new look...One morning I found a tiny little deceased finch on the bottom of the cage. I was mortified! Not too long after, another tiny birdie body was on the cage floor. George was building another nest on top of the original nest!

I ran to my finch book to read up on birdie infanticide. Sure enough, George is part of a demented group of male finches who indulge in "nest sandwiching." Sound appetizing? It's not. With this rather sick syndrome, the male takes his job of providing for his family a little too seriously and continues to build nest upon nest in his little wicker shell. He, because he's a bird brain, overlooks the fact that he may be smothering the little denizens of his nest by throwing stuff in on top of them. So, how does George deal with this rather morbid situation? He removes the little expired birdie bodies that are cluttering up his nest.

About now you're probably saying "YUCK!!" HOW COULD SALLY THINK THIS IS A NICE STORY TO TELL ME? Well, as this is a true story, you will have to bear with me. Life is usually more bizarre that fiction. And, in George's defense, he was just doing what comes naturally, but he was a little over-zealous. And what about Martha? Why wasn't she giving him a few pecks on the head to straighten him out?

Pecks on the head...ah yes, if Martha only knew what was coming!

Okay, back to the drama: Life seemed to calm down for the chick-less couple for a few weeks. Mayhaps they were in mourning, or just resting after the flurry of activity surrounding their first pregnancy. The young couple spent more time flitting from perch to perch, leaving the nest rather vacant. It was more like their younger, more carefree days. But then, Martha began to gain weight, George began to forage for string. The nesting scenario was upon them again! However, this time I, the ever intelligent human, decided to intervene! (BIG MISTAKE) I decided to take the experts' advice (in the finch book) and monitor the nest building frenzy. When the nest was built, and the eggs were present, (three this time!) I did the humane (or human) thing and took the string box out of the cage. No more string, no more nests! Happy babies, happy parents!

I don't know if you have ever had this experience with how-to books, but I have found that the "how-to" only goes to a certain level, then, you're on your own. Then when you mess up the "on-your-own" phase, you have to go to the expert to fix the situation. The expert either says, "sorry, you're still on you own," or "well, I can fix this but it's going to cost you." That's why they wrote the inadequate books

176

in the first place: to get you to ultimately come to them with your incredibly messed up (and expensive to fix) problem. Moral of the story? Don't do-it yourself.

But I did it myself: I took out the string box so George would stop building the nest.

I am going to stop here, because I know your time is precious, and you don't need to waste it all reading about dead birdies. But stay tuned for the next episode in the "Young and the Nestless," as the story rises to a new level of suspense and drama—maybe I should say the story "sinks" to a new level...

Have a good afternoon and I promise (unless Tisa goes into labor) to write the next installment soon!

Love, your friend and storyteller, Sal

Subj: another TOMORROW?!!!
Date: 12/4/2000 5:49:27 PM Central Standard Time
From: debbiesb13@aol.com
To: sarahjf50@hotmail.com

Dear Story Teller Sal,

You know of course that I'm loving this story thing! I don't even mind the waiting, well not, too much!

Happy birthday to Anthony! Sounds like all went well with the party. How do you make the macaroni and cheese?

When Travis was in the 4th grade his teacher said something about teenage boys having worse hormonal mood swings than girls. I thought "not MY boys." Sometimes they can make PMS look like life's greatest joy. It has gotten better, but we are moving rapidly towards 18 now so I'm expecting a whole new set of issues— no curfew, spring break road trip, etc. But we will survive.

Glad to hear your girls liked the stuff, I didn't realize you hadn't let them open them before! Also glad Zachary liked the book.

Friday, I went back to see the doctor, his recommendation is a minor surgery to biopsy the 3 solid lumps. My ob/gyn strongly recommended I not let this be done by a handles-all-different-kinds-of-cancer doctor. I opted for waiting to see the breast specialist. I will go with all films and reports from both mammogram and ultrasound for his evaluation of future treatment. I would prefer it to be a definite yes or no procedure.

Speaking of joy, my mother just called, asked me to take her to buy new shoes, and hung up on me when I said that I can't take her wheelchair in my car. Her behavior has changed—she hates everything. She thinks she can walk and live on her own and that I am taking her money. She calls me at least twice a day now to blame me for something. This does seem to be much more her own mental failing than manipulation. Sunday she said she did not want to be with us Christmas.

Tom was so sweet and very concerned that her berating me was going to again send me over the edge with depression. I'm not beyond being hurt, but did not feel out of control either. In fact, later in the day, I found some nice things in the *Joy* book about how we choose to have positive attitudes. This tells me her unhappiness is not of my making.

I cannot imagine what is going to happen next to George and Martha!!! Poor Martha! Was there no finch "psychotic drug" for obsessive-compulsive behavior? And yes in our house, do-it-yourself has often led to the need for a professional!

Well, I have had four phone calls, and a hiatus to pick up Austin during the course of this e-mail. If something doesn't make sense please blame it on the interruptions not my mental state! Hope you have a wonderful evening!!!!
Love, Deb

Subj: directly to the point
Date: 12/4/2000 9:12:43 PM Central Standard Time
From: debbiesb13@aol.com
To: sarahjf50@hotmail.com

Dear Sal,

Do you sometimes find that God thinks a subtlety may be lost on you so he has to be very direct and to the point? This definitely happens to me from time to time.

I will refer you to *Joy for the Journey*:

"Then what if you find, for instance, a lump in your breast?…"

Sometimes He's beyond direct, and just hits me over the head with a hammer!
Love, Deb

Subj: Male hormones
Date: 12/5/2000 9:18:03 AM Central Standard Time
From: sarahjf50@hotmail.com
To: debbiesb13@aol.com

Dear Deb,

I think that males have just as strong a hormonal mood swing as women. Anthony does suffer from mood swings, and his favorite thing to do right now is ask us if he can do something and fly off the handle if we say no. He defends himself by saying he at least asked us, but sees red if the answer is no—and usually doesn't accept that answer. Anyone who tells you teen girls are harder to handle has not lived in my home. Anthony is turning out to be the piece de resistance! But I adore him.

178

Macaroni and cheese:
>*Boil up pack of large elbow size macaroni.*
>*Drain and put half the macaroni in a baking dish*
>*Add 1½ c. grated cheddar cheese (I use mild but sharp is ok too)*
>*Top with remaining macaroni*
>*Add another 1½ c cheese*
>*Make 2 cups of white sauce (I just do the butter, flour, salt, milk recipe)*
>*Pour over macaroni mixture*
>*Grind pepper over top*
>*Bake covered at 350 for 20-30 minutes.*

Thanks for filling me in on the biopsy procedure. You most likely explained this to me before but I am easily confused...losing brain cells at a disturbing rate. I will be so interested in what the doctor says on Thursday!

On your mom, she reminds me of my dad in his last days of lucidity. He became very paranoid about my mother and my brother, plus he thought he was going to prison, and that there was a conspiracy against him. In talking to other people who have gone through senile dementia in a loved one, paranoia seems to be a common trait, and often directed at those closest to the patient. I am sorry she is doing this to you, but it is probably very normal for her senile condition. I am thinking if my mom were to become paranoid about me and her money: it would be hard to separate myself from the reaction of being hurt that she would think I would do this to her.

Hasta Luego, mi amiga! Sal

Subj: Amen
Date: 12/5/2000 9:31:43 AM Central Standard Time
From: sarahjf50@hotmail.com
To: debbiesb13@aol.com

Dear Deb,
>*His word, His wisdom, His way of reaching us is rather like a velvet sledge hammer, is it not?*
Love, Sal

Subj: The Young and the Nestless, Part III
Date: 12/5/2000 12:57:28 PM Central Standard Time
From: sarahjf50@hotmail.com
To: debbiesb13@aol.com

Happy Noon!
>*Newsbreak: Tisa's doctor said they did not want to induce Tisa as little Lyndsey is in a posterior position and it would cause Tisa's previous c-section*

incision to possibly burst. Since Lyndsey is still little (7 lbs) they are going to wait and see if she moves into a more favorable position, if and when she does, they will break Tisa's water. If she does not move, and Tisa has to be induced, then chances are she will have to have another c-section to prevent damage to the previous incision.

Okay, I have my hot, steamy tea, how about you? Constant Comment today.

The Young and the Nestless: Part III

When we left our little feathered friends yesterday, they were on the verge of becoming parents again. They were also on the verge of repeating the previous tragedy of smothering the babies with too much stuff crammed into the nursery. At this point I became directly involved, taking away George's ability to build, build, build, nest, upon nest, upon nest, by removing George's supply of string.

What I did not take into consideration is that George is a brilliant decorator. Have you ever noticed in model homes how ingenious the decorators are? Also, they are masters of creativity and improvisation, taking unlikely objects and turning them into functional, attractive objects.

This is exactly what George did: found a new, innovative, inexpensive way to feather his nest...and I do mean "feather" his nest: One morning I saw him with beige feathers in his mouth...Martha looked fine, so I thought he was picking up discards on the cage floor. I kept an eye on him, and kept the cage fairly devoid of feathers, which should have slowed down his nest building—but, then Martha started looking a little bald on the top of her tiny head...

Sure enough, George was going to the source of the feathers: Martha. So, what to do? By this time, there was no hope for the newest flock of babies. I found a discarded egg shell to testify to the fact that in George's eyes, babies were just an irritating facet of nest building. And Martha continued to go bald—which isn't good for little birds as they will catch cold.

Now it was time for us to leave on vacation. Went to Hawaii. We left a person in charge of feeding our birds. And in final desperation, I took the whole wicker nest out of the cage, thinking to distract George onto other projects. Parenting was not his thing. And poor Martha, she didn't have anything to say about all this. So, when we returned, I would read some more on finches and try to work out this unpleasant situation.

We returned from Hawaii, had a nice time, by the way, and looked into the rattan cage, at George jumping around, chirping. But where was Martha? She was nowhere to be found! Then we noticed a little tissue covered shroud placed on the kitchen counter with a note beside it which read: "She died and we didn't know what to do with her."

I opened the tissue, and there was Martha, very composed, but totally bald AND totally devoid of any breast feathers. I looked at George who was so happy to see us, chirping and hopping around...: you dumb bird: how can you practice survival of the species when you keep killing off your chances for your species to survive?

The girls and I took Martha out to a remote corner of the grass park by the hotel and gave her a lovely resting place, alongside our tropical fish, and gerbils. Yes, we had quite a full pet cemetery...

Now, I could tell you the story ends with Martha's demise, but sad to say, it doesn't! George was alone in his cage, which is not good for a finch (even a killer finch like George) as they are community dwellers. This was a dilemma! Should I get another female? Or how about getting a male? Would that work? Would he not respond to any other bird, because Martha was his chosen mate? Remember at the beginning of this story I got the wrong Martha and they were very incompatible. What would you do?

Finally, I made, what I thought was a brilliant decision: the answer to all the little birdie dilemmas of the past. I would take mother nature into my own hands (I have since learned that the adage "you can't fight mother nature" is true in my life). Tune in for the final episode of the Young and the Nestless on Wednesday. It is not only surprising, but also predictable (I wish I could have predicted this, as things may have turned out a lot different). Until tomorrow.
Love, Sal

Intermission (or remission?)

Subj: can't pick just one
Date: 12/5/00 7:22:19 PM Central Standard Time
From: debbiesb13@aol.com
To: sarahjf50@hotmail.com

Hi Sal!

There are so many items of interest today!! How was Tisa about the news from the doctor's appointment? Could not tell from your description if she was concerned about the prospect of another c-section or just taking it as a part of the process.

Poor Martha!!!! I would have let George be a bachelor, as he seems to be lacking something mentally to fit in as a community dweller. On the other hand, I can see where George may not have realized the consequences of his actions. (Have you seen the stuff in the newspaper and on morning news programs about men only listening with half their brain while women use both sides? Isn't it interesting how it always takes a study for someone to figure out what we women have known for years?) Well, I am sad for poor Martha, but quite curious to know how you solved this dilemma for poor obsessive-compulsive George—cages side by side?

Food glorious food: thanks for the macaroni and cheese recipe. I'll try it on the weekend when we are all present and accounted for. Yes! I've had Constant Comment and like it. On food/expanding waistlines — do the antidepressants make you crave sweets? I like desserts, but am not normally one to crave sweets (bread, yes!). Lately I just can't get enough.

Spoke with the hospice nurse and have the doctor coming to see my mom on Thursday to assess if this recent change is due to medication or her brain tumor.

You have so much fun with Zachary. I wish Tristan could come to our house more often, but know it is difficult for Tracey to balance all the demands on their time. She really does amazingly well all things considered. When they were here last he was going to tell me something and in his excitement he said "D Grandma!" We all laughed as in "a, b, c, d," which is not far from the truth as he has 5 (counting real and step grandmas!)

Oh speaking of Christmas… the lady I volunteer with in the college room has four kids between 6 and 17 (you can identify with her, yes?) She told me today she told her husband there is just not enough time for decorating outdoors. Her solution: one light on a tree outside with a sign that says, "Simplify!" Of course she won't do that, but it does seem to speak to the heart of the matter!

Like the idea of the velvet sledgehammer!

Well, I must close this now as my house is in musical overload. Travis is now in a rock band and is in his room (directly above me) practicing his songs with the PA system he bought recently. Austin is in the family room practicing his trumpet. I can listen to one or the other but both together is a bit discordant no matter how adorable they may be! I'm going to my room and close the door!

Have a peaceful evening! Feliz Navidad!

Love, Deb

Subj: bah humbug...
Date: 12/6/00 5:25:42 PM Central Standard Time
From: sarahjf50@hotmail.com
To: debbiesb13@aol.com

Dear Deb,

Thanks for your cheery message!

No Christmas spirit for me today. I have not had time, but I really need to do some scripture study. Need to get back on the right track. How's that for Christmas cheer? Sorry Deb, I hope I'm not spoiling your lovely spirit! Throw some of it my way, I'm stuck on the dark side. Parenting is not always my best attribute in life...

Will send you the final installment in the birdie story a little later. There is one very important fact about the ending of the story that I cannot remember! I asked Bob and he didn't remember. Next I will ask Tisa if she remembers. Bob said if I couldn't remember to make something up, but I can't do that! We're talking about a REAL story here, and it wouldn't be right if I made up part of the ending. Anyway, I will write later!

Love, Sal

Subj: Tis the season
Date: 12/6/2000 8:45:23 PM Central Standard Time
From: debbiesb13@aol.com
To: sarahjf50@hotmail.com

Dear "Blue Christmas" Sal

Hi there! Sorry to hear you are not feeling too "ho-ho-ho" today!

Don't let Darth Vader lure you to the dark side. The force (faith) is strong in you, my friend.

I was telling Mary Jo today about your sending me the *Joy* book and how quickly I had found things that were speaking directly to my current trials. The scripture is a source of peace. How about I remind you of your favorite Philippians verses 4:6-10 (isn't that it?)

Glad to know Tisa is OK with the goings on with waiting, etc. Keeping her in my prayers.

Yes, by all means the REAL story on George and Martha!!!! Or at least as close as you can remember. I'll be happy to wait for the real thing! I won't even make any remarks about TOMORROW! (That one doesn't count!)

Well, must go for now. I think I hear … chestnuts roasting on an open fire and jack frost is nipping at your nose……If none of the above has helped at all — there's always the hot toddy!
Love, Deb

Subj: Joy to the World
Date: 12/7/2000 8:05:54 AM Central Standard Time
From: debbiesb13@aol.com
To: sarahjf50@hotmail.com

Good Morning My Friend!
  "Joy to the World" is the song for the day! It is my favorite — a fully orchestrated version with lots of brass (gee, I wonder why she likes the brass?)
  Thought for the Day:
  Set your mind on things above, not on things on earth. Col. 3:2
  I'm going to leave a little early for my appointment with the breast specialist to check out this new little park at St. Joseph's Hospital. Saw it on the news on the weekend. They evidently tore down the old maternity ward and invited all the people born there to come for this park dedication on the grounds. I was crushed I had not received an invitation having graced the world with my presence there on May 9, 1952, at precisely 12:42 PM. During delivery my mother told the doctor she had changed her mind, as she was too old to have a baby. The doctor said, "Give her the gas!" Now you have heard the story I have heard every May 9th, for the last 48 years!
Love, Deb

Subj: update
Date: 12/7/2000 4:43:56 PM Central Standard Time
From: debbiesb13@aol.com
To: sarahjf50@hotmail.com

Hi Again!
  Just a quick stop to say what happened at the doctor's appointment. He said I definitely need the three lumps examined. So I go on Tuesday, Dec. 19th for the biopsy.
  It's called a stereotactic biopsy. They x-ray from different angles and insert the needle through small incisions so they can see it is going into the correct location. I'll have the results a couple of days later. Just in time for Christmas!
  This is the clinical description — will write later with the editorial comment. Hope you are doing something joyful today. Possibly witnessing a miracle?!
Love, Deb

VI

Joy to the World

*

Rat Tales and Cancer

The Caroling Season

Beginnings and Endings

Breast Biopsy: Ho-Ho-Ho!!!

*

Rat Tales and Cancer

Subj: *Nightcap*
Date: *12/7/00 11:42:38 PM Central Standard Time*
From: *sarahjf50@hotmail.com*
To: *debbiesb13@aol.com*

Hello from beyondandthensome!
    This is the first time I have sat by myself all day! I left the house at 8:30, drove Anthony to school (11 miles), picked up my Mom (11 miles back), picked up Gina (20 miles), we went down to see Tisa (35 miles) and take her to run errands (20 miles). Four generations in one car…Ran more errands. Zachary and I had fun running around Wal-Mart while everyone else shopped. We bought some chalk and M&M's. Went to lunch—girls ate tons! Took Tisa home, took Gina home, took my mom to look at a tree, got gas, car wash, dropped off Mom, went straight to Anthony's school (5pm by now) picked him up, went the other direction picked up his car ($400 later: brake job). Came home made dinner (7pm).
    My mom calls at 7:30: She has a black rat in her apartment. We take our little dog Keoli over as her breed was bred to catch rats on barges in Belgium. Anthony and I couldn't find the rat, and all Keoli did was poop on Mom's tile floor…So much for being a ratter—maybe we have to take her back to Belgium to sniff out Belgian rats. Asked Mom if she wanted to come and stay with us, she said yes. Called the apt guy and he said for us to put out rat traps w/peanut butter. Anthony and I bought a trap, which we lovingly named big bertha—Anthony set trap. Brought Mom back here, put her in one of guest rooms. Now it is 11 o'clock.
    I HAVE BEEN THINKING ABOUT YOU ALL DAY!!! Wondering how things were going with your appointment. Happy Holidays? December 19 sounds a little uncomfortable for you.
    Will have to tell you another story—or maybe I won't be done with this one! Will get back to George and Martha soon.
    What timing! Biopsy results right before Christmas…guess it's better than waiting until after Christmas? I can't believe we're having this conversation about you. I am so glad you have been good about having breast exams. We will take this one step at a time. So far so good! You're on the right path.
    Thank you for kicking me out of the dark side. I did my scripture study last night, Emilie [Barnes], the one on being feminine at the end of the book. It was a good one for my frame of mind.
    Let me know what I can do, Deb, to make your life a better place right now. (I know: finish the stupid birdie story!). Tomorrow should be a little calmer, once we take care of the rat thing…My mother thinks it will chew off her leg in the middle of the night, poor thing. I tried to tell her it just wanted her kitchen but she's totally yucked out about this. She's the one who sees a spider, sprays it with bug

spray, sucks it up in the vacuum and then sprays inside the vacuum cleaner bag...we're talking daddy long legs here...not brown recluse.

So, how do you feel about rats and spiders? Okay, I'm laughing now. I am such a sappy friend! Here you are, going through some very, very difficult times, and I am telling you stories about birds smothering and plucking to death other birds, and rats and spiders.

Aren't I just the cheeriest thing???? Okay, how about this: you pick a subject (rats, spiders, shopping, college, hairstyles, diamonds: go for it...) and we will talk about it! I'll try not to bring the subject down in the gutter (my favorite dwelling place of late).

Maybe I could even make you laugh? (Just read my typos, then remember I applied for a job with an attorney: there's a good laugh...I kept misspelling his name Boothe—kept dropping the "e".)

Well, it's late, and I have to get up early put on my exterminator's gear (gardening gloves and a broom) and march back to Mom's and tell that rat to find a new home.

Sweet dreams and Hasta luego, baby, or maybe that was hasta la vista...ask Arnold S.
Your pal (I'm praying for you) Sal

Subj: Silent Night
Date: 12/8/2000 11:16:25 AM Central Standard Time
From: debbiesb13@aol.com
To: sarahjf50@hotmail.com

Dear Overdrive Sal,

At the time you were finally finishing your e-mail to me last night, I had already been sleeping 4 hours! I fell asleep reading before 8:00; got up at 9:15 and went to bed. Guess it was a combination of the cold, period, and probably mental exhaustion. But you are the one who should have been sleeping!!!! At that rate you will be getting oil changes every couple of weeks, and your body will be running on fumes! When you have a day like that, though, don't you sort of feel like you notched a little victory — I think there is a certain satisfaction in amongst the exhaustion at having accomplished so much for so many.

Did you catch the rat?

Here is our personal rat story: When we lived in Beaumont, Tom and I were sleeping soundly when something that sounded like a small herd of elephants ran across the attic above our bed. Seems we had a whole thriving little colony up there. They had burrowed little freeways through all the insulation and had set up individual townhouses for themselves etc. They entered through a hole conveniently eaten in the wall in the garage. The exterminator put out poison, which they ate and then ran outside gasping for air. So, pleasantly, they did not die in the house — that time.

About a year or so later, Tom got a phone call saying he was being transferred to Florida and was to leave immediately. In the first week he was gone several things went wrong with our house, of course, one of which was something dead in the attic. So here I was supposed to be getting our house ready to sell, and it smelled like dead things. The exterminator told me to put out oil of wintergreen. Do you have any idea how bad dead rat masked by wintergreen can smell?! This was worse! Eventually the smell went away. When the movers were bringing stuff out of the attic they were courteous enough to bring down the offending furry critter, which by then was a stiff.

Yes, you are the cheeriest thing!

OK, here are my thoughts on the breast situation. After finding myself in a panic at various medical miscues, my doctor (who has the sign in his office that says, "God does the healing, physicians get the credit") calmed me. He sent me to the RIGHT doctor who will do the RIGHT test that will give the RIGHT answer (whatever that may be).

If they tell me it is malignant, it will not be the worst thing — having someone tell me our kids or Tristan had a problem would be much worse. Although I don't believe in focusing on the negative, it wouldn't be right to be an ostrich sticking my head in the sand and fail to consider my options either.

If faced with choosing lumpectomy or mastectomy, I would just want them to take the boob now instead of facing a possible second time around. I have asked Tom, who has been so concerned and supportive, if it came to that would he want me to have reconstructive surgery. He said it's up to me. I think not.

I want you to feel free to tell me anything you think about any of this and hope you don't mind if I do the same. I guess I probably feel the need for that most of all, just to be able to share thoughts in that completely open honest way. Do not think I am assuming bad news — not true. But the options to consider for a "NO" (jumping for joy comes to mind) are a lot easier than the ones for "YES."

Remember how you said in college Greeks were Geeks? TCU was the same. I lived in this great dorm built in 1908, had huge rooms, and only about 150 residents, very anti-Greek. I was a resident advisor (big joke), which meant, among other things, manning the front desk a few hours a week. One day I was there playing bridge, wearing my debate team shirt, which had Pi Kappa Delta (in Greek letters) on it. This guy came in and, knowing this was not a sorority, asked if that was Greek for boobs. One of my friends said, "No, it's Greek for no boobs!" So, if I lose one, who will even notice! (Hopefully you will not be reminding me I said that!)

Tonight is Austin's Christmas concert. That is one of the things I appreciate so much about being here — that you can actually have real Christmas music. Anyway. I love to go to his concerts and am so proud of what he has accomplished with his music.

Will go for now as there are a few things to do around here. Hope you are feeling rosy and bright and that you had success in your zoo keeping efforts.
Love, Deb

Subj: Joy to the World!
Date: 12/8/00 12:44:11 PM Central Standard Time
From: sarahjf50@hotmail.com
To: debbiesb13@aol.com

And Halleluiah!
      I just found out a few days ago that "Joy" was done by G. F. Handel. Did not know that!
      Anyway, "Joy to the World!"
      Yes, let's discuss all sides of your breast situation! It's not as if you aren't thinking all those thoughts, anyway! And that's not being negative or morbid, it's just examining options realistically. One step at a time. And, let us not miss the opportunity to find some humor (however sick) in the situation if it makes you smile or laugh! I have a friend I e-mail who has no identifiable breasts like me and we refer to each other as bosomless buddies.
      I understand about your comment about this happening to you is easier than if it happened to your children. I can think of nothing worse than losing a child...yes, Lord, take me, not them.
      Of course, if you do have cancer, we will have to explore all avenues of everything that has to do with this condition. We will not go through this, cancer or no cancer, without a good sense of not only humor, but style!
      If a thing is worth doing, it's worth doing right. For example, if I go into a coma, would you come up to the hospital room every couple of weeks and use Nair on my menopausal chin hairs? I would hate the thought of friends and loved ones coming to see me and I become a female Rip Van Winkle...And also, how about spritzing me with my favorite perfume, please? Hospital rooms are so devoid of ambiance. How about a little music and candles? And periodically, just for me, rearrange the furniture in the room. A nice wreath that changes with the seasons would be a nice touch. You know, I love to entertain...how about a periodic buffet of treats from the vending machines, arranged tastefully on the foot of my bed. Sort of an "open house/room" affair. And please, encourage people to cry and sob for me. I don't want to be the only one lamenting this deplorable condition!
      A year ago today, I saw my Dad for the first time in over a year. He was gone, mentally in so many ways already. Plenty of dementia and paranoia. But periodically he would become lucid, and know where he was and what was happening. The expression on his face during those moments was the most painful for me. This was also his last day in his own home. We committed him to the hospital on Dec. 9. In the hospital one of his most calm times was when the nurse played Kenny G Christmas music on the CD player. He almost looked at peace, I know he loved the music as he always played Christmas music at home.
      The last time I was ever to him awake was two days later when I was leaving the ward, and he was sitting in a wheelchair, by the nurses' station, watching me leave. When I went back in January he was in a coma. I'm telling you this because it is easy to write it, but I can't actually say it out loud without breaking down. And I know I can tell you anything and you will be by my side, in

190

spirit. This is sort of performing a special memorial to my dad, honoring not only his memory, but also honoring his last days, even if they were painful for him. Thanks for giving me the opportunity to do it this way.

You are certainly in the right region for excellent cancer care, with MD Anderson close by. Hopefully that will not be the case, hopefully you will be benign, (didn't I read that 98% of lumps are benign?). Not to upset you too much, but the odds of you having cancer are not very good...we may have to invent something else to complain about, Deb!

We did not catch the rat. We're thinking that maybe it skittered back outside when Anthony took Keoli out. We found not even one rat dropping. So, Mom just has to keep the traps armed, sleep with a can of mace to ward him off when he starts chewing on her ear lobe—JUST KIDDING...She is afraid of the real possibility it may crawl up in something and die and stink.

I have to do some stuff now. Will sit down with coffee later and finish up George and Martha.

Hope you're doing some fun stuff today, maybe something Christmasy!
Love, Sal

Subj: *The Young and the Nestless: Ending (sort of)*
Date: *12/8/00 1:48:24 PM Central Standard Time*
From: *sarahjf50@hotmail.com*
To: *debbiesb13@aol.com*

Sorry Deb,
Only I would write a cliffhanger story, which has no ending, as you will see...at least an ending that I can remember. I have e-mailed our daughter Andrea in hopes she remembers.

The Young and the Nestless: Ending (sort of)

In our last episode, we were struggling with what to do with the guilty widower, George. He was not supposed to live alone, but was not an ideal mate, by any stretch of the imagination. Actually, I liked your idea better than any of mine, Deb: put the two in separate cages. That would have worked much better than what I did.

I bought a male parakeet. My reasoning was that he was physically twice as big as George, and he was a male. I thought because they were also different types of birds, the competitive element would not be an issue. George would have to be crazy to try to pluck one feather off a bird who was a male, twice his size.

Oddly enough, they really liked each other! I have had a few parakeets in my lifetime and I knew that if possible, they should be let out to fly periodically. So I tried this with George and Winkie. They would flutter out of the cage, flit around together and have a great time, then eventually retire to their cage to sleep side by side. One of their favorite perches was on top of the drapes where they could see out through the window above the drapes. They would sit there and sing and nudge one another. How sweet! How smart of me!

This happy behavior went on for a few months, then the day came when I had to reexamine my facts, and realize I had made another fatal mistake. Firstly, yes, I was right, George would have to be crazy to pluck anything off a large, male parakeet. Therein lies the fact: George WAS crazy. Also, it should have dawned on me that when two males get along so-o-o-o well, that there is a gender issue here. Rather like two male humans who cohabit amicably, one takes on a male role and one dons the female role...guess which bird took on which role? Oprah could have done a show on this back in the nineties. It all became clear to me when I saw George and Winkie sitting on the drapes and George had blue feathers in his mouth. I thought, surely, Winkie would only allow this a couple of times then he would peck George. After all, shouldn't it hurt if someone pulls out a feather? Yes!!!!! As I watched, George did get a response from Winkie: Winkie not only pecked George but he scolded him. Alright! Things were finally balancing out, George was receiving an appropriate response to his action. He should have been discouraged. He SHOULD have been. He was not. He kept on plucking at this one area on Winkie's breast, which was as high as he could reach on the big birdie. Soon we could see Winkie's bare skin. I knew this was bad. But I still felt that Winkie would hold his own.

He died rather quickly! I think they die of cold and he succumbed a lot faster than Martha had, I think. Of course I was in Hawaii when Martha was on her last days, so again, I did not examine all the facts well enough.

Two birds! George had killed two grown birds, not to mention all the little chicklings. George was a crazed killer. He was about as big as a cocktail weenie, and he was worse than the Marquis de Sade. Needless to say, I decided George would have no more feathered friends. If he died of loneliness, it was certainly well deserved.

We took him with us when we moved to Chico, CA. He lived happily by himself, chirping and flitting about. At Christmas he loved to sit in our real Christmas tree. I have the most darling picture of him nestled on a perch in the tree. If you weren't aware of his life story, you would almost be totally charmed by this Christmas scene!

Now, here comes the ending: I cannot remember what happened to George!!! Bob can't remember what happened to George. Tisa can't remember what happened to George. I will ask Andrea next. Gina and Anthony weren't born yet, so they would be no help.

I just can't remember him dying...I can't remember giving him away. You'd think with such a violent story, that I would have really paid attention to how he ended his days, to see if he received what was coming to him. But I don't remember.

This is a story without an end. All I remember is the Christmas tree scene in 1981...Bob said make up a great ending, but I am too stuck on trying to remember...think it's too much for my aging brain to dredge up from the past.

So, let me just close this story on the note that even though George did have a dark side to him, he did leave a lovely memory of being a living decoration in our Christmas tree. Maybe that was his way of evening up the score...maybe that is just enough justification to make it a story not only of fractured relationships, but it was also a story of new beginnings. George was good at that.

The end. Sort of.

Dear Deb, this is not the kind of Christmas story that you sit your grandchild on your knee and tell, is it? But at this holiday time of year, when you see Christmas trees decorated with birds, think about tiny, demented George and how even he got into the spirit and added to the beauty of our tree.

Subj: A Hug
Date: 12/8/2000 3:03:27 PM Central Standard Time
From: debbiesb13@aol.com
To: sarahjf50@hotmail.com

How interesting about "Joy to the World." I never knew it was Handel either!

I am glad you feel free to laugh about boobs along with me. I have already decided my "small busted women" sign could be changed to "single" if necessary. And yes, in the event of a coma, I will be happy to take care of your chin, move furniture etc. knowing you would graciously do the same for me. After all we must keep up appearances at all costs — no Billy goat chins here either, please!!!

Here is another mouse story (this will not give your mother comfort). When we were first married we lived in an old house with only one main bathroom. Sitting on the toilet one morning before work, I noticed this little field mouse scurry into our bedroom. I closed the door, and put a towel along the bottom to be sure it didn't sneak out. That evening we put out some traps and left to go out to eat. When we arrived home, there was the little mouse deceased in the trap. End of story, go to sleep peacefully, right? Yes and no — we were awakened by the sound of a second trap catching yet another darling rodent. You may not want to tell your mom, her rat may have a friend!

I haven't accomplished anything for Christmas today, but did listen to Christmas music.

The story of George is amazing!!!! I would not have thought of the parakeet! Cannot believe no one remembers what happened to poor George! Even poorer George! Or perhaps that is best — remembering Christmas George adorning your tree.

In closing, having watched my father's battle with Alzheimer's, know that I understand your feelings as you look back on your dad's illness. It's hard for us to go there, but we have to in order to heal. Hope you know we both are honoring our fathers every day by keeping their memories alive. My prayer is that as you reflect on the past, you will find peace, trading the painful memories for joyful ones.

Love, Deb

The Caroling Season

Subj: Oh, the rising of the sun...
Date: 12/9/2000 9:29:23 AM Central Standard Time
From: debbiesb13@aol.com
To: sarahjf50@hotmail.com

Good Morning!
    OK, maybe it's been a few hours since the rising of the sun, but it's still morning. Just wanted to wish you a day full of God's joy.
Love, Deb

Subj: And the running of the deer...
Date: 12/10/00 5:45:01 PM Central Standard Time
From: sarahjf50@hotmail.com
To: debbiesb13@aol.com

Love that carol, Deb!
    Hi there, it's happy hour and we're going over to my mom's for a glass of vino. Just read your e-mails and wanted to say hello!
    I spent the day doing our Christmas letter (I'm becoming one of "them") and making our menus for Christmas. I send the menus to our visitors when they come for the holidays. Keeps me organized, too!
    Will chat with my coffee in the morning.
    The Lord is with you, dear friend.
Sally

Subj: The playing of the merry organ...
Date: 12/10/00 9:24:11 PM Central Standard Time
From: debbiesb13@aol.com
To: sarahjf50@hotmail.com

Dear Sal,
    Can't help but thinking what a sharp contrast between your home and ours on a Sunday.
    You have your family gathered round, no doubt with lots of hustle and bustle, and wonderful aromas in the kitchen from your grand feast. Here on the other hand, Sunday is usually quiet with the boys off doing their own things. Travis at work, Austin with friends over (yes, even that's quiet today!), bit of yard work, game of Scrabble, etc.

Can't help wondering if Tisa is still waiting or if little Lyndsey has made her arrival.

Have been thinking about George. He could be the poster boy for "survival of the fittest" if not "the species"! And poor Winkie! You would think the larger bird would take charge, but then perhaps that gender issue thing was an obstacle...maybe you needed Samson or Hercules. I really enjoyed the stories and appreciate tremendously the effort you put into giving me something to smile about. It worked. You did really good!

For my mom's birthday a couple of years ago I gave her a parakeet. I thought it would give her something to enjoy since she liked the one we had when I was growing up and it would give my dad something to take care of. He loved animals! Since they couldn't have a dog and he enjoyed feeding the ducks at the apartment the parakeet seemed a good choice. The day after her birthday I went by to visit, and my dad says, "Do you want a bird? I don't know where the hell this damn thing came from!" (This scene was repeated many times!). It still makes me smile to myself every time I think of my dad trying to give me back that bird.

Have spent some time on the internet trying to find out more about stereotactic biopsies. I have to buy a sports bra so they don't have to "wrap" me afterwards. Did find an encouraging fact to go along with what you had said about benign lumps: 80% of suspicious lumps are not malignant!

On Saturday Tom said something about "after your autopsy..." Pardon me? Isn't that rushing things a bit! We had a good laugh!

Well, it's time for the evening bedtime rituals. Hope you had a great weekend! Stay warm tomorrow!!!!!
Love, Deb

Subj: *And the singing of the choir*
Date: *12/11/2000 12:43:26 PM Central Standard Time*
From: *sarahjf50@hotmail.com*
To: *debbiesb13@aol.com*

Hi Deb!

Br-r-r-r-r-r-r-r-r! I won't be writing terribly long novellas to you today because I have to go outside with my sled, and sit at the top of the slope of our front yard, and wait for snow! The wind chill right now is 0!

Tisa and I have decided that Lyndsey will be true to form for the character of the women in our family, and come in the middle of a blizzard tomorrow. Of course "blizzard" to us means 1-2 inches on the ground for more than 6 hours.

Hey, I loved your description of our home on a Sunday. Lately, however, our Sundays have been more like yours, as the girls are staying home more. Tisa is not supposed to travel up this far so near her due date—she broke the rules when coming for Anthony's birthday last Sunday! I find myself in a different lifestyle with three girls out of the house, and Anthony seldom here.

I thought to myself on Saturday that I need to develop some new traditions for Christmas, as all our traditions involved group projects. Our Christmas this year has each daughter in her own home, baking her own cookies, decorating her own tree with her husband/boyfriend. I am pleased that the girls are making their own homes special and do not still rely on Bob and I to provide the traditions. Positive passages.

Today, I am doing Christmas cards. I did do a newsletter as we had so many milestones this year. I really can't stand the newsletters that brag about the gifted children and all the professional successes...but here I am, going on about my family! Bob says, "You become what you mock"—I have always hated that philosophy, but I find it is true more often than I care to note...

Hey, while I'm writing this I'm listening to the radio—we have a station that plays 24-hour Christmas music—and "The Holly and the Ivy" is playing.

I loved your story about the parakeet and your dad! Sounds like this little birdie had a pretty good story to tell, also!

Well, time to go grease the runners on my sled and get my mittens on. If you see a picture in the paper of a middle-aged woman frozen to her sled, with icicles hanging off her double chin, you'll know we had more freezing rain than snow, and I never made it down the hill! Pray for snow, snow, snow!!!! Charlie Brown Christmas is on tonight! One of my favorites.
Love you, Stay warm! SallySnowflake

Subj: Hark! The Herald Angles Sing!
Date: 12/11/2000 3:57:02 Central Standard Time
From: debbiesb13@aol.com
To: sarahjf50@hotmail.com

Dear Sally Snowflake,

Yes, the Peanuts Christmas special is tonight and it's one of our family favorites! I love Linus telling the Christmas story, Tom had a shiny aluminum Christmas tree when he was growing up, and our boys do the kids "oooh-ing" at the end, bobbing their heads to "Hark! The Herald Angles Sing" (of course, they wouldn't admit it!). We used to watch something like Charlie Brown while we decorated, but as the boys have grown, so have their tastes, so now we watch *National Lampoon's Christmas Vacation* while decorating. Positive passages?

0 wind chill!!!! Yikes! You will have to let me know how you do with the downhill racing on your sled. Wouldn't it be wonderful to have a little white Christmas even if it's early.

I put something in the mail for you today that should be there on Wednesday or Thursday.

I got a good bit of shopping done this morning. Think I will go do some wrapping now. While you are freezing on the sled at the top of this hill, it's still 70 here, but we'll get ours tonight and tomorrow (But hey it could be worse, south Florida is in the 80's!)

Will pray for you some snow! What a story for Tisa and Nana to tell Lyndsey when she's growing up—you were born in the blizzard of 2000!
Love, Deb

Subj: Cascabeles! Cascabeles!
Date: 12/12/00 10:27:34 AM Central Standard Time
From: debbiesb13@aol.com
To: sarahjf50@hotmail.com

Good morning to you!

Well, how were the sledding conditions? No bumps or bruises I hope! It's gotten cold here now. During the news last night it was in the 40's here and still in the 70's across town at Hobby airport. Strange Houston weather! The wind was blowing so hard when I opened the door for the dogs a little pile of leaves came in with them! We are supposed to get freezing rain tonight. Hope you get your wish for snow.

Besides your sledding update — how are things on the baby front?

Last night Austin and I were parked by the fireplace dutifully watching the Peanuts special. Did you see the Garfield special is on Thursday? That's another favorite of ours. I love it when he gives the grandmother the old love letters and when they light the tree.

Got a call from a friend of my parents' from WWII to see how they were getting along. It was hard to tell her about my dad, but it was hard to tell her about my mother's declining health too. That took me a bit by surprise. I guess it's sort of like you said about having to verbalize certain things being more difficult. It was nice to know she still remembered them in better days.

I was thinking about what you said about your daughters starting their own traditions in their own homes being a positive passage (I think that's the term you used). What a good mom you are, Sally! I wanted that kind of acceptance of my growing up and becoming a woman from my mom for so long. Even when she had been in the hospital and I was having to go put her to bed each night, she would argue that I couldn't be out alone after dark to go home. Oh well...

Well, I will go for now to stuff myself with all the holiday delicacies with the ladies from our gourmet group. Hope you're enjoying the cold, but staying cozy and warm as well, maybe even sharing in the miracle of life. Almost forgot — I think cascabeles is jingle bells in Spanish. Feliz Navidad and Vaya con Dios, mi amiga!
Love, Deb

Subj: Oh, the weather outside is frightful!
Date: 12/13/00 8:48:02 AM Central Standard Time
From: sarahjf50@hotmail.com
To: debbiesb13@aol.com

Good Morning!
        It's pretty cold all over the state, is it not? I am sad to report that I had to drag my little sled inside, as the snow never came. Got a lot of ice though!
        Just talked to Bob, he slid into a guardrail on the way into work, but he's okay!! My husband is always the car you see on TV as the only car on the freeway in terrible conditions. Said he went across three lanes on the freeway, but the cars behind him slowed way down and gave him room. Thank you Lord!!! The car is a little dented, so will have to have that fixed. Said he would take a taxi into Dallas to catch his flight: good idea. Better idea: stay home. But he never has. He has always braved the snow, ice, hurricanes…must be his pioneer spirit…personally I'd rather stay home warm and cozy, but his manly drive is the same as the cave man had: go out and hunt the mastodon for dinner…Bob has a good guardian angel, thank the heavens, who works overtime on him. Please say a prayer for him.
        Back to our e-mails, yes, I love the Garfield Christmas. I also like the puppet animated ones about Rudolph and Santa.
        Stay warm and stay home! Might be a little icy on the way to Mary Jo.
Adieu, Sally, the icewoman

Subj: But the fire is so delightful
Date: 12/13/00 4:02:21 PM Central Standard Time
From: debbiesb13@aol.com
To: sarahjf50@hotmail.com

Dear Sledding Sal,
        Don't put your sled up yet!! Our weather here this morning said you're supposed to have real snow this afternoon!! Hopefully that won't turn into more ice!!!!!!! It sounds like Bob had quite a treacherous time this morning!
        So how are the cookies coming? Are you doing a lot of different kinds, shapes etc? The boys and I used to make cookies together, but they just want to eat them now. We usually have chocolate chip and sugar ones with sprinkles. I have given up on shapes as everyone is just interested in eating them as quickly as possible.
        Mary Jo had me schedule next week's time so it will be after I get the biopsy results. It was good I was going today, as there were some of my peripheral issues that had been on my mind. Friday was the anniversary of my aunt's death. That was such a sad day.
        Yes, let's talk about Christmas shows. I like the puppet ones too. Travis surprised me the other day. He voted for *Rudolph* as the best Christmas show of all time on some on line survey. He likes Yukon Cornelius!

Are your ears pierced? I don't remember. I want to get a second set of holes in my ears. Tom has given me sets of studs over the years that I don't wear because I like dangle ones and hoops better (which are also his gifts). So I was thinking a second set of holes would be a good solution. What do you think? My mother will be horrified — she thinks I'm barbaric as it is. Hmmmmm...maybe a navel ring instead! Hey, I could turn this into a whole midlife crisis issue if I work long enough!

Do you open your presents Christmas Eve or Christmas Day? We always had ours on Christmas Eve until Tom and I married. He insists on waiting till Christmas Day. This has become a nice tradition of our own. We still do Santa gifts and fill the stockings even though the boys are big.

Glad your mom has not had any more rat sightings.

Well, I think I've gone on too long. Will go wrap the gifts from today's shopping efforts and possibly work on the menu for Christmas dinner for who ever shows up. Will look forward to news of your sledding if the snow shows up. Blessings and cheer of Christmas my friend...
Love, Deb

Beginnings and Endings

Subj: *So if we've no place to go…*
Date: *12/13/2000 10:35:11 PM Central Standard Time*
From: *sarahjf50@hotmail.com*
To: *debbiesb13@aol.com*

Dear Deb,

On your lumps: God is wrapping you in plenty of friends and professionals to make sure Deb gets the best care. We will all be in this together! Chances are (sorry to disappoint you) we won't have much to talk about after surgery, as the doctor will probably say "Take your lumps and get off this table woman! Make room for the gals that have SERIOUS lumps." Like I said before, oh well, we will have to find something else to complain about.

Seriously, though, how are you feeling about this whole breast thing? Any poopy things to get off your chest? (sorry for the pun). I am here to hear you vent and rant on and on about anything that ticks you off. Maybe you're just fine—WHATEVER!?!? I'm here.

Ah, why is it in our parallel universes we go through traumas at the same time? Did not grasp that your aunt died at Christmas time. Sorry you had to go through that along with all the other stuff with your parents. Life is hard, is it not? Live and learn? What have you learned, friend? I have learned more than I care to know…

Yes, my ears are pierced. I am the WORST when it comes to keeping earrings, which is why I don't have anything worth more than $25 hanging from my lobes…I take them off where ever and never find them again, or only find one. If I had two holes in each ear, it would be twice the number to lose…I also have this problem with rings. However, I do have a ring, which belonged to my great-grandmother, my namesake Sarah Jane.

Okay, Deb, another favor: when I'm lying in a coma, and my daughters come in and try to rip the ring off my finger, just slap them. They have all begged me to give them this ring, and I have told them they can kill each other over it after I'm dead, but while I'm in a coma, it's mine.

Not having known my grandmothers, and having something from my namesake is very special.

Getting back to your ears, GO FOR IT!!! I can be on a quest to find you earrings—I would like to buy them for someone who would wear them and not lose them (unlike moi).

My big cosmetic thing this month is to go back into acrylic nails. I am ready for some nice manicures again. My nails are splitting and looking like I do dishes for a living…actually I do, but don't tell anybody.

As for snow—no, we had melting streets and sunshine! So I put my sled up and I ran out to Lowe's and got some stakes. Tomorrow I do outdoor Christmas lights, so when Bob comes home on Friday, he drives up to something Tim on Home Improvement *would be proud of. May cause a statewide blackout when I turn it on.*

We open our presents on Christmas Day. Bob's family did it on Christmas Eve, and they all sat in a circle and opened them one by one, with everyone watching. Wow! I was appalled! I was used to total chaos, where my brother and I ran downstairs yelling and tore through the presents having a great time, paper and ribbons flying. I loved not sleeping all night, thinking about Santa and all the presents. My parents never put the presents under the tree until Christmas Eve. So Bill and I were gift starved and when we saw all those gifts on Christmas Eve, there was no way we could go to sleep!

One year my mom tied our bedroom doors together with rope because she had overslept and needed to put out the Santa gifts. So, every time I'd open my door, my brother's door would slam shut. He got so mad at me because I kept opening my door when he had his hand stuck out, trying to undo the rope—yes, we were little barbarians.

Tisa is in such a foul mood. She goes to the doctor tomorrow and she's so afraid the doctor will let her go a few more days and then she'll have to have a c-section which will put her in the hospital during Christmas. I told her to cry her eyes out in front of the doctor tomorrow, really lose it. That doctor needs to let her have this baby NOW.

Tomorrow I will watch Zachary while she and Dave go to the doctor. I'm going to tell Dave not to come home without a baby—no pressure! Anyway, Zachary and I will have fun sticking stickers all over each other—I got him some new choo-choo stickers. We also play "get me" where I run around after him wiggling my fingers and he screams. Ah, I love that two year old mentality—it's so me!

Also, I am a motor mouth! Wow, how long is this e-mail? Sorry, Deb, I just started rambling.
Love, Sal

Subj: Let it snow, let it snow, let it snow!
Date: 12/14/2000 9:39:35 AM Central Standard Time
From: debbiesb13@aol.com
To: sarahjf50@hotmail.com

Good Morning!
I should be getting about my day, but decided I would much rather have a cup of tea (orange spice) and sit down with my friend who sadly did not get to use her sled.

Tisa has to be going nuts with the wait. In fact I was thinking yesterday that it was coming up on two weeks past the Dec. 3 date she had expected. At least you can have fun today with Zachary while you await the news. He can help (?) you do your lights! The time from 18 months to 4 or 5 I think are just the greatest years.

Everything is such a wonder to them, even the simplest little things like chasing them.

On the subject of lights…We have a little herd of those white light deer. I used to like them, but now they are everywhere, and I have grown tired of them. Will keep them though until they croak probably. Anyway, last year one morning I went out for the paper and the daddy deer was engaged in what should have been a private moment with the mommy deer. Right in front of the child too! Shameful!

I love the story about you and your brother and the door! How funny!!! Your Christmas morning sounds more like what our boys experience. This will be our 6th Christmas in this house and it's our first two story. One of my greatest joys has been watching them charge down the stairs to the tree on Christmas morning.

A couple of news items that require comment:

1. At last the Presidential election is over! I found it very objectionable yesterday on one show that they had psychiatrists on analyzing how this was going to effect Tipper and her depression. GIVE THE WOMAN A BREAK! Why anyone would marry a man in politics is beyond me!

2. A Canadian medical journal reported everyone in the Hundred Acre Wood has mental issues and that even Winnie the Pooh should be on Ritalin. What is our world coming to?

There, it felt good to get that off my chest! Speaking of my chest, or getting things off of it… I have really been OK about the upcoming biopsy. At times I am almost the Queen of Denial going about my life as if it's no concern. At other times, my mental process is already into the treatment phase and thinking about things like if I lose the breast will I want to sleep on the other side of the bed. Either way "whatever" has become a bit of a mantra (sp?).

Mary Jo and I talked yesterday about how I will react if it's cancer. I told her I doubted I would be thanking God for this challenge right off the bat. She said she would be worried about me if I did. Of course, if not, which as you have said is far more likely, I will be giving thanks immediately!!!

You also asked me what I have learned from my experiences this last year. Like you, way more than I ever wanted to know! But the most important thing I have learned is how to give myself and my problems more to God and let that be a comfort. It doesn't mean I'm "pain free" only that it takes the edge off, making it manageable.

I must really get going. But being a motor mouth myself, I have gone on and on. Will e-mail you again later this afternoon or tonight to address other important issues like jewelry and nails. In the mean time, you have a very fun day with your little man Zachary.

"Love and joy come to you…"

Deb

Subj: Rudolph the red-nosed reindeer…
Date: 12/14/2000 8:51:10 PM Central Standard Time
From: debbiesb13@aol.com
To: sarahjf50@hotmail.com

Well Howdy Do!

Last year somebody put red dots on the noses of all the deer on the deer crossing signs around Kingwood. They still look so festive!

How did things go with Tisa at the doctor? Hope it was good news.

I will be more than glad to keep an eye on your ring if you are ever in a coma. Perhaps I should be sure to keep up your new acrylic nails too so that it will be shown off to best advantage. Maybe bring a rose for you to hold in your hand as well. What color polish do you want? Or do you want little designs and rhinestones? What if we are in comas at the same time? Who will keep my fake right boob in place? Maybe we could share a room and have moments of lucidity to take care of each other's cosmetic requests and replenish the buffet.

It is odd as you said that we have had so many of our traumas in the same time frame. Not necessarily the same ones at the same time, but similar. Here's a thought: don't get your own breast lumps!!!!!!

Did you watch Garfield? "It's not the giving, it's not the getting. It's the loving!"

I will close for now. Maybe I will go outside and see if the glow from your outside lights is drowning out the stars on the north side. I'm sure you'll do way better than Tim the Toolman. After all, you're a woman!

Love, Deb

Subj: Chestnuts roasting by an open fire…
Date: 12/15/2000 8:04:05 AM Central Standard Time
From: sarahjf50@hotmail.com
To: debbiesb13@aol.com

Good morning!

I have learned that my day is peppered with thoughts of writing to you and sharing things with you—then when I don't find time to write, I get mad at myself. You are the faithful, more disciplined of us two, methinks!

News: updates on Tisa—her doctor said she would induce her next Friday the 22nd!!!

Well, we women will persevere, and God made us to endure when we did not think we could endure anymore, so even if we storm the halls of the hospital to bring Christmas to Tisa and Lyndsey, Tisa will have a family Christmas and a baby!

Until this afternoon, when I can respond to other things you wrote…
Love, Sal

Subj: Jack Frost nipping at your nose…
Date: 12/15/00 1:46:19 PM Central Standard Time
From: debbiesb13@aol.com
To: sarahjf50@hotmail.com

Dear Sal,

Poor Tisa! I can only imagine her frustration level. Hope you were able to console her some today, but imagine she is almost beyond that point. If you hadn't said her doctor is a woman, I would assume it was a man who had no idea how it feels to be pregnant for so long.

I am so glad today is Friday. It's making me nervous that we haven't really shopped for all our boys and girls yet. So that is our project for tomorrow.

Will look forward to hearing from you when you can relax!

Love, Deb

Subj: Thank you!
Date: 12/15/2000 6:05:16 PM Central Standard Time
From: debbiesb13@aol.com
To: sarahjf50@hotmail.com

Dear Sal,

At the risk of stressing you by finding a second e-mail from me today…Thank you so much for the wonderful card! You are always there to remind me I am not alone, that I have God lighting my way in the dark.

Plus now I have an original Sally Fugazi — you drew a perfect picture of our candle! A treasure!!!

Wishing you an evening filled with God's peace and the joy of Christmas!

Love you, Deb

Subj: Yuletide Carols being Sung by the Choir…
Date: 12/17/2000 10:53:26 AM Central Standard Time
From: sarahjf50@hotmail.com
To: debbiesb13@aol.com

Good morning!

It's Sunday and I am making my lists for the next few days. I hope you got my forward that Tisa had sent me about the schedule for next weekend.

Tisa has risen to the occasion, once again, putting all her ducks in a row. Did you catch the part about them changing the name of their little girl? Tisa and I had a conversation on Friday, and I said she should change the name to Mary Holly…kidding of course, but I talked about the name Mary and how I liked it, but nobody uses it anymore. So, my hope is the new name might have Mary in it—but I've been known to be wrong 99% of the time. Anyway, this adds a little fun to the waiting, as we are all making up names. My other choices were Mary Carol, Holly Berry, Ornamenta, Tisa liked Mistletoe...Dave liked Yulelogga...How about: O.Joy, Tinsel, or Star?

Gina said if their little girl comes at Christmas they will name her Noelle.

A Zachary moment: Zachary came up to me and said, "Nana, do you want to hear a story?" I said, "Yes!" He said, "Won upond a time der was boy nem Zacky in he wad a gud boy a-a-at de door so he get won, du (holding up his fingers) kissmiss dockins. De in"—and he bowed!

Translation: "Once upon a time there was a little boy named Zachary and he was a good boy at the store so he got one, two Christmas stockings. The end."

Thank you, Lord. I am blessed with the most darling little boy.

Okay, if you are in a coma (notice how I changed the subject?) I will make sure both of your breasts (fake and real) are lying in the appropriate spot. We can't have any of this slippage! Also, I will make sure your mouth doesn't gape open...how unflattering...oh, and don't worry about the drool either. If by some happenstance we end up in a coma together, our kindred spirits will pick up the task, and occasionally I will drift into the real world, stagger over to your bed, dragging my IV of the best chardonnay behind me, and rearrange your boobs, and check to make sure your IV of your favorite beverage is also functioning well, then go back to dreamland. I will send you some Nair and tweezers so you will be prepared for my coma. What kind of music would you prefer?

Well, it's off to the North Pole for more gifts!
Love, Nana Sarah

Subj: And folks dressed up like Eskimos
Date: 12/17/2000 3:18:41 PM Central Standard Time
From: debbiesb13@aol.com
To: sarahjf50@hotmail.com

Dear Nana Sarah,

I can see Tisa is putting all her energy into making this Dec. 22nd date work out no matter what! Go girl! Does this mean she has redirected her frustration into organization? Maybe little Mary or Holly or Star or Joy or Lyndsey will come even sooner, but when ever she arrives or whatever her name she will no doubt be the most welcome arrival to your family!

Your Zachary story is so cute! You are blessed with an adorable little boy!

I'm going to try making your macaroni and cheese tonight to go with dinner. It's pretty bad when your husband and son would rather have the Kraft stuff out of the box than homemade, but they will be guinea pigs tonight anyway! Tom's grilling some steaks so they won't go hungry.

The grocery store had Constant Comment today. Perhaps that should be our "official" tea as we are so good at "commenting," don't you think. Have a great Sunday!
Love, Deb

Breast Biopsy: Ho-Ho-Ho!!!

Subj: *Everybody knows a turkey & some mistletoe*
Date: *12/18/2000 8:43:45 AM Central Standard Time*
From: *sarahjf50@hotmail.com*
To: *debbiesb13@aol.com*

Happy Holidays To You, Deb!
    This is the official beginning of the week of madness, known as the week before Christmas. To begin it on the right note, here is your first Christmas trivia question:

> *What is the average number of gifts a child receives for Christmas, 8 or 12?*

    And since you have been a good little girl this year, you get to have a bonus question:

> *In what state is the city of Mistletoe—Kentucky or Idaho?*

    If you get one answer right, you get to sit with a cup of Constant Comment tea (official tea of fe-mailers)—no interruptions—for one hour today!
    If you get both answers right, you get to have a glass of wine an hour earlier than usual!
    If you get both answers wrong (like I did) then you get to try to do all the things on your list today—in other words, business as usual.
    NO WAIT—I'M GOING TO CHANGE THE RULES—because it's Christmas and we need to be kind to ourselves in the midst of all this hubbub. If you get both answers wrong, you get to rent your favorite Christmas movie and watch it whenever you want! No need to punish ourselves, right?
    Okay, top of the agenda—give me, por favor, your schedule for tomorrow, so I can stop and pray for you at each moment during this difficult day. I will be near to you, dear friend, throughout the day, and be telling everyone I meet to pray for my friend who needs all our prayers today. Please remember

> *"The Lord will guide you continually, and satisfy your soul in drought, You shall be like a watered garden, And like a spring of water, whose waters do not fail."—Isaiah 58:11*

and

> *"He shall hide me in his pavilion, ...He shall set me high upon a rock." —Psalm 27:5*

    I hope that you will not be too uncomfortable after this surgery. But in any event, TAKE IT EASY. Let your body and mind ease back to a normal rhythm, from the trauma of surgery (big or small). God gave you this lovely earthly vessel to harbor his spirit, and it should be nurtured and honored. Take care of yourself, dear friend.
    Don't forget to send me tomorrow's schedule…
    Okay, now, about your e-mail:

Another change—Gina and Stephan had a long discussion about the baby's name. But it is now settled: Juliana. Gina can call her Julie, and Stephan can go for the more formal Juliana (pronounced) Juli-AH-NAH—(we would have to get a cultured son-in-law...)

Tisa is up to the task—we are going shopping on Wednesday to buy her "apres-birth" ensemble: comfortable but cute day outfits that withstand the rigors of those first weeks of breast feeding, burping, soggy diapers...but still look great!

Here's my week: Today MAILING YOU A LITTLE CHRISTMAS GIFTEE! It's not much but I love you! Taking my mom shopping—this will take all day. Making next batch of our secret recipe of Christmas cookies.

Our family Christmas cookie recipe is in no cookbook. Everyone loves our Christmas cookies and they ask for the recipe. We always say, "We would have to kill you if we told you."

Only your best friend would do this for you: if you get an unfavorable result on your biopsy of the lumpolas, YOU WILL QUALIFY FOR GETTING HALF OF THE SECRET RECIPE!!!!

There is only one way I will divulge the second half of the recipe: diagnosis: terminal. I really hope you won't think it necessary to go to that extreme. I mean, our cookie recipe is precious, but not worth getting breast cancer for...and—no trying to make me feel sorry for you!

If you do have breast cancer, you are NOT the first woman to ever get it, and you won't be the last! Furthermore, it's too curable these days, so you might not even DIE! There, I said it: "You might not even die, Deb!" Chances are you will have no surgery, or maybe a little surgery, or maybe a lot of surgery, or maybe you will have chemo (new hair possibilities—we will have to explore that...) but I'm sorry, the cookie recipe can only be divulged totally if there's no hope.

I hope I haven't been too blunt here. But we are talking about MY cookie recipe (and maybe a little about you...).

Now you can tell me to go to hell! Anger at this point would be appropriate. I can take it, I'm your friend no matter what! Except when it comes to my cookies...

Where was I...? Oh yes, my week (who cares about yours?) (Mad yet?) Today I take my mother shopping, tomorrow Gina and I get our nails done (don't worry—I can pray during a manicure) then we go shopping. Wednesday I take Tisa shopping. Thursday I clean my house, get ready for houseguests. Friday I am at the hospital by 6:30 am (per General Tisa's instructions) to welcome the Christmas baby! Saturday, Gina and I have hospital duty from 9-3pm. Then I take Zachary home with me. That evening, Bob, I, and Zachary go to DFW (shouldn't be to-o-o busy, right?) to pick up Bob's dad and brother. Then the fun begins! I have prepared the menus for Christmas weekend, and everyone has them, now I will shop and start preparing. I'll send you a menu, but don't think about coming, because I just don't have room (mad yet?).

Must let you go, do you wear contacts or reading glasses? I have both. Still have trouble seeing the light...HO-HO-HO!

I have such a busy day compared to yours, and my life is so stressful compared to yours, (mad yet?) I really have to go. Think of me as you are lounging on your hospital bed, contemplating surgery, and just be thankful you are lying down (mad yet?).
Your pal Sal

Subj: Help to make the season bright
Date: 12/18/2000 10:06:49 AM Central Standard Time
From: debbiesb13@aol.com
To: sarahjf50@hotmail.com

OK, I'M PISSED!!!!!
How can you expect me to wallow around in self pity with a friend like you?!!
And about this cookie thing — you realize that cookies are my biggest weakness when it comes to sweets (well, with the exception of Brennan's bread pudding souffle). So how am I to decide? Dying of cancer vs. the cookie recipe… hmmmm… tough choice! Of course I could just have cancer and not DIE from it. Then I'd get half the recipe and spend the rest of my days trying to figure out the other half. Now there's a thought, and probably a safe bet for you given my cooking skills!
You are going to have such a busy time from now till the first part of January after JuliANA is born and Gina settles into motherhood. I'm really impressed at how Tisa is focusing her energy so positively! Despite the fact that you don't have anything to do during the upcoming weeks, I'm still planning to send you harassing e-mails so just plan to set your butt down and read them!!!
On a more sincere note…I had a really hard time sleeping last night even with two glasses of wine with dinner. Reality has started to sink in that the time for an answer is here. I was scared. I wanted to cry and couldn't; I prayed, but still felt at loose ends. This morning I woke up and felt that nagging anxiety hanging over my head. Went for my walk and had a very long talk with God which was comforting at last.
Was thinking I would be missing your correspondence as you will be tres busy with births, births, births. But there you are this morning, asking for a prayer schedule! An eternal candle!
OK here is my week: Tonight dinner out with Tom. Tomorrow we'll leave a little after 10. I have to be there at 11:00 and the procedure is scheduled for noon. Don't know how long it will take, but they will make separate incisions for all three lumps. On Wednesday I'm supposed to take it easy. Thursday, they are supposed to give me the results by phone. Friday (and along the way): praying for Tisa, baby-to-be-named-later, and you and yours.
Here's what I'm doing in between: thinking of something to make this Christmas fun. No one is coming to our house for Christmas dinner but my mom. I'm so disappointed. It will make my dad's not being here so much more difficult

(for me anyway). And then I have these two boys who can't seem to be in the same room anymore without a fight let alone agree on something they are both willing to do. I am going to have to use ALL my creative energy to make this day be harmonious and festive.

Oh, I almost forgot your trivial — oops! I mean triviA questions. My guess is 8 gifts and Mistletoe, Idaho (it must be right, it rhymes!). So how did I do? Do I win the BOOBY prize?!

Yes, I wear glasses. MUST have them to read anything closer than 36" away or to find my boobs. Have slight distance correction as well, but can do fine without that (rarely hit anything with my car).

Must go for now. Will be counting my blessings that I have a friend who is so dear she is willing to give me not only her prayers and scripture, but HALF a cookie recipe in return for cancer. God, am I blessed or what?!
Benignly (I don't even know how to spell that!) yours, Deb

Subj: *(two) tiny (girl) tots with their eyes all aglow…*
Date: *12/18/2000 4:05:49 PM Central Standard Time*
From: *sarahjf50@hotmail.com*
To: *debbiesb13@aol.com*

Okay,

   Stop Christmas, stop the babies coming, stop life. I have 431 things to do this afternoon but I'm sitting on my fat butt—fatter after the holidays, sigh, e-mailing with you!

   Here's my latest tacky thought about breast cancer…if I had to have both my boobs cut off, no one would notice…in fact, I'd have holes in my back.

   Okay, on the trivia answers, I have good news and bad news: good news is, you don't have to go out and buy your kids four more gifts, they only get eight— Yeah Deb!! The bad news is it's Mistletoe, Kentucky…so have a cup of tea!

   Okay, for one million servings of Brennan's Bread Pudding Soufflé: In Ireland, what must your name be to snuff out the candles on Christmas Day?

   You know, I caught that little slip of Christmas TRIVIAL you made…you think I should be nice to you and forgive you just because you have lumpy breasts? No way! And just for that, the questions are getting harder, until you will scream for mercy on Christmas Day. That's how good a friend I am!

   On a serious note, Christmas is a little harder this year without our dads, is it not? It's good we have good, loving memories of them to soften the loss a little…

   Okay, have to go, I'm with you all the way Deb!!!!
Love Sal

Subj: will find it hard to sleep tonight…
Date: 12/18/2000 6:29:16 PM Central Standard Time
From: debbiesb13@aol.com
To: sarahjf50@hotmail.com

Ho ho ho, Merry Christmas!

Actually the above subject is the next line from the song not a statement of complaint about my personal agenda. (I would come up with something far more dramatic than that!)

Here is a thought — if both boobs are cut off, at least symmetry is maintained. But then again "nothing from nothing is nothing" as the song says.

You may not find this amusing, but too bad you get to hear the family story anyway. My cousin Connie lives in Pennsylvania and over the years we have teased one another about local good luck traditions at New Years. One year I sent her several cans of black-eyed peas at Christmas. That year she had breast cancer the second time. Later that same year she was being fitted for her prosthesis (sp?) and she had to bend over. She herniated a disc in her back and had to have surgery for that. She blames me for sending the black-eyed peas. At least she laughs about it!

OK, how many guesses do I get for the Ireland question? Patrick and Nicholas are too obvious. Mary and Joseph are a thought. Then there are Spud, Clover, and Lucky. But I think I will go with Shannon for the perfectly logical reason that I like the movie *Far and Away*. Yes, Sal, that's my final answer for the million servings of BBPS. So when shall I expect delivery?

Well, I must go refresh my appearance for my big date tonight…la Mad's fireplace, wine, and something delectably fattening.
Love, Deb

Subj: *they know that Santa's on his way…*
Date: *12/19/20008:12:52 AM Central Standard Time*
From: *sarahjf50@hotmail.com*
To: *debbiesb13@aol.com*

Good morning!

This will be quick, as I know you do not have a lot of time today! As for sending you your one million servings of bread pudding, I'm sorry, they are closed for the winter…but they referred me to a local supermarket, which is having a terrific special on black-eyed peas! So, thought you might enjoy a little good luck, instead. Ho-Ho-Ho!

Okay, everyone who is anyone is praying for you! You may be lumpy, but you are being blessed with lots of prayers!

"Now may the God of hope fill you with all joy and peace in believing, that you may abound in hope by the power of the Holy Spirit"—Romans 15: 13
Our fires burn together today, Deb.
Love, Sal

Subj: he's loaded lots of toys and goodies on his sleigh
Date: 12/19/2000 9:02:48 AM Central Standard Time
From: debbiesb13@aol.com
To: sarahjf50@hotmail.com

Good Morning!
  Thanks for your prayers this morning and during the day. No matter how today goes I know I am truly blessed. There are things a lot worse than you and I having to make more boob jokes.
  Told Tom when I came home from my walk that I should have just left my boob hanging out and it would already be deadened from the cold. My nose hasn't thawed yet.
  You have your manicure planned for today — another delicate procedure to be concerned about. Keep a close eye on those cuticles and be sure they sterilize all their equipment! So what kind of look are you going for — a little international ambiance with a French manicure, something red and festive for the holidays, or perhaps something in rose?
  You have fun today!
Love, Deb

Subj: and every mothers' child…
Date: 12/19/2000 4:26:59 PM Central Standard Time
From: debbiesb13@aol.com
To: sarahjf50@hotmail.com

Dear Sal,
  Hope you had a really good day. How was the manicure? What color did you get?
  The biopsy was not so bad as I expected. The doctor said to call him tomorrow afternoon in case he gets the results sooner, but it's a maybe.
  I thought of you while I was waiting as there were two other women there waiting for ultrasounds that were talking about God's blessings. One lady said you can't explain godly things to people who don't believe in God. It made me think of how God came into your life. I am not sure she's right. Sometimes I think there is no other way to explain godly things except by speaking of God.
  Now I know what I will look like without boobs as they have bound me so tight I'm even flatter than a pancake and cannot take a deep breath at all. It feels a little like armor! Have to wear this binding and cannot shower for two days, and even then not a hot one (also no pushing, pulling, weightlifting, etc.)
  They had me lay on my stomach on this table with a hole in for the suspect boob to "hang" down. Then they mash it like a mammogram, deadened it, and x-ray while using the needle to extract samples from various parts. He only needed one incision for the two lumps that are together and did not do the other one as he said it

211

looked fine. Had to wait a long time after with pressure and ice packs to prevent bleeding (also the reason for the binding). It's sore but not terrible. So all in all, not too bad.

So tell me what is the latest on the baby front?

Will go lie down for a while and finish my book.

Love, Deb

Subj: can hardly wait to see if reindeer…
Date: 12/19/2000 7:33:11 PM Central Standard Time
From: sarahjf50@hotmail.com
To: debbiesb13@aol.com

Hip-hip-hooray!!!

You have survived the surgery! I knew you were up to any task—Hey, as long as we can make fun of something or each other life is manageable.

Okay, my new nails are dark red and are really getting in the way of my typing. Have got to find a different angle. In the meantime, forgive the typos til I adjust. Had a nice day with Gina, and got some errands run…we met Anthony for lunch. Dropped off a new hair dryer with mom and had a glass of wine. I have no personal life, except for you and Bob…I just help everybody else. It's okay, because they all need it right now.

Trivia answers: The Irish name was Mary! Sorry, you are not doing so well on Christmas trivia…but we'll keep trying!

Wow, you have bound boobs—that's what mine look like naturally. You are being awfully brave and calm about all this. Doesn't it hurt? Why aren't you yelling or at least demanding that Tom drive to Brennan's for bread pudding souffle? It is so great that you get to know possibly tomorrow. I will be going to take Tisa shopping in the morning than driving back up here to take my mom and I foo shoping. I really need t work on these nails. foo shopping is when you go shopping for food without vitiamin D. Really, I am not drunk, I just have long nails!

You mentioned your boys arguing—My boy is being such a stinker. He wants a motorcycle, so he's going to all these stores, calling insurance companies. He thinks we will co-sign and he will make the payments. We are already buying him a car and paying the insurance. It's really getting a little unbelievable, that he expects so much. Oh well, time for a reality check, bring him down to earth, he'll hate us for a few days, then move on to some other quest.

As for how the girls are doing—they are both feeling like Mary about now, very pregnant and very tired of being pregnant. But both of them are troopers and are not complaining, just slowing down and shifting their massive stomachs into comfortable positions. Both of them are to the point where regular maternity clothes are too small. They are not heavy in other parts of their bodies, just these big tummies. I have to admit, I am ready to have those little babies here. Gina may have Juliana as soon as Jan. 5th if the doctor continues to be concerned about the size of the baby. Since Gina weighed 10 pounds at birth, it is all too possible Juliana is growing the same way.

As to you and your experiences, I am not going to ask any more questions—we will just talk about it at a later date—you have probably had enough boob stuff today! But I do hope you will be comfortable and sleep well!

Okay, ready for your new trivia question? Too bad—you have to have one anyway! It's part of your personally designed rehab program!

In Miracle on 34th Street, *what does Susan teach Kris to do?*

I had a thought: don't even think about hoping that you might have breast cancer so you can have the cookie recipe. You are going to be just fine, sorry, old girl!
Love, Sal

Subj: really know how to fly…
Date: 12/20/2000 5: 17:49 PM Central Standard Time
From: debbiesb13@aol.com
To: sarahjf50@hotmail.com

Hi there!
    The verdict is no news for today. The lady finally called me back and said to check with her tomorrow afternoon. Oh well…whatever?
    A few boob notes…it wasn't hurting at all this morning till I drove. Straight was OK, it was turning that pulled as the incision is only about two or three inches diagonally down from the arm pit.
    Here's a thought:
    A merry heart makes a cheerful countenance. But by sorrow of the heart the spirit is broken. Prov. 15:15
God answers our prayers…candles.
    How was the shopping? Is Tisa all decked out to welcome and care for her little Christmas angel in style?
    I hope you are spending lots of time in the sun since you are buying all your food without vitamin D! Doesn't it take longer to shop that way?
    Well, that's it for now. I snuck (that looks weird! Someday I MUST learn to spell) this in between Austin and Travis doing their things. Have a glass or two of wine. I'll have one with you. Have a merry little evening!
Love, Deb

Subj: not yet
Date: 12/21/2000 2:39:29 PM Central Standard Time
From: debbiesb13@aol.com
To: sarahjf50@hotmail.com

Dear Sal,
    Waiting stinks!
A la Scrooge, Deb

Subj: hallelujah!!!!!
Date: 12/21/2000 8:44:22 PM Central Standard Time
From: debbiesb13@aol.com
To: sarahjf50@hotmail.com

Dear Sal,

      Celebrating my BENIGN news with you over a glass of wine was a special treat!!! Pinot grigio never tasted so good!! Even though we couldn't "clink" our glasses over the phone, pouring the wine and sharing a toast with you made it a celebration nonetheless!

      Appreciate so much your being there for me day in and day out, with a willing ear and quick wit. Nobody but you could make waiting for news of breast cancer a "fun" time. Sharing scripture, keeping me on the edge of my seat with a story, stumping trivia questions, all of your prayers and the prayers of people around you are the most awesome of gifts.

Love, Deb

VII

From Birth to Death

*

Mothers and Daughters

Blessings of the Season

Pregnant (meno) Pause

The Other Pisces: A Poem

Memories of Dad

Birth Days

All God's Children

Fe-mail Hormones

Happily Ever After

*

Mothers and Daughters

Subj: And so I'm offering this simple phrase…
Date: 12/20/2000 11:41:41 AM Central Standard Time
From: debbiesb13@aol.com
To: sarahjf50@hotmail.com

Good morning again!

I have settled down with my cup of tea (c.c.) and a corn bread muffin. The corn bread was left over from the other night and was just sitting there saying, "Please warm me up, slather lots of butter all over me, and eat me!" Who am I to deny a muffin it's final wish!

By the way, did you get your present?

Dark red nails — very festive! It is hard to type when your nails change isn't it? My mom still has beautiful nails, which look like acrylic, but are real. She still keeps them long and polished. So, do you think you will keep doing them on a regular basis?

Trivia is one of my passions, but I am distressed to find your Christmas questions are hard. Having seen both the old and new versions of *Miracle on 34th Street* I cannot for the life of me remember what Susan teaches Chris. Don't even have a good guess.

How about something easier — like name the reindeer! Here is one for you — what state has a city named Santa Claus?

Gina weighed 10 lbs! I just assumed Anthony being the boy was your biggest baby. Just shows though that birth weight has very little to do with your final grown up size!

By the way, did you get your present?

Good luck on the motorcycle thing. Aren't we lucky that they are not yet of an age they can just do these things on their own? Last summer Travis was adamant about getting a Camaro (never mind that his truck was only a year old and we are making the payments; he pays insurance). To him it is very simple — just give the truck to Austin and take up another payment. Why of course! Why didn't I think of that — yeah, right!

I want to share a story with you about my dad. My grandparents immigrated here from Slovenia (part of Yugoslavia) just before my dad was born in 1915. I was always begging him to say something in Slovenian. So from time to time he would teach me a word — cat, rat, devil, church mouse, horse "poop." (Daddy was a man of few words, but had a tremendous sense of humor!) About this time last year we were having lunch in the dining room at their assisted living. He always sat with his back to the room looking out the window to the courtyard. He wasn't talking much in those days and sometimes you didn't know if he was really aware of what was going on around him. At the table behind him were six women complaining non stop about something with Bingo. My dad looked at me, cocked

217

his head at them, pointed his thumb over his shoulder and said "Starababas!" (sp?), and went back to his own little world. I just laughed out loud. He had told me, in his singular way, that a bunch of gripey old women were sitting behind him!

Yes, Sal, it's good we have many fond memories of our fathers. And I feel doubly blessed to be able to find some from even his worst times. A toast to our fathers and a prayer of thanks for these wonderful men!

By the way, did you get your present?

Did you buy out the stores?

Festively, Deb

Subj: for kids from 1-92...
Date: 12/20/2000 11:27:48 PM Central Standard Time
From: sarahjf50@hotmail.com
To: debbiesb13@aol.com

Good evening!

I just sat down to read your e-mails. Took Tisa around for errands. She cannot handle more than thirty minutes, then she has to sit down, poor thing. By the time we checked out of Target, her hands were trembling. We found her five nice, cute and comfy outfits, which should get her through these first couple of months. Zachary was his usual cute self.

Left her place at 3:30 went to Mom's took her food shopping—got home around 6. Had big fight with Anthony because he hates his truck and wants a motorcycle but he can't understand why we won't co-sign. I told him he was spoiled and he said I insulted him. WHATEVER...Bob found cat poop behind his piano...I want all of them to go away now. Leave me in peace—love them but...

I sometimes marvel at the way the Lord puts me in places where I am needed and allows me the freedom to help others. All my adult life I have been a mom and a volunteer at schools and church. It is not an unnatural thing for me. I have a feeling this constant flurry of family is going to diminish. Having two daughters pregnant at the same time is unusual and my mother's affairs are settling down for now. The next couple of weeks are going to be rather exciting, but it's all good things that are happening!

Yes, thank you, I got your present. I'm sorry I didn't mention it before. I have put it under my tree. I am not good about presents. I feel awkward when I get them. Yeah, I know I'm weird!

Gina is coming over tomorrow so I can highlight her hair. It is really bothering her that she cannot use hair dye because she's pregnant. She's a little afraid to come to the hospital and see Tisa in labor and then in pain after the c-section. Her young mind is a little overwhelmed by facing Tisa's labor, delivery and recovery and seeing what she may be in for in a couple a weeks. I told her she could come just when she felt comfortable, Tisa would understand.

Enjoyed the story about your dad! My father did a similar thing in the hospital last December, he all of a sudden made a very lucid comment, identifying the name of a song we were talking about that had been popular in the forties. My dad was such a teddy bear! Your dad sounds like a real character! I did not realize he was from Slovenia!

My nails...I usually go for a few months with them, then get tired of them.

Think I'm, starting the night sweats...wake up hot then cool off after a couple of minutes. Menopause soon?

Your gal Sal

Subj: *and so it's been said...*
Date: *12/21/2000 8:35:29 AM Central Standard Time*
From: *sarahjf50@hotmail.com*
To: *debbiesb13@aol.com*

Hello!

Before I get going on my clean up day, wanted to take care of some TRIVIAL business! Also wanted to wish you a warm, happy, fun day!

Okay, where is the town of Santa Claus? Hm-m-m can I use a lifeline? Okay, no help...how about New Mexico. That just popped into my head as probably the most unlikely, (therefore likely) place! After all, Santa Fe is there, why not Santa Claus?

Susan taught Kris to blow bubble gum. I didn't know that either.

Now, since you've been whining about tough questions, I'll ease up on you, keeping in the spirit of Christmas.

Who was Santa's lead reindeer in Rudolph the Red Nosed Reindeer *(your boys' favorite Christmas special)?*

Have a great, and good day, dear!

Love Sal

Subj: many times, many ways...
Date: 12/21/2000 8:49:11 AM Central Standard Time
From: debbiesb13@aol.com
To: sarahjf50@hotmail.com

Good morning!!!

I have to leave shortly to pick up some medicine, take it to my mom's and resolve a little mini crisis with her this morning. Will tell you more on this later.

Just so you don't think I'm cheating, I'll answer your trivia before Travis gets up: I think it's Blitzen. Also New Mexico isn't the answer to the state with a town called Santa Claus, but since you still have a lifeline left you can try again!

OH! I saw on the news this morning possible snow for north Texas Christmas Day! Is that you or the panhandle?

Love, Deb

Subj: Merry Christmas to you!!!!!
Date: 12/21/2000 11:29:03 AM Central Standard Time
From: debbiesb13@aol.com
To: sarahjf50@hotmail.com

Happy Day!

OK before we talk about anything else, let's discuss tomorrow. I will be praying for Tisa and baby-to-be-named-tomorrow to have a healthy, easy delivery. I have YOUR schedule and will be keeping you all in my prayers through out the day as you await the appearance of your first granddaughter. It sounds as if Tisa has been a very strong woman dealing with all the frustration of waiting and the physical drain of a pregnancy that goes on and on.

Speaking of mothers and daughters. My mother had decided yesterday she was too sad for Christmas; it didn't matter anymore; the boys don't care if she's here; and direct quote, "My daughter doesn't matter anymore either." I did not take offense at this as I know it is dementia talking. She is sad and I sympathize with that, but don't think it's healthy for her to just be alone. Tom went by to see her last night. I'm sure he gave her some what-if-Deb-had-cancer talk that went right over her head. My approach this morning was more direct: If, you don't want to come, fine; we'll come to you. After thirty minutes she decided to come. Case closed.

We're going to have a giant breakfast and open presents while she is here. Then take her home in early afternoon. We'll have our Christmas dinner as an evening meal (something we have not done before, and don't faint, something both boys requested). We may also go see a movie and play a game of Guesstures. I will be wearing a black and white striped shirt and whistle for the day. Not too bad of a plan.

Thank you for the Christmas present. It came last night, but I'm saving it to open on Christmas. As usual you are too kind! Suppose in a way every one is a little shy about the recognition a gift represents.

Did you make a second guess yet at the trivia? The answer is Indiana.

Here's another one from *Rudolph:* What does Herbie want to be instead of an elf? (Is that too easy? I don't want you to be whining too.)

Well, that is probably enough for now.

Love, Deb

Subj: The Holly (?) and the Ivy (?)
Date: 12/22/2000 2:50:26 PM Central Standard Time
From: debbiesb13@aol.com
To: sarahjf50@hotmail.com

Dear Nana Sarah,

Have been thinking of you all day!

Sending prayers your way…

Love, Deb

Subj: *Re: The Holly (?) and the Ivy (?)*
Date: *12/22/2000 11:01:39 PM Central Standard Time*
From: *sarahjf50@hotmail.com*
To: *debbiesb13@aol.com*

Dear Deb,

     Could feel your prayers. Don't have much time but wanted to let you be the first:

     Lyndsey Anne was born at 3:57 pm, 9 pounds, 10 ounces, and 21 inches long. She has her mother's dark curly hair and big eyes. Absolutely the most beautiful little girl born today. Mom is fine—had a tough go: did a c-section after 6 hours hard labor—doctor said she was minutes away from rupturing uterine wall where first section incision was. Tisa and I panted together. She's a champ. Lyndsey and Nana spent some quality time together.

     Happiness.

Love, Sal

Subj: What Child is This!!!!
Date: 12/23/2000 10:39:30 AM Central Standard Time
From: debbiesb13@aol.com
To: sarahjf50@hotmail.com

Good Morning!

     Congratulations on the arrival of little Lyndsey!!! A wonderful Christmas blessing!!!!!

     I was thinking about you all day. You mentioned on the phone taking the Christmas trivia book as a labor room distraction and I couldn't help wondering how many times you went through it. Watching Tisa labor for so long must have been hard. Thank God, the c-section was done in a timely manner, as that sounded a little close for comfort!

     How did Zachary react to his new little sister? I am sure the days ahead will be mind boggling for him with Christmas, a new little doll in the house, Tisa's recovery, and all the comings and goings.

     Lyndsey sounds like a lovely little girl and I don't doubt for one second that she was the most beautiful baby there! And big! Your daughters are taking after you in that regard.

     The next few days will be incredibly hectic for you. I have no idea how you're going to do all the cooking for the holidays on top of being Nana, mom, wife, daughter, etc. I hope you get to have a few minutes at least to stop, take a breath, and enjoy!

     Our plans for the day are a little cooking (cookies from a WHOLE recipe from some boring cook book, thank God!) and picking up the lift van for my mom. Piece of cake!

     I'm so happy for you and your family!!!!!

Love, Deb

Blessings of the Season

Subj: It came upon a midnight clear…
Date: 12/24/2000 10:11:13 AM Central Standard Time
From: debbiesb13@aol.com
To: sarahjf50@hotmail.com

Dear Sal,

    Want to wish you Merry Christmas!

    Hope all is going well with the homecoming plans for Tisa and beautiful little Lyndsey. Thought that under the circumstances, even though you aren't in a coma (you haven't been driven there yet have you?!) it might me a good idea to go ahead and hook up that chardonnay IV to get you through the holiday madness. Will save you the time of lifting the glass to your mouth anyway!

    We are going to dinner tonight with Tracey, Tristan, David, his mom and dad, Tracey's mom, and Tiffany. Then to Tracey's house for presents. Should be fun.

    I am hopeful to keep the peace tomorrow. As of yesterday my mom is refusing to come because she is mad, but I am counting on her to have forgotten by then. On that score I feel a little like Chevy Chase in *Christmas Vacation* when he is ranting on Christmas Eve about everybody having a good time like it or not. We WILL enjoy it!

    A blessing for this season:

    We (meaning you and I) are so blessed to be able to celebrate the joys of this season having come through the many ups and downs of this past year. We are blessed to have our families with us, the memories of those lost, and the wonders of those just arrived. We are blessed to have special friends, candles in the darkness. With prayers of joy and thanksgiving, I wish you the very merriest Christmas! Peace on earth, goodwill among men!

Love, Deb

Subj: What shall we sing now?
Date: 12/26/2000 11:35:18 AM Central Standard Time
From: debbiesb13@aol.com
To: sarahjf50@hotmail.com

Good Morning!

    Know you are still busy with nursing Tisa and entertaining house guests, but I'm hoping you at least get an occasional minute to read e-mails so that they haven't piled up on you and take literally hours to catch up on! (Of course you can see I'm willing to take that chance!)

Want to thank you for the wonderful stationary set and the ornament. The stationary is the kind of thing I love to have and never spend money to buy for myself. Maybe I will come up with something to write to you so you can enjoy it too! And the ornament is beautiful. Thank you!

Our Christmas turned out to be really nice, and busier than I expected. We had a great time Christmas Eve with Tracey et al. Tristan was adorable of course. At dinner he ran around to sit in my lap just to give me a hug. Kids can make you feel so special! He had a great time setting up this Tonka town thing with Grandpa Hotel. It was really special to have Tiffany there: the joy of all four children together! First time in years.

Christmas Day was more fun than I had anticipated, and surprisingly I didn't even need my whistle! We did "Santa" with Travis and Austin which was a joy, and then brought my mom over for a big breakfast and presents. Took her home for a nap then brought her back for evening dinner. We watched *Gladiator* while she was gone (gory, not very festive, but impressive to the male element, so good). Tom's sister, Trudy and her husband, Steve called at the last minute to say they were coming for dinner. All in all, very fun.

At dinner we had a great time reading trivia questions that were in our crackers. One Christmas question: What does Santa ride on in Finland? a. Rudolph the red-nosed Reindeer; b. a sleigh; c. a goat named Ukko; d. a flying carpet? (answer below)

I am writing to you from one of my presents. No it's not my laptop (yet). But it's a great little workstation that will hold laptop, printer, and some storage space. It can go all over the house. Not sure I ever told you but the thing that aggravates my back the most is sitting. So I do as little of it as possible. So while you are sitting at your computer sipping your tea thinking of me doing the same, picture this instead: In the past, I've been standing up, with the keyboard perched on top of two pots to bring it up to my level (necessity is the mother of invention). Well not any more! Now it's at the perfect height on my new little stand. I'm very excited! And there is a place to put my tea. So now you have the real picture.

Have been thinking about you. Cannot wait until you have some leisure time to tell me about Lyndsey's birth and how you were able to orchestrate Christmas for everyone.

My plans for the next couple of days involve very little. Tracey and Tristan are coming over New Year's Eve so we won't be going out. It is just as well we are staying home as Travis IS going out. This way I can worry and Tom can criticize me for it in the privacy of our own home. What are your plans? Possible "special delivery," a night out, or just a welcome respite?

The trivia answer is C.

Will close for now, so that you don't have to read in installments. Hope you had a wonderful Christmas!

Love, Deb

Subj: Ice, Ice, and more Ice
Date: 12/27/2000 1:55:13 PM Central Standard Time
From: debbiesb13@aol.com
To: sarahjf50@hotmail.com

Hi Sal!

Hope you are staying safe and warm! It sounds like you are getting more than your fair share of winter. Am assuming (falsely?) that since Bob is on vacation I won't be seeing him on the road during the news broadcasts. Hope all the ice is not making it too difficult for you between hostessing, nursing, mothering, etc. but think that's probably a little optimistic. Perhaps a pinot grigio IV for a change?

This is not very flattering, but I thought of you this morning. I woke up drenched in sweat (see, not very flattering), which reminded me you said something about starting night sweats. I have had them for a couple of years now and still no menopause (be careful what you wish for!). My guarantee to have them is a big dinner or two glasses of wine (so you can imagine I have them often!)

Here's another trivia question: What are the only two mammals that sunburn?

Betsy is going crazy trying to get to the dog in *Toy Story 2* through the TV. She's running around barking, and sniffing the screen when he comes on. Austin keeps rewinding it to aggravate her. My dog is soooo smart!

Guess that will do for now

Love, Deb

The answer to the trivia is humans and PIGS! Oink. Oink.

Subj: whew!
Date: 12/27/2000 10:22:06 PM Central Standard Time
From: sarahjf50@hotmail.com
To: debbiesb13@aol.com

Dear Deb,

Hello and I take it from your e-mails that Christmas was full of pleasant surprises and fun!

I am very tired—we went non-stop. It is rather difficult to start out the holiday in the labor room and zoom into house guests and then zoom into Christmas! But it was done, and fun was had by all! Bob's dad and brother had a lot of fun and laughter and smiles. We all enjoyed our gatherings. Lyndsey gets more beautiful each time I see her. She took an hour nap on Bob's shoulder yesterday, while he, his dad, Kent, Dave and Zachary watched Toy Story 2. *All my meals came out well, we had lots of warm treats to tide us through the cold weather. Tisa was able to go home on Christmas Eve, and in between weather blasts, we took a Christmas dinner and presents to their home.*

Gina goes to doctor tomorrow to find out when her delivery will be scheduled. Her due date is Jan 5. She has been very brave and interested in all of

Tisa's experiences and is entranced with Lyndsey. She is very anxious to have their little girl.

Anyway, Bob and I went to the club for a nice quiet dinner tonight to celebrate a good holiday and toast to calmer times in the future (and that would be when?).

As always, Deb, you are here with your funny, cheery, newsy notes! Thank you for the lovely book! It is full of so many treasures! I am looking forward to savoring its nooks and crannies during the freezing days of January! I have been getting to bed between 12 and 2 since last Friday, then leaping up to have more fun, so I am going to say good night for now, and will reread your notes tomorrow and attempt to answer your trivia questions! Also want to comment on your holly jolly days!

Sweet dreams, Sal

Subj: Feliz Ano Nuevo
Date: 12/28/2000 3:05:09 PM Central Standard Time
From: debbiesb13@aol.com
To: sarahjf50@hotmail.com

Dear Sal,

Hope you got to enjoy the coziness of a warm bed a little longer this morning! The hardest part about having house guests is not the entertaining, feeding, etc, it's being the last one to bed and the first to rise. And that's not even counting the baby activity you had going! Know you're exhausted.

Well, how was Gina's doctor's appointment today? Got the impression from your e-mail that she is perhaps a little more at ease about her upcoming delivery, yes? Will be keeping her and baby Juliana in my prayers.

Glad you and Bob got to have a little calm between the storms with your dinner last night. I smiled at the thought of toasting to calmer times. What a nice idea! I would like to toast to that as well.

Tom and I are going to dinner tonight at the Outback for our private little New Year celebration. We will be having Tracey, Tristan, and now a group of Austin's friends for the real thing. Should be interesting.

For Christmas I got Tom a big Civil War battle set complete with all the little soldiers, buildings, etc. He can't wait for Tristan to come over so they can play on Sunday. I assume my responsibility will be keeping the big boys out of their fun and putting out mass quantities of food. Including black-eyed peas of course. Since you have lived so many places what is your traditional food for luck on New Years?

You mentioned about my being in a good mood. Yes, I have been. Christmas really helped me turn a corner I think (of course finding out I wasn't getting half your cookie recipe helped also!). Tom even commented at how good I am getting at taking things as they come and living the "if it's meant to be" philosophy. This has come in handy as my mother is again playing the spoiled little child if I don't make a daily appearance, which I don't. What a wonder and a relief to say as you have said "whatever" and turn my hands up for God to fill the cup.

Just wanted you to know it was really good to get your e-mail today. Understand what a busy time this has been and is going to continue to be for quite a while yet — toasting to calmer times! Would love to see a picture of Lyndsey.
Love, Deb

Pregnant (meno) Pause

Subj: 2001: a new beginning
Date: 1/2/2001 1:25:17 PM Central Standard Time
From: debbiesb13@aol.com
To: sarahjf50@hotmail.com

Dear Sal,

Hard to believe 2001! Seems like it should still be just a movie about the future, but it's here. I am praying for this to be a year better than the last two. Although I must say that on the whole 2000 was such a growing, learning year I'm not sure I think of it as "bad" in the end, even though there were certainly bad times.

In the day when I cried out, You answered me, and made me bold with strength in my soul. Psalm 138:3

Our New Year's was far more hectic than Christmas. It was all a lot of fun but it seemed like all we did for three days was get food out, put it up, wash dishes and start all over again. I'm kind of glad to have my quiet house back.

Just got the picture of Lyndsey and Zachary. It's absolutely adorable and she is beautiful!!! She has gorgeous eyes! And Zachary looks like a little prince holding her. Sal, you must be such a proud Nana!

Will send this now and write more later. Travis is up and needs to contact his friend. Will never understand why they can't use a phone — it's a whole new world out there!

Love, Deb

Subj: *a voice from the past…*
Date: *1/2/2001 2:21:40 PM Central Standard Time*
From: *sarahjf50@hotmail.com*
To: *debbiesb13@aol.com*

Good afternoon!

Remember me? My name is Sally, I met you at the company conference in June. We began e-mailing back and forth and found out we were destined to be bosom (or bosomless) buddies, through thick and thin. Then the holidays exploded and it has been a runaway train through New Year's. Now the train has pulled into the station, for refueling, and the time has come to talk to my faithful friend. I have read your e-mails and must comment on 1679 different things…not necessarily in chrono order, but most important:

You: hurray!!! On your ongoing journey with dealing with depression. Yes, the drugs work and it is a long process of gradually feeling better and stronger. You find you do have the emotional strength to handle things. Guess what? It was

227

always there buried in your heart, under the oppressive, smothering weight of depression/anxiety.

More important, you have learned that the weaknesses you felt during the summer/fall were chemical imbalances and have a chemical cure. The therapy is focused first on showing you how to deal with the illness of depression. Then it focuses on how to prevent yourself from overdoing the emotional strain to the point your body slips into depression.

Bob still doesn't fully understand depression and treatment. He still will refer to my anti-depressant medication as happy pills. But, unless one has experienced clinical depression: an emotional betrayal by your brain (that's how I saw my depression) then one does not understand how the whole thing works, and how it is controlled.

Well, in order to answer some of your questions and make more fabulous and profound comments, I will close this e-mail and start a new one so you can rest in-between filibusters.

Happiest of new years.

Pal Sal

Subj: Humans and Pigs
Date: 1/2/2001 3:17:48 PM Central Standard Time
From: sarahjf50@hotmail.com
To: debbiesb13@aol.com

Okay, bear with me here, I am making a true attempt to catch up on our e-mails, and in this letter I will talk all about myself, and not mention you at all. Let me be self-centered and focus inward...I'm so good at that!

As for the answer to what two mammals sunburn—I qualify for both species, as I am: The Human Pig. I have eaten so many crackers, cheese, dips, chips, candies, chocolates, pies, cakes, potatoes, stuffings, bean casseroles, lasagnas, cookies, nachos and maybe a tiny bit of salad...I am truly the human pig. I think I was oinking in my sleep...I have this urge to constantly stick my nose in the trough (frig) and root around for more slop (leftovers). Then there's the urge to roll in the dirt/mud (my house after the holidays) and do nothing.

As for night sweats and hot flashes: PLEASE don't tell me you have had these lovely physical conditions with no further signs of menopause for two years! I have to recant my diagnosis of your depression: no longer is it a case of too much emotional strain on your brain for too long. The new conclusion: arrested menopause. What a depressing situation! Would you like me to rip out your ovaries now? Then you can come and do mine.

How, in heaven's name, am I going to be when I have night sweats in the summer? Right now it is an inconvenience, but I just uncover myself to the cold night air for two minutes and it subsides—just a minor clamminess. But summer nights and night sweats? I will have to put waterproof pads on the bed, Bob will sleep on the floor with the dogs, I will be the first woman to drown in her own bed.

This is not to mention how my bedroom will begin to reek like the boys' locker room. I will spend a fortune in washing sheets and fragrance oils and candles.

Oh, I get it now! This just came to me! This is God's way of making men stay away from (unreliably) unripe, dried-up, old women. Having us mid-life women rubbing deodorant all over our bodies before bedtime (instead of handing over the massage oil) would be a little of a turn off. And don't forget to factor in the human pig syndrome...Oh my Lord, I'm becoming like those thick, frowning women I see, with perspiration on their fuzzy upper lips.

I missed my period this month....so I'm pregnant or going through menopause—no wonder we gorge ourselves and get cranky. What kind of life is this? And you say wine increases your night sweats? I'm in trouble.

Have you considered Hormone Replacement Therapy (sounds like a brain transplant)? Last spring my gyn said I wasn't in menopause yet, but gave me a HRT pill to curb my rather severe periods. I never took it because I thought it was not that big of a problem, and I might gain weight on an HRT program. My philosophy? If you're going to gain weight, make it a worthwhile endeavor like I do: become the human pig during the holidays.

Anyway, enough about me (by the way, my new name is Petunia, as in pig) and I will close this e-mail all about me with a trivia question to which I do not know the answer: Do pigs sweat?

(next e-mail is about my daughters and their baby stories—much more fun!)
Love, Petunia

Subj: *Three in one day!*
Date: *1/2/2001 4:39:09 PM Central Standard Time*
From: *sarahjf50@hotmail.com*
To: *debbiesb13@aol.com*

Dear pal Deb,
I'm beginning to feel a little better about our e-mail situation, am getting caught up, sort of!

As I begin to tell you the latest about the girls, let me tell you I am sitting in the study, looking at the snow around the pool and loving this winter weather during the holiday. Luckily, the weather has not gotten in the way of the baby parade, and looks like Gina will not have weather to deal with when she's ready to go in the hospital.

First update on Tisa, etal. Lyndsey continues to get prettier every time we see her—and you know I am not biased. She looks very much like her mother did at that age, dark hair, dark pink skin, curly eyelashes, delicate features. Gina and I went over to see Tisa on Friday, so I could clean her home and do the laundry, and Gina helped Tisa with the two little ones. Gina is really interested in everything Tisa is doing and experiencing. She also loves to care for Lyndsey, change her diaper, burp her, etc. The good Lord is looking out for young Gina by having her near her big sister at the time she has needed her the most.

I wish you could see Tisa with Lyndsey. She has a special way of kissing her children, which is so tender and loving. When she picks up Lyndsey, she always kisses her. She does the same often with Zachary. Between Tisa's motherly love, and Dave's gentle, good spirit, those children are blessed!

Yesterday, New Year's Day they came over for dinner (and we had black eyed peas as a side dish to our lasagna and chicken cacciatore) and we took a lot of pictures. At one point Bob took Lyndsey and went into our room for about an hour and a half. He was watching football with Lyndsey fast asleep on his warm shoulder, with two cats surrounding him, also asleep. Zachary spent a lot of time sitting on a chair in Nana's warm kitchen, eating snacks and watching Arthur and Clifford on Nana's Christmas present: a little TV for the kitchen. I don't have cable but I still get quite a few channels, like PBS, so Zachary was happy. Tisa and Dave were able to relax around the fire with Gina (Stephan was working), so it was a nice break for them.

Gina has so much energy (and continues to work out, much to my dismay) and she just pops in the kitchen and says, "What can I do?" So all the food prep was a little easier, and a lot more enjoyable, with her here. Baby wise, her doctor has told her he will not let her go past 41 weeks, which is next Friday. She's ready!

I have come to the realization that not only do I love my daughters, but I truly like them. They, as many teenage girls, were very trying at times. But as they grow into young womanhood, they become these very nice, very accomplished, very responsible young women. I am truly impressed with how they conduct their lives.

Better go, I keep getting kicked off the internet. Must be a lot of ladies out there sharing holiday stories with fe-mail friends!
Love, Sal

Subj: Yes! I remember!
Date: 1/2/2001 6:02:00 PM Central Standard Time
From: debbiesb13@aol.com
To: sarahjf50@hotmail.com

Dear Petunia,

How could you think I'd forget?! After all, it is the short-term memory that goes with age. And you are giving me a real treat (the low calorie kind) today catching up on everything.

Move over at the trough, honey, there's another pig here. What is it about the holidays? I couldn't stop eating either. If I could have grown another belly, I would have happily filled it as well. I read once that people aren't satisfied with liquid diet drinks because they don't get to chew. That must be me. I need to chew, chew, chew! But as you said, as least the weight gain was fun.

As for missing your period...hmmm. That could be really interesting. I don't think I could take being a pregnant grandma. When I finally "lost it" back in

Sept., I was watching *Father of the Bride 2* on TV where the mom is giving birth at the same time as her daughter. I started crying and didn't stop for hours.

As to night sweats in the summer — maybe your mom will loan you her fans! Don't know if pigs sweat.

I think you gave your girls probably the greatest compliment a mother could give to say that you like them and are impressed with them as women. Wow! Sal, I don't know if you have told them that or not, but I hope you do. It is a compliment I would have given anything to hear my whole adult life.

When Tracey was here the other night she mentioned how scary it was for her facing Tristan's birth being so young (20 when she got pregnant). She had a lot of support from family and friends, and is a credit to herself as a mom.

Glad to know you finally got snow by the way! I read in the paper yesterday Dallas had an inch on the ground. Probably not enough to sled, but maybe you got to make a snowball or two! Also glad to know it's going to melt before Gina is slip sliding to the hospital.

You must be so tired of looking at a computer screen!!! Take care and have a restful evening.

Love, Deb

Subj: *On the road again*
Date: *1/3/2001 9:37:31 AM Central Standard Time*
From: *sarahjf50@hotmail.com*
To: *debbiesb13@aol.com*

Well Deb,

Funny you should mention Father of the Bride II*...I watched it last night. I love that movie, as I do* Father of the Bride I.

As for being pregnant, I would truly make medical history if I was...more than likely I am doing just as you have been doing and skipping a period or two.

You mentioned telling my daughters how wonderful they are. You are right, and I do try to remember to tell them. I also send them cards telling them how great they are.

Have a peaceful, fulfilling day.

Love, Sal

Subj: Ready to Run
Date: 1/3/2001 4:16:32 PM Central Standard Time
From: debbiesb13@aol.com
To: sarahjf50@hotmail.com

Dear Sal,

OK, I have to skip past all the important stuff and go to the very important cosmetic problem I'm having. What do you do for the dry skin on your heels in the

231

winter? I have been putting a moisturizer on them everyday and they are just getting more cracked and rough. Though I rarely go without socks because it's too cold, I find that when barefoot I'm sticking to the carpet like Velcro. If it gets any worse I am going to find myself stuck until somebody bigger and stronger pulls me loose.

On the topic of appearance, I have a huge pimple today over my left eyebrow. Shouldn't there be an age limit on these things? Also got the second set of holes in my ears today!

How did things go with Gina at the doctor?

Mary Jo made an analogy today about coming through difficult years like we have had to a stronger better place. In the spiritual realm, it is a little like carrying the cross and then transitioning to the resurrection. Even though the pain is immense, you wind up in a better place. She also was saying that the people who have trouble letting go of the therapy are the ones who have gotten the most out of it. The ones who get nothing can let go with no trouble. Interesting, huh?

Travis sent college aps yesterday – University of Texas, Florida State, and Texas Tech. Thinks he wants to major in film with a business minor. He has a good chance of getting his choice of schools as he hangs on the border of being in the top 10% of his class. We are really proud of him!

Glad to hear you are not making medical history in the baby department. I would not want to see you plastered all over the front of the grocery store tabloids. They always use the most unflattering poses!

Guess I will see if Travis will give me a brief moment in the space time continuum to send this off to you. (Why am I not the one in charge here? Nice mommy who isn't into control?) Hope you have a lovely evening.
Love, Deb

Subj: Almost Indian Summer
Date: 1/4/2001 4:40:16 PM Central Standard Time
From: debbiesb13@aol.com
To: sarahjf50@hotmail.com

Hi Sal!

It has been the most beautiful day here!!!! So sunny, warming up a little bit but still cool. I'm upstairs and can see down to the back yard from here. A few plants look a little the worse for wear from the cold but most are fine. The one larger Mr. Lincoln looks like it's actually been growing vigorously all along. How are your plants surviving?

Here's what I found out about my mom today — when she went to bed at night she was taking acetaminophen with a sleep aid, an anti-depressant and an anti-anxiety medicine! No wonder the woman never wants to get up in the morning! When they started the anti-depressant and later the anti-anxiety drug nobody thought to take away the sleeping pill since the other drugs would make her sleep anyway. And here's a thought: I wouldn't have known that was wrong if I hadn't been on an anti-depressant myself.

I read the chapter in Barnes last night on "The Spirit of a Woman." Have you read it? Probably so. I really liked it because it showed balance between being feminine and being capable. That the two are not mutually exclusive. I like anything that says there is value in being a wife and mother.

Will be taking Austin to his trumpet lesson shortly. On the soapbox for a moment. This child loves his music. He analyzes every note of the band's performances. He wants to give private lessons to beginners (6th graders) when he's a senior if possible. I think he'd really like to teach music but always says he won't because the pay isn't good enough. I tell him to go for the thing that will make him happy and he can make it work.

I will never understand why we pay teachers peanuts and men (who are nothing but overgrown little boys) ridiculously obscene sums to play sports. Even mediocre ones make millions now. What does that say about screwed up priorities!?

Well, guess I will go for now.

Love, Deb

Subj: *Sunny days*
Date: *1/5/2001 10:18:41 AM Central Standard Time*
From: *sarahjf50@hotmail.com*
To: *debbiesb13@aol.com*

Good Morning!

It's brisk and chilly here this morning but will warm up into the fifties so I can take down the outdoor Christmas decorations. My roses are standing tall but dormant (as they should be in this weather). Much to do in the "back forty" this spring. My first (notice I say first) project will be to build an arbor across the walkway that leads to the rose garden, which is located behind the garage. I have looked at iron arbors and the white resin ones, but decided to build my own.

News briefs: Gina's doctor set up 7am Monday to induce her. She is so excited about having this baby.

Lyndsey and Tisa are doing just fine. Zachary has become a little louder and more physical (throwing his toys) but that's to be expected, and we keep him busy.

I was interested in your comments on your boys. They sound like they are great kids! The teen years are so important and it sounds like they are busy developing their talents and looking to the future.

Just talked to my mom, told her I wanted to come over later to have a glass of wine and toast to Dad, as this is the day he passed away. I am sending you an e-mail about my dad—a little tribute—it is a poem I wrote for him last year, and sent to his dearest friends and family. I thought on this first anniversary of his death, it would be appropriate to send it out again, in his honor. My mom's comment on today was, "I was trying not to think about it." His last days are difficult memories for her. I told her Dad would appreciate a toast in his honor, and I would be over later.

233

Your feet—I have the same problem. Mine stems from the fact that I love to go barefoot in the summer and get great calloused feet, which I shed in the winter months as I, like you, don socks. Neutrogena puts out a great foot cream. Rub it on at night put your feet in socks and sleep tight. Do this every evening for a while, and you'll see improvement. I have cracks so bad sometimes they are painful to walk on.

As for pimples—My favorite remedy is to—again in the evening before I go to bed; wash off the head; then with cotton q-tip swab the offending mass of putridity with alcohol. In the morning the bump has lost its fire and is drying up. Hey, with all these evening rituals, there will be no time for sex—in fact, who would want to have sex with a naked woman with socks on, with runny sores on her face, smelling of alcohol—that is why God created darkness (you think?).

Must let you go—look for the poem about my dad and please say a prayer for his salvation.
Love, Sal

The Other Pisces

Subj: The Other Pisces – by SJF
From: sarahjf50@hotmail.com

     As you go about your day today, take a moment to think about Miles Palmer, my dad, and the happy times you had with him. I can think of no better memorial to any man, than to have his friends and family remember the good times. He still makes me smile...

The Other Pisces

As you gaze up to the heavens on high,
Tonight you'll see a new star in the sky.
On January Fifth this world was born,
At the dawn of the Third Millennium morn.

For on this day our Dad received the grace,
Of being transported to a heavenly place:
A gift from God for a life well-done,
Look to the sky to see where he has gone.

It is a world of Dad's fish stories
That all come true...
And a world of music and dancing
All the night through...

It is a world of great football games
Won in the last two minutes of play...
And a world of rounds of golf
Where he doesn't hit a bad ball all day...

It is a world of sweet grandchildren
Laughing and gathered near...
And a world of old friends and family
Like George and Grandma Kear...

As you gaze up to the heavens on high,
Tonight you'll see a new star in the sky.
Think of Dad and his lake full of fish,
Then look to your heart and make a wish.
—SJF

Miles Russell Palmer
March 7, 1916 - January 5, 2000

Memories of Dad

Subj: Honoring Your Dad
Date: 1/5/2001 11:59:23 AM Central Standard Time
From: debbiesb13@aol.com
To: sarahjf50@hotmail.com

Dear Sal,
    Borrowing a chapter from you, this e-mail will be about your dad and then I will send you a separate one of our things.
    I wish so much I had had the opportunity to know your dad. I feel like a I learned a lot about him reading the beautiful poem you wrote to honor him, not so much because it tells me he liked fishing or golf or being with grandkids, but because it tells me how much you loved him.
    From your descriptions there is a lot of Miles Palmer in his daughter Sally. For in you is his obvious zest for life, happy outlook, and loving caring ways. I will certainly be thinking of him today, praying for him, and offering a toast with you as well. A toast for your dad is a nice honor. One thing I have learned from Mary Jo, it's to honor your dad's memory because it's important for YOU, for YOUR healing.
Love, Deb

Subj: our things
Date: 1/5/2001 1:14:40 PM Central Standard Time
From: debbiesb13@aol.com
To: sarahjf50@hotmail.com

Dear Sal,
    Can imagine it's very exciting for Tisa having Lyndsey look so much like her. I can tell it's definitely been a pleasure for you. Speaking of Zachary, throwing toys etc. sounds so normal. Tristan does that when Tracey brings her goddaughter Haley over lest she get some attention that should be his.
    I was thinking the other day that your kids were really spread out. Was that easier or harder you think? Travis and Austin are just over two years a part, which I liked at the time, but now think it makes them way too competitive. In fact in many ways they are mirror images of their respective older sisters.
    Thanks for the beauty tips. Will look for the foot cream.
    Your arbor sounds like a great idea! Tom may have some books with design drawings if you'd like to borrow them. He had planned at one point to build one where you go from the garden to the grass in our yard.

The nurse from the oncologist is supposed to call me today and tell me what type of lump I had in my breast.

Will close for now and go have some lunch. More pulling up to the trough!

Love, Deb

Subj: A claret
Date: 1/5/2001 7:44:32 PM Central Standard Time
From: debbiesb13@aol.com
To: sarahjf50@hotmail.com

Dear Sal,

Did your Dad enjoy red wine or white? My dad was definitely a red wine man. But he would drink it almost like a shot. Sometimes Tom would get frustrated when he would give Daddy a very fine wine to enjoy and see it gone in a matter of seconds. He'd say, "Frank, you didn't even taste that." My dad would say of course he had but let him try it again. So in honor of both our fathers, I am enjoying a nice claret from Santa Barbara.

One more wine thing and then we'll move on. In shipments from the wine club they always include a newsletter. The one for this month had an interesting thing about calories in wine. It said that they are metabolized by your body differently than the same number of calories from chocolate cake. So not a weight problem. Sounds good to me!

Remember when you told me some day I may have to help someone with depression. Well, my time has come. One of my cousins is in a crisis. I felt so bad for her. She called today in tears. Her doctor has put her on an SSRI anti-depressant for PMS symptoms telling her just to take them during her period. They are making her cry and have panic attacks every time. But she's afraid to take them and at the same time, afraid not to take them. I'm trying to get her to see another doctor. I promised her I'd help her work through this, so now I pray I can keep that promise. So my friend, please say a prayer for her (and for me to help point her in the right direction).

Well Sal, hope you have a peaceful, blessed evening.

Love, Deb

Subj: Monday's Child is full of Grace
Date: 1/7/2001 2:44:09 PM Central Standard Time
From: sarahjf50@hotmail.com
To: debbiesb13@aol.com

Hello there, Deb!

I have been working outside in my garden, pulling up annuals, and herbs. Also making designs for arbor and such. The wind is a little too cold to be out there and just peruse...

Hey just got my nails done, and she cut them way down so I can type better.

Gina and Stephan are enjoying a quiet weekend. Gina put the hospital bags in the car last Thursday. She has her bag, the baby's bag (with fashionable ensemble), and Stephan's bag, which she packed for him with really thoughtful stuff, like a phone card so he can call Germany. I told her to call me when she wanted me to come to the hospital on Monday. I also gave her and Stephan a gentle way out if they decided they wanted to do the labor by themselves: I told Gina I would come when she felt she needed me there and I would not be offended if they wanted to do this alone. So, tomorrow will be very exciting, will let you know ASAP!

Had a nice couple of hours with Mom on Friday, having a couple of glasses of wine, talking not only about Dad, but also about everybody else.

On our teenage boys: they are interesting, are they not? Anthony went from the motorcycle thing to wanting a ferret. We said no, he argued for a couple of days, then came home with a 12-inch long king snake.

Would you like to hear some of my statistics as a mother? This is in reference to your question about how it is having kids so far apart:

- *Anthony's first day of kindergarten was Tisa's first day of college.*
- *I went 18 years straight with a preschooler at home.*
- *By the time Anthony is done with adolescence, I will have gone 19 years straight with a teenager in the house.*
- *For the first 34 years of marriage, Bob and I will have had a minor child in the house.*

I think this qualifies me not only as an experienced mom, but also as an eligible candidate for the funny farm.

My dad preferred red wine to white, but his favorite drink was Vodka. He did drink too much, at times, as did many in that generation. My mother really hated his drinking. When he had had too much to drink, he became Happy and Sleepy (like the seven dwarfs). It caused my mother to become Grumpy (about his drinking). P.S. I was Snow White (happily ever after!)

What was the verdict on your lump(s)? It's interesting to think they are made up of different things: Like maybe the stuff we ingest that is not used for fat or fuel, like dog hair or dirt or tin foil or rocks or nail polish (do you bite your nails?) or plastic or whatever. Now, I'm not saying you eat these things on purpose, they just kind of sneak in on other bits of food. Ever see the science show about all the bugs who live in your eyebrows? Or about the bug that only lives on your eyelashes and nowhere else? Are you hungry anymore? This will be my new method of losing weight: thinking unappetizing thoughts before eating.

Alrighty! Have to go get my hoe! Have a pleasant evening with your boys and enjoy the solitude of Mondays! Will give you Gina's baby news when I can— first baby may take her awhile. Prayers would be nice!
Love, Sal

Birth Days

Subj: A Blessed Day
Date: 1/8/2001 6:49:07 AM Central Standard Time
From: debbiesb13@aol.com
To: sarahjf50@hotmail.com

Dear Snow White,

Sending prayers to Gina, Stephan, and their little girl. I will be thinking of her as I go about my day at the resale shop and look for news as soon as I get home this afternoon (which as you said will probably be early for a first baby).

With your daughters you always seem to strike the right balance of loving, being there for them, but giving them the space they need without being offended if they want it. You are not only their mom, but such a good friend. We ate Chinese last night. My fortune cookie said, "Friendship is the answer to peace of mind." That's what you've been giving your girls as they go through these pregnancies — peace of mind. What a gift!

Well, I must go and do all those morning beauty rituals to get ready for the day.

Love, Dopey
(I'm not really dopey, but Dopey is my favorite dwarf)

Subj: Morning Muse
Date: 1/8/2001 8:53:53 AM Central Standard Time
From: sarahjf50@hotmail.com
To: debbiesb13@aol.com

Good Morning!

Just a little note to say have a lovely day! The weather here is sunny and brisk and full of energy!

How many days a week do you work at the resale shop? My wandering memory does not remember the charity that benefits from the proceeds. Do you always volunteer for various school, civic or church activities?

News flash: Stephan just called and Gina is hooked up to the pitosin and she's in room 107 and the green light is on for me to go. I think I'll stop and pick her up a beautiful pink rose. I am becoming experienced with this new role as "labor room comfort specialist." I am taking in my bag: body splash, lip balm, extra pair of warm socks, hair brush, tic-tacs, two videos: Anne of Green Gables *and* Little Women *— her favorites, some Winnie the Pooh thank you notes, her bedside prayer book (in which I found a romantic poem Stephan had written to her and a pressed rose!) and her baby book and pad of post-its for lists. Anthony is* *coming straight from school to home then to the hospital. He and Gina have always been very close: 2 ½ years between them.*

Little side note on Anthony: when he was a little boy, 4 & 5, Tisa would come home from high school and then college and he would be so excited. He told me he was going to marry her when he grew up. Tisa loved it. Unfortunately, he didn't have the opportunity to go to the hospital to see Tisa when she had Lyndsey because he was either working or visiting with his grandfather. This time however, with Gina, he is making plans to call work to tell them he cannot make it this evening in order that he can make it to the hospital.

Okay, back to "Labor Room Ambiance" — I think there is a real need for an extra woman to be around, discreetly, to relieve the husband, to freshen up the mommy with a cool scented cloth on her brow, and to calmly talk about something other than contractions, don't you? I would like to create a spa ambiance in the labor room easing Gina's concerns about her personal appearance. So, I feel my focus today will be to alleviate Gina's fears of being a gross, laboring cow, but instead merely a young woman in ENORMOUS discomfort. I always felt like the laboring cow, myself, but there was no one to help me freshen up until I could take that first wonderful shower.

Must be off! Nana Sarah has hospital rounds to make.

Dear Lord, please let my daughter and new little granddaughter be safe and blessed with your holy grace on this special day. Amen.

Love, Sal

Subj: Sending Prayers
Date: 1/8/2001 4:21:15 PM Central Standard Time
From: debbiesb13@aol.com
To: sarahjf50@hotmail.com

Dear Nana Sarah,

You know I've been thinking about you all day, stopping to offer a prayer now and then.

You are so thoughtful! I would have never thought to take all that neat stuff to Gina (which is probably why God gave me boys!)

Whoever receives one little child like this in My name receives Me.

Matthew 18:5

With love and prayers, Deb

Subj: *Juliana Marie*
Date: *1/9/2001 8:22:14 AM Central Standard Time*
From: *sarahjf50@hotmail.com*
To: *debbiesb13@aol.com*

     We have a new little darling in our midst! Her name is
                       Juliana Marie
She was born at 8:30 pm Monday, January 8th, to her very happy parents, Gina and Stephan. She weighs 8 lbs 13 oz and is 21¼ inches long. She has blonde hair and big dimples! Stephan will be taking Gina and Julie home tomorrow as they are both doing very well.
    Update: Lyndsey, Julie's cousin (and best friend), is 2½ weeks old and looking more beautiful every day. Zachary, at 2½, is a great big brother, but seems to have developed a new penchant for throwing his toys…
    All three are adorable and perfect in our eyes.
Nana Sarah and Grandpa Fugazi

Subj: Nana x 3
Date: 1/9/2001 9:05:34 AM Central Standard Time
From: debbiesb13@aol.com
To: sarahjf50@hotmail.com

    Congratulations!!! How quickly you went from Nana of one to THREE!!! Your description leaves no doubt Juliana is a beautiful little girl — and long!
    I'm sure Gina was grateful to have you there and all the wonderful things you brought in your bag. I could envision you a bit like Mary Poppins just pulling out all the right things as they were needed.
    Know you will be at the hospital and doing all the Nana things in the days to come, so enjoy, enjoy, enjoy.
    My day will be a bit crazy today, but will write more later. I wouldn't want you to come back to the computer in a few days and not have mail waiting! I'm so happy for you!!!!
Love, Deb

Subj: *three is a good number*
Date: *1/9/2001 10:14:55 AM Central Standard Time*
From: *sarahjf50@hotmail.com*
To: *debbiesb13@aol.com*

Dear Deb,
    Am sitting here (the only time I will sit today) having my tea and I wanted to tell you a little about the labor etc. and how Gina fared yesterday. I am a Nana to three little cherubs!

They started her induction at 8 am, I didn't go to the hospital until around 1 pm as she was barely in labor. Gina, throughout the whole labor and delivery was composed, graceful and so sweet...She said thank you to all the nurses, etc., rarely complained about pain and other than throwing up a few times, did not have any complications. Stephan was a doting, solicitous husband and took care of her very well. I was the brow mopper, perfume sprayer, hairdresser, comic relief and experienced mom. Gina at one point looked at me like she was five years old and said, "Is this going to really hurt?"

Gina was fabulous. Today she is very tired but nursing well with little Julie. Tisa is heading up to see her this morning, I'm taking the afternoon shift, and Anthony will join us after school. Stephan will be in and out, as proud father, family photographer and e-mail historian.

Bob did what he has done when he has first seen all his grandchildren, kisses his daughter, pats her and starts laughing softly and carries on a conversation with his new grandchild about staying away from the people with needles. He always says, "I'd run if I were you!" when the nurses come in the room.

Tisa and Dave arrived at the hospital last night thinking they were just coming to say hello and wish Gina luck on the rest of her labor and then they were going to go home. But Juliana was born 5 minutes after they arrived. Tisa and I got in trouble with a nurse because we were listening at the door of the labor room for the baby to cry. I had told Gina I would wait outside while she pushed and delivered, as that is serious business for the mom and dad, not for Nana to be a part of. Bob arrived a little later, we took pictures and will send you some.

Right now I'm doing some Monday laundry, picking up the house, then it's off to the hospital for the afternoon shift. Also need to do some preparing for Tisa's birthday which is Thursday, she'll be 30! We'll have a family dinner with everyone on Saturday. After that, our family can relax, no more family milestones for a month or so.

Our middle daughter, Andrea and her boyfriend, Darin will be flying out in mid February to see the new nieces. Tisa's birthday has always been the official end to our holiday festivities and I think this year we are all ready to hibernate for the rest of the winter!

Hope you have a good day, dear pal. Thanks for all the prayers and good wishes. The Lord has blessed us for a third time with a lovely, healthy grandchild. Love and Peace, Sal

Subj: the joys of Nanahood
Date: 1/9/2001 4:52:42 PM Central Standard Time
From: debbiesb13@aol.com
To: sarahjf50@hotmail.com

Dear Sal,

    I have so enjoyed your e-mails of the last few days! It sounds as if Gina made it through like a champ. I know you are so proud of her and Tisa both. They are a credit to themselves and to you. In the inexact science of delivery timing, I'm sure it was exciting that Tisa was able to be there for the birth. Anthony is a great kid too to be there for his sister. And how wonderful both of your girls have married men who can be doting husbands and fathers.

Will look forward to seeing a picture of baby Julie. Does she look like Stephan or Gina? Who does she get the dimples from?

You and Gina both thought of so many things to bring to the hospital. Maybe you should go into this "labor room comfort" thing as your part time job. For all the young women who have otherwise overbearing mothers or mothers-in-law you could just go and fill in for them. With Christmas and your company being there you didn't have an opportunity to share your little Lyndsey birthing story. Maybe next week or when you have some quiet time, I would love to hear it.

It's good you think 3 is a nice number of grandchildren, but you realize of course, there will be more at some point. If you think your motherhood statistics are staggering (which they are!!!!!) wait till you start assembling Nana statistics in the years to come. And speaking of your motherhood statistics — remember when you said maybe the cause of my depression was misdiagnosed? Well, now there's a thought for you too! Though trying at times, what greater joy is there than seeing the fruits of your labor (literally and figuratively) blossom into truly admirable adults.

Will close for now, as I have to do a few things around here. Hope you got in some quality cuddle time this afternoon!

Love, Deb

Subj: musings on musings
Date: 1/9/2001 8:36:17 PM Central Standard Time
From: debbiesb13@aol.com
To: sarahjf50@hotmail.com

Hi there again!

Was Gina feeling OK today? Hope she knows that by just being a mommy she is radiant!

You mentioned that Tisa has a birthday coming, are you doing anything special since it's one of those milestone years? What a great opportunity for you all to be together — they can put your rocker to good use! Which reminds me — this is why there are no cable hook-ups in the kitchen — men don't cook.

My poor mother! Seriously, I never know what to expect any more from day to day. Today she was nice as could be, but planning a trip to Germany to a record shop; on the weekend she was hostile and accused me of keeping her from my dad just to be mean. She still has a mink she bought when I was in high school, and it is shedding worse than our old dog. During some of those really cold days she insisted on wearing it even though she doesn't go out. She was telling people it cost $13,000!

243

To answer a few questions you asked — the breast lumps were fibro cystic but appeared solid on the films. What ever I "eat" (no, I don't bite my nails) that is fibro-cystic has got to go! And yes, I hate those little eyelash bugs most of all! They live on your mascara too you know.

In answer to your question about volunteering: I usually volunteer at the resale shop two Thursdays a month Sept - April for the Houston Junior Forum. Also volunteer Tuesdays at the high school in the college room (resource room for applications, catalogs, scholarships, etc).

Perhaps you could give me a little guidance on this depression situation with my cousin. She has been calling me about three times daily since Friday. Here is my dilemma — she keeps asking what to do and then not doing it. I even checked doctors on her insurance for her on line. She's afraid she's going crazy, but won't take action to fix it. So, any ideas?

I go to the psychiatrist myself in the morning for the two-month follow-up on my medicine. I guess it's working good now because Tom keeps telling me how much better I am than this time last year. Anything would be better than that.

Well, Nana Sarah to the third power, it is time for me to give you a rest. Tomorrow will be another exciting day for you with little Julie making her way home. What a happy day!!!!
Love, Deb

Subj: *Wednesday's child is full of woe…*
Date: *1/10/2001 9:21:06 AM Central Standard Time*
From: *sarahjf50@hotmail.com*
To: *debbiesb13@aol.com*

Hi!

Thanks for all the newsy info on your mom, your kids, and the volunteerism. So close to my own lifestyle…

Yesterday I spent the morning doing laundry, picking up, enjoying some quiet time. Went to the hospital around two. Gina looked very tired and Julie was sleeping like a baby! Did not want to nurse. I encouraged Gina to "play" with her, examine every part of her, kiss her tiny face with the idea of trying to wake her up. I warned her the nurses would come in and use some strong-arm methods to get Julie to nurse if we were not successful beforehand. We were not successful. Two different nurses came in and pulled Julie and Gina's breast every which way, but Julie just wanted to sleep. Gina was not liking any of this but sat there obediently. After an afternoon of womanhandling, Gina finally settled down to get some sleep, but in comes another nurse to take vitals. By last night Gina had only had 8 hours sleep in two days.

Gina was fading fast. She just sat on the bed cuddling Julie and looking like a tired little girl/mother—which is basically what she is. Hopefully Gina got some well needed rest last night—but not likely. Stephan will take her home today and I told her she would have plenty of opportunity to rest then.

Tisa's birth experience—she was in a much more painful labor than Gina. They induced about 9 am, she was dilated to two. By 1pm her contractions were constant and she was still dilated to 2. They did not want to give her an epidural until she reached 4. At 3pm she was still dilated to 2 and in serious pain. I was mopping her brow, and keeping her on a breathing pattern, as she was having trouble controlling her breathing—too much pain! She never complained or screamed, but she was suffering. Dave was so calm and so comforting—truly a rock for her. She threw up a lot also. The doctor came in around 3, examined her, looked at her graphs, said, "I don't like the looks of this, let's do a c-section."—Tisa said, "FINE!" As they prepared her to go to the O.R., she turned to Dave and just sobbed.

I took that opportunity to go out and give Dave's dad and sister the news. Dave's dad was sweating bullets, he was so worried. Then off she went to have this baby. This was not an emergency section as with Zachary, so Tisa was in no discomfort at all during the surgery (with Zachary, they had to cut her open before her anesthesia had taken effect, ouch!), everything was much calmer. However, when the doctor went into to retrieve the baby, she saw Tisa's incision from the first section had stretched to the consistency of cellophane and was minutes away from rupturing. What that meant was the baby would have slipped into the abdomen and death was a likelihood within 5 minutes...

Yes, the good Lord was merciful and the timing was impeccable. Another 30 minutes of labor and Tisa and the baby would have been in serious trouble. As it turned out, when Tisa and Lyndsey came back from O.R. they were both healthy and peaceful, Tisa felt great. The pain Tisa felt during labor was probably her incision stretching to the point of rupturing. All's well that ends well!

As for your cousin and her depression, I have a couple of suggestions and since I do not know her, you would be a better judge of what would work. Basically, a strong approach or soft approach.

Strong: Ask her if she wants to win or lose this fight. She does have a choice in this battle! In order to win, she has to stop focusing on her pain, she has to do the courageous thing and get help. In order to lose, she just needs to keep doing what she's doing now. It's a matter of choices.

Soft: tell her you have been there and know this is very painful and seems very hopeless and frightening, but there is a way out, if she will trust you to guide her in the right direction.

Give her one task and ask her not to call you until she has completed it: call a therapist/doctor and make an appointment.

If she calls back and says she can't, then offer to make the call for her. If she calls back and says she can't go, offer to go with her (if she lives close by), or help her to find a friend to go with her.

Just keep reminding her of the choice she has to make: win or lose this battle? Win means to get professional help—Lose means to continue to do nothing.

Thanks Deb, for being with me. You are my spiritual guardian angel.

Love, Sal

All God's Children

Subj: Cold Hands
Date: 1/10/2001 2:49:10 PM Central Standard Time
From: debbiesb13@aol.com
To: sarahjf50@hotmail.com

Hi there!

It is too cold here today!!!! The temperature isn't that low, but it's windy and wet and feels like 20. My hands are still freezing from being out so maybe if I type faster they will warm up (beware of more than the usual number of typos).

The story of Lyndsey's birth is so frightening! I would find it very difficult not to concentrate on all the "what if's." Sal, you did not say but I know you must have been so scared yourself! Poor Tisa is obviously destined to not have run of the mill birthing experiences. She's incredibly strong to weather these trials as if they are the norm. Thank you Lord, for watching over both of them!

Assume Gina has been able to go home by now. It is so much nicer when you can get home and rest in your own bed and explore your little one for the first time without nurses popping in and out and poking and prodding. I always felt like the nurses were in charge, and the baby wasn't really mine until we got home.

I have a new theory on my mom and the "grief" she gives me from time to time. I am now taking the place of my father as her outlet. I think she has a certain amount of anger she must unload in a given day, but she must do it with someone who is "safe" (won't desert her) and since my dad is gone from that role, I must pick up the slack.

Sometimes however, her outspokenness comes in handy. They started doing two seatings for meals at her place due to high occupancy. My mom is a late riser so she has the second seating, which means lunch at 1:00. Evidently on Monday she pitched a major fit about not being allowed in the dining room before that. End result, lunches are now at 11:30 and 12:15 instead of 12:00 & 1:00. Makes more sense because they all show up half an hour early anyway, but I had to laugh.

What day's child are you? I am Friday, but don't remember what the poem says about Friday.

My cousin just called me. I have been using soft so today I gave her kind of a combo hard/soft approach. After an hour I think she is finally going to call for an appointment.

I learned an interesting fact at the doctor today. LAW requires psychiatrists to see their patients at least every three months. Did you know that? She said it's so you don't go into crisis without proper medicine management. Interesting.

In the "you have to laugh" department … my mom just called to tell me that even though I tell her I love her, it doesn't mean anything because I don't do anything for her. That was all she wanted and then we hung up. Why do I even answer the phone?!!!!

OK, I started this e-mail at 12:30 and look at the time! Tom will come home tonight and think I really was eating bon-bons and watching TV all day! Do you watch soaps?

Do have to say one last thing though before closing. Something you said to me once:

Two are better than one, Because they have a good reward for their labor. For if they fall, one will lift up his companion, But woe to him that is alone when he falls, For he has no one to help him up. Ecc. 4:9

That is us — together, side by side, kindred spirits, candles in the darkness, friends.
Love, Deb

Subj: my new toy!
Date: 1/11/2001 3:10:22 PM Central Standard Time
From: debbiesb13@aol.com
To: sarahjf50@hotmail.com

Dear Sal,

I'm writing to you today from my new toy!!!!!!! You are my very first e-mail (now there's a surprise!) My laptop came late yesterday but I didn't have time to hook it all up until just now.

Now I will have to become more computer literate (hopefully there will still be hair left on my head when I'm done!) That reminds me ...do you color your hair? Mine is turning more white by the day but I'm telling myself it looks like highlights.

How is Gina today? Was she able to get some much needed rest. Does Gina remind you a little of yourself when you had Tisa? You weren't much older than she is. I was 30 when Travis was born — big difference, although nervousness is probably universal for a first child at any age.

Was thinking again about Tisa's delivery...did the doctor restitch the old incision since it was stretched so thin? What do they do to make it stronger in the event she gets pregnant again? Happy Birthday to her today!

My cousin finally made her appointment yesterday. Told her to quit taking the anti-depressant because every time she does she gets hysterical and she's not taking it daily anyway. Do you think that's wrong?

Well, I'm going to go for now and straighten up the mess I've made here with boxes, instructions etc.

Have fun with your party preparations tomorrow. I'll be home most of the day, a welcome little quiet respite.
Blessings, Deb

Subj: *Friday's child*
Date: *1/12/2001 11:24:09 AM Central Standard Time*
From: *sarahjf50@hotmail.com*
To: *debbiesb13@aol.com*

Good morning, Friday's child!
     You are loving and giving:
     Monday's child is fair of face, Tuesday's child is full of grace, Wednesday's child is full of woe, Thursday's child has far to go, Friday's child is loving and giving, Saturday's child works hard for a living, But Sunday's child is...I can't remember the wording of this one, but it is the child who is closest to or graced by God. I am a Sunday's child. (surprised?)
     Today is scullery maid day—my house needs major cleaning—but I am looking forward to this—a little peace and no driving! I love my girls, but it takes 30 minutes to drive to Gina's and 45 min to get to Tisa, through metroplex traffic.
     Yesterday I left the house at eight, picked up Mom, drove to Tisa's watched kids while Tisa went to doctor. I did some laundry for Tisa, then we all went to lunch, then dropped off Tisa and crew, got call from Anthony on cell phone, he's sick, went home early. Took Mom to Linens 'n Things to use her coupon, dropped her off, raced home to check on Anthony—he gets terrible stomach aches—fixed a meal for Gina, raced to Gina's with meals, helped her to give Julie a bath, raced home around 7, fixed dinner...read a phrase by Absolom Greer in the Mitford *book about being too useful to the point of becoming useless.*
     Bob's dad had open-heart surgery on Wednesday, he's okay: two bypasses. He's 80 but in very good health. This past year has been an enormous strain for him: being a 24-hour caretaker for his terminally ill wife. They had been married over 55 years. It was at times a rocky marriage, but these two remarkable people were strong in their convictions to weather the hard times for the sake of marriage and family. Together to the end: an invaluable family legacy.
     To answer your questions:
Gina is so in love with her little baby. But she (Gina Marie) has been crying (when nobody's looking) and is so concerned about doing the right kind of care for Julie. I am staying nearby, and so is Tisa, to give Gina the support only a mother can appreciate: telling her we've all been where she is, and she will be fine, but in the meantime, go ahead and cry, as it's frightening to be a new mom and hormones are raging—but it will pass. Julie is precious!
     As for your comment on your mother channeling her abuse to you: I agree with you. The anger has to come out someplace...how sad for your mom, and how sad for you!
     The only reason I ever watch a soap is to see what the women are wearing and their hairstyles...I cannot abide the subject content of the ridiculous scenarios...but I do appreciate their fashion sense!
     Wow! Your own laptop! I think that is the perfect gift for you as you are such a great e-mailer and your aching back gives you trouble. The laptop will allow us to continue our "sisterhood," by making it easier for us to communicate.

Tisa's doctor's appointment yesterday was to check her incision and she's doing fine. As for me being scared for Tisa while she was in labor—luckily I did not know she was in such grave peril, none of us did, until the baby had been born and both were okay—as for thinking about the what-ifs, I try very hard, with help from above, to not go there.

Not that we haven't learned from this, but I don't take my mind into the realm of losing a child or grandchild, as it is unfathomable to imagine the pain of that kind of loss...don't need to imagine it...Her doctor said any subsequent children would definitely be c-section.

On your cousin and the anti-depressant: She needs to be taking an anti-depressant every day, or everything else in her life will not improve. It is the second most important step, after being diagnosed by a doctor. All you can do is point her in the right direction and stand by her. The really tough work she has to do herself.

You have many times thanked me for being such a help to you. I was a signpost, redirecting you, encouraging you along the way. But YOU are the one who made the decisions to seek help and heal. YOU worked on yourself to strengthen your tired, weak body. I am your biggest fan, and know how hard it was for you. It was your determination and your faith that saw you through. I hope your cousin has the same courage to help herself. You and fifty doctors cannot help her if she doesn't take personal responsibility for herself.

Yes, I do color my hair. This keeps my hair a little more lively, as my face seems to grow grayer as I age, too! My trouble has been finding an eyebrow pencil to match my gray eyebrows...I tend to find these pencils that have too much brown in them and when I fill in my eyebrows it looks so fake...glad my life does not depend on my looks!

It has been so great to sit and chat with you, my friend. You may not know it, but you keep my brain chemicals in balance!
Love, Sal

Subj: Sunday's Child
Date: 1/12/2001 3:47:42 PM Central Standard Time
From: debbiesb13@aol.com
To: sarahjf50@hotmail.com

Dear Sal,
      No I'm not surprised you're Sunday's Child!
      Was Bob's dad's surgery unexpected? Glad to hear he is OK. Tom always said my dad's heart by-pass added 15 years to his life, which is probably true. After his recuperation he felt great. Hope Bob's dad has the same kind of rejuvenation. He sounds like such a dedicated husband and father. In this day and time, few people put forth that kind of effort to keep a marriage growing. A great example for generations to follow!
      Another hair question—if you are checking soaps for hairstyles, have you changed yours since we met? Mine is basically the same, but the layers on the sides

and back are longer (almost page boy like) and I put it behind my ears. Still keep the bangs just so my mom will have something else to complain about.

Understand what you're saying about my cousin and the anti-depressant — the cumulative effect question. I'll call her later and see what she did about that. She's worried about what people will think if she gets psychiatric help. I asked her what she thought people were thinking now. Not nice, but it was effective.

Did your parents save everything? My parents and my aunt saved everything they ever owned even stuff like empty bottles, and thought it was worth a fortune. My theory is it came from growing up in the depression. When my aunt would give me her "valuables," I had to keep them because she had a tendency to ask for things back. Plus, she would look for them when she came here.

Know your weekend will be busy. What fond memories you are creating for your kiddos and their little ones of coming to Nana's house!
Love, Deb

Fe~mail Hormones

Subj: Sunday Blessings
Date: 1/14/2001 5:27:31 PM Central Standard Time
From: debbiesb13@aol.com
To: sarahjf50@hotmail.com

Dear Sal,

Not sure what kind of day you're having there but it's so beautiful here. Sat in the hot tub for a bit, and am enjoying writing to you from outside! After all the gray drizzly days we have had I could not let the sun be shining and me be in the house.

Yesterday a man came to give us a bid on doing the bed for the roses and plant a tree. Tom just doesn't have the time to do these tasks and I can't do any of it, so...

We are planting the tree, a red oak, as a tribute to my dad. Hopefully it can be here by his birthday on the 26th and we can have a little toast or something. Tom wrote me a beautiful letter at Christmas likening my dad to an oak. It brought tears to my eyes. I had never really equated his love for trees to being like a tree himself, but he was.

On the subject of birthdays...how was your party for Tisa? Is she taking 30 in stride? Now 30 is so young in comparison to what it was when we were say 20! Ah perspective...

Travis' birthday is two weeks from today. Our birthday "tradition" is that the birthday person picks a restaurant of their choice for dinner.

Back to your crew, how is Gina feeling?

You will be glad to know my cousin didn't take my advice, and did continue taking the anti-depressant, which she seems to be tolerating better with the help of an anti-anxiety med. Again, I will thank you for your gentle way of saying, "You're doing it wrong!" without ever saying, "You're doing it wrong!"

She told me on Saturday this has been going on for 4 years!!! (It became intolerable the last several months.) Her pastor had told her in counseling a year ago she had a chemical imbalance. Unfortunately, she was afraid to get help. From her experience and my own, I can't help wondering how many women are out there who need help but are either afraid to ask or they think they must pull themselves up by the bootstraps and soldier on alone. At least I am someone for her to talk to and to pray for her.

This eyebrow thing you mentioned is interesting. Hadn't thought about gray hair in eyebrows. What about coloring them? I have always wanted to dye my eyelashes (which are so light you can't see them) but don't have the courage to let anything dye related get that close to my eyes. I don't use eyebrow pencil as I could never make it look right. In fact I am a minimalist when it comes to makeup—using

251

eye makeup and blush. Only use base when going out for something special. But I am religious about moisturizer and mascara.

We took my mom to Sonic yesterday for lunch. A drive-in is the best we can do as she wants to go places, but does not want to use the lift van. Keeps insisting she doesn't need it (maybe she doesn't, but Tom and I do as she can no longer stand at all to transfer between the chair and car). Anyway, the boys even went, so she had a good time.

She has started another new thing. I came in one day and she was eating sausage at breakfast. I had a bite and said it was really good (I never buy it). So now she's saving sausage for me. The only problem is it can be days old and she thinks that's OK. Isn't old age fun?

We have so much to look forward to! What do you think about us reserving rooms in the same nursing home in our later years? You & Bob and Tom & I could have adjoining rooms or something so that we won't be forced to stop communicating when our typing abilities, and thus our e-mails, fall victim to arthritis. We will have to get hearing aids of course so that one of us won't be going on and on about one thing and getting an answer on a completely different subject. This way too, we will be available to each other to help with things like chin hairs etc. Bob and Tom could spend their days inspecting the property just like they do now with their hotels (we'll give them maps so they don't get lost). So, what do you think? It's never too early to think about the future!

Guess that's about it for now. I'm going in to send this, pick up Austin at his friend's and figure out something to fix for dinner. Hope you had a great weekend and that you will have a peaceful, pleasant Monday. Maybe you will even get to stop and take a breath!
Love, Deb

Subj: *Woof-woof*
Date: *1/15/2001 11:14:05 AM Central Standard Time*
From: *sarahjf50@hotmail.com*
To: *debbiesb13@aol.com*

Hello Deb!

Can you hear this over the barking of Keoli? The cable people are installing a new line in our back yard and she is so infuriated that there is an intruder in HER back yard.

I had a great weekend with our kids. The babies are so precious and Zachary is too cute. The most beautiful aspects, however, were the expressions on Gina's and Tisa's faces as they looked at their tiny girls: weary but so happy! Gina is having great success with her breast feeding and is feeling a little stronger day by day—it's only been a week today and I cautioned her about doing too much too soon. Gina, who has always been very maternal, is a natural mother and is so in love with Julie. Stephan has two and a half weeks off, starting with a few days before Julie was born. He is being such a big help to Gina. He adores Julie in a way few men care to show in public—maybe it's his European ways—anyway, he fusses over her and coos at her, and pets her. Gina says she loves having him home. I will now be referring to the invading hordes as the lactating hordes—I've never seen so many big boobs!

    My hair: still looks the same as when I saw you last: short and a mind of its own!

    Menopause question: Do you get hot flashes during the day? I do. I'm fruitlessly hoping it's sweating off pounds, along with hormones...I go to my gyn in March for my annual appt, but in the meantime, have you got any pointers for how to alleviate or lessen these flashes, night and day—drugless pointers? Or is Hormone Replacement Therapy the only answer? I know I could look all this up somewhere, but I'd rather ask the professionals: my friends. Haven't had a period since Thanksgiving.

    Aha...(says Father Tim) I sense a new ministry for you. You say your cousin has little self confidence, which means, little self worth, which means she doesn't know how special she is in God's eyes, which are the only eyes that truly matter. If she would but focus on God's plan for her own life, she would begin to see the self doubt fall away, and a new path open in front of her. Does she have a faith life?

    Children of the Depression: my dad led the pack—saved everything, always had ten jugs of water, 10 cans of beans, forty rolls of paper towels...Mom had it a bit easier as her mother, came from one of the first families (Herman and Sarah Jane DeMund) in Phoenix, and they were fairly well off—so even though my mom's dad may have had some work difficulties, they had a rather wide and firm safety net in the DeMund estate. The house that Herman built for Sarah Jane in Phoenix in the early 1900's is now an attorney's office.

    Sarah Jane had a lovely rose garden in the back, which is now a parking lot, I do believe...next time I go to Phoenix I will go and visit. Maybe my roses are doing well thanks to Sarah Jane's intercession for them in heaven, since her own rose garden was replaced with concrete...

    To everything there is a season...: a time to wash, a time to clean, a time to do paperwork, a time to pray—think I'll start with prayer.

    Have a content and fruitful day.

Love, Sal

Subj: Nana on Hormones
Date: 1/15/2001 1:28:20 PM Central Standard Time
From: sarahjf50@hotmail.com

Hormonal Musings from Sal:

    My last period was at Thanksgiving, I have night sweats every night and occasional hot flashes during the day...either this is the beginning of menopause or I am a sweating, pregnant grandmother (this conjures up an attractive picture, does it not?)

Actually, being pregnant is not possible, so I opt for menopause. I have my annual physical in March but in the meantime, other than using a deodorant soap, I am scanning cyberspace for drug free tips on how to alleviate these symptoms. Not having a period is great, but one could do without the summertime blues in the winter!

Not that this winter has been without its highlights: 6 birthdays, 2 granddaughters born, 4 holidays, 8 celebration feasts for 8-12 people at our home (not to mention the usual weekend hordes which descend for the normal Sunday buffets).

I belong on the Food Channel (or in the nut house) as an expert on how to serve a lot of people, a lot of mediocre food, and still have a fun time! The key is to serve good wine...

Speaking of hormones (was I?) our Pregnant Hordes (Tisa, Gina and husbands) which used to descend on us every weekend, foraging for any kind of food, turning down the air conditioner to 65 this past summer, and turning off the furnace this winter, putting their swollen ankles on the coffee table, (not the men...) groaning and holding their large bellies...have been replaced by
LACTATING HORDES.

These buxom new mothers turn our home into an infant nursery, with tiny used pampers in the trash, spit up on the couches, pink blankets everywhere, booties (usually only one) on the floor, pacifiers on every flat surface, cozy baby infant carriers parked in the mud room, tiny, soft cotton caps (to keep those precious little heads warm), baby wipes, diaper bags, nipple shields, bouncy seats, tick-tocking baby swings, discarded tiny pajamas, and more bare breasts than I have ever seen, since 1974: when I attended a La Leche (nursing mother's) League meeting in Sacramento.

Enjoying the process, Bob and I hold court over the proceedings, as Nana and Grandpa, more than willing to hold little Lyndsey or tiny Julie at any time, or take sweet Zachary to go "tee-tee on the potty." It is, simply, survival of our species and wonderful to watch!

So, I do not lament the loss of the function of my own hormones, as my daughters' hormones have replaced mine in importance. This is my concept of Hormone Replacement Therapy: Grandchildren...Personally, I'm ready for this next phase in my life, glad to hand the hormonal baton to our girls. Blood, sweat and tears...whoever came up with that phrase was a woman who knew about childbirth and menopause—and let's qualify the "tears": those are tears of joy.

And on that joyful note, I close this musing on feminine rites of passage, and head for the shower.
Love to all my women friends,
Sal

Subj: Monday, Monday
Date: 1/15/2001 2:07:26 PM Central Standard Time
From: debbiesb13@aol.com
To: sarahjf50@hotmail.com

Hi Sal!

How is the decibel level at your house now? Those utility people just have no respect for animals.

Glad to hear you had a nice weekend with your lactating hordes.

About your menopause question, I can't really say I get day time hot flashes. A time or two but nothing regularly. I do all my sweating at night. As to drugless pointers…foods high in estrogen, usually this is anything soy (yum, yum).

Vitamin E is supposed to be very helpful as is vitamin C with biflavanoids, and some experts say the B's also. Where I go for my mammogram they recommend 800 units of E a day. Lots of herbs are supposed to be good like ginseng, but personally I find most of them a little scary as some can have worse side effects and may interact with the anti-depressant.

Exercise is also supposed to be helpful (but what kind of sense does it make to sweat to alleviate sweat?! — actually increases endorphins or something)

Then there are the what to avoids, mostly the fun stuff — alcohol, caffeine, spicy foods, sugar (after that, what's the point?)

Got your "Hormonal" e-mail while writing this — you always make me smile! Like you I am reluctant to take hormones. There is no easy answer.

Your family history is really very interesting. Did your mom grow roses? Did you know about your namesakes rose garden when you got interested in them or was that after the fact? Isn't it ashamed they didn't keep the rose garden of her house!

Nancy Reagan was on the *Today Show* this morning. In talking about the book of her husband's love letters she commented that letters are so much better than email: That in an e-mail you don't get the "flavor of a person." She obviously doesn't know us. I think we have a tremendous amount of flavor! I want to be pralines and cream. How about you?

One other item and then I must go visit my dear mama. Do you give up something for Lent? I know it's early, but I'm already thinking on this subject. I haven't earnestly done this in years. I was thinking of giving up sweets as I am still craving them like crazy which is not my norm (do you think this is the anti-depressant?). Thought maybe that if I broke the cycle for 40 days the craving would go away. Food for thought.
Love, Deb

Happily Ever After

Subj: *Response to Sunday*
Date: *1/15/2001 3:20:46 PM Central Standard Time*
From: *sarahjf50@hotmail.com*
To: *debbiesb13@aol.com*

Hi—again~!

Okay, I am doing nothing but sitting on my proverbial butt, answering e-mails today and doing a lot of blah-blah-blah. It's two pm and the laundry is still on the floor in the laundry room. Just read your letter from Sunday that was delayed with "technical difficulties."

I was just thinking, maybe our e-mails reflect our personalities in another way: You send me e-mails faithfully almost every day. Always there when I need you! My e-mails sent to you are more sporadic: nothing for days, then 3 in one day…discipline vs. chaos. I may not get to the computer, but my heart's always with you, pal!

On the flavor of our emails I, too, think we are very palatable. As for pralines and cream, since you have done dessert, I will go for the main course. I like turkey as a description of our style: flat breasts, big thighs, rich in tradition and flavor.

I, too, was outside yesterday, cleaning out various pool filters, looking around and surveying the winter carnage (3 large gardenia, 2 margharites dead as doornails). Also started the trimming of the wisteria tree. It is my nemesis in summer: growing three feet a week, trying to attack and conquer the fence— In summer I have to trim it with the hedge trimmer every week or the fence disappears in a flurry of green vines. Yesterday I pruned it wa-a-a-y down, hee-hee-hee! It may become a well-mannered tree yet? I have it on probation now.

Tom is a great husband and friend to write you such a letter about your dad. Can you frame it? I keep old notes from kids, letters etc. in an album called "Letters from Home." I slip the notes, etc. into plastic page protectors. The letters, etc, date from my college letter to home (in 1967) to one from the present from Zachary. It has notes to Santa and Easter Bunny by kids, letters from camp, from grandparents—all that look like they should be kept for family history. Tom's letter sounds like a very special treasure—what a guy!

Makeup? Honey, I am a natural beauty (another term for lousy cosmetician).

From hairline down:
- *I wear a little "erase" to cover my burn scar on my forehead.*
- *I wear eyebrow pencil to fill in my balding eyebrows.*
- *I wear light shadow under arch of eyebrow, brown shading above eyelid, light shadow on lid…all of this usually wears off after 20 minutes, as I either have a hot flash or my oily skin absorbs the color.*

256

- *Sometimes mascara—depends on whether I want to show off my stubby eyelashes or if I want to look like the Mona Lisa: sans mascara.*
- *Blush on cheeks and chin—no foundation, as it seems to magnify the growing number of crevices on my alabaster complexion.*
- *Lip liner and lipstick*

Bare minimum, to walk out the front door: at least lipstick and eyebrow pencil, other wise I look like someone who has pulled panty hose over her face: all features are blended together into one flesh toned, lumpy mass.

Let's hear it for the natural beauty!!!!!!!!!!!!!!!!!!!!!!

A SIGN OF THINGS TO COME! Okay, this is the real reason I had to respond so responsibly and on time to your e-mail: I love the vision of the four of us in the home together: WHAT A FABULOUS CONCEPT!!!!!!!!! Not only have you eased my fears about no one being available to control my chin hairs from taking over my face (how disgusting: a senile, bearded, old woman), but you have given new purpose to our "up a creek without a paddle" retired husbands! Every Christmas, we could give them matching planners, which they could carry around to write down all the infractions of the nursing home. Of course the Home must serve wine with lunch, so we can take a nice long nap in the afternoon, then get up in time for cocktail hour, a dinner of soft serve T-bone steaks (I think the chef's name is Gerber) and top it all off with a dessert of jell-o jigglers, shaped like different replaceable organs: such as liver, kidney, and heart.

After a lovely meal, we shuffle into the game room (a process which will take some time as we forget where we are going a few times) and sit down to play some therapeutic games, such as

- *Scrabble for seniors: the tiles are the size of beverage coasters. The object is to make as many four-letter words as possible...*
- *Trivial Pursuit for seniors: questions only about what happened 80 years ago because we can't remember what we did three hours ago.*
- *Scattergories for seniors: write down ten words that start with any letter of the alphabet, totally ignore any category. Goal: to spell one out of ten correctly.*
- *Monopoly for seniors: Bob and Tom just take all the hotels and hoard all the money. We proceed to "Go" and wet our pants—oh, sorry, Depends! Do they have pink for us and blue for them? If not, maybe we need to design some. How about control top Depends—I would need those.*

Then the orderlies restrain us in straight jackets for being too rowdy, but what they don't know is that this is an act so we can get them to give us heavy drugs. They wheel us to our adjoining suites where we all are put into bed happy and sleepy. In an hour we awake because we all have to use the bathroom. Then we can't get back to sleep, so you and I get out the tweezers and magnifying glass to groom each other. Meanwhile Tom and Bob try to remember what the date is so they can get to the right page in their planner, as they need to take some notes on the cleanliness of the door handles and quality of the service provided by the cats that visit them every week.

Whew! Back to the real world (darn...) adieu for now, have a great Tuesday!
Love, Sal

Subj: love your notes
Date: 1/15/2001 4:29:13 PM Central Standard Time
From: debbiesb13@aol.com
To: sarahjf50@hotmail.com

Dear Sal,

You have no idea how wonderful it was to come home and have a laugh just now!!!!! I don't know why you worry so about when you write, your timing is always impeccable!!! Will answer you more in depth later or probably tomorrow after college room.

Was thinking on my way home I pray to God your mom never feels like my mom feels right now. It is my prayer for you as well.

Thanks so much for the sunshine in my day!!!
Love, Deb

Subj: Rainy but cozy!
Date: 1/16/2001 11:54:47 AM Central Standard Time
From: sarahjf50@hotmail.com
To: debbiesb13@aol.com

Dear Deb,

My life: I called Tisa and cancelled coming to see her and take her on errands, as the weather forecast was cold and rainy today but Wednesday was dry. Get up and find out now Wednesday will be worse than today... this is my life! It is nice to just stay in, though.

Thanks for hormone info!!! Very interesting...I would rather sweat than give up my three absolute favorites: caffeine, alcohol and sugar. What fun is life, anyway, without those foods?

And yes, I do have sweet cravings on the anti-depressant. I actually start to drool when I see chocolate. Chocolate peanut clusters are my favorite, next are turtles...I am drooling again...

Funny thing about my roses and my great-grandmother, Sarah Jane. I started growing roses in 1986. Never tried them before. I had success and came to love the rose gardening. In 1997 my Uncle Richard (with whom I have a lovely e-mail relationship) came to see me in Houston. He had rented a camper-van and was driving from Phoenix to east coast, up east coast to Maine, then west to Seattle, then south to San Diego, then home. He was eighty when he did this by himself! Anyway, he dropped in to see us just so he could tell me some of the family history, as I had sent him a letter asking about my great grandmother. He sat and told me stories, including the fact that she grew prize-winning roses. I had not known this about her! I guess it's in the genes.

Another spooky story about us two Sarah Janes: When looking for a statue to be the fountain for our pool, Bob and I looked at dozens of statues. Everything from dolphins to Poseidon. We finally decided on a simple, yet graceful statue of a girl balancing a jug on her shoulder. As the man was hefting her into our car (she's four feet tall) he said, "Enjoy Rebecca!" We asked who Rebecca was and he said this was Rebecca from the Bible, Isaac's wife. I looked up the story about how she was discovered at a well drawing water and offered water to the servant of Isaac. It is a lovely story and I smiled inwardly as I discovered, once more, that God uses my material objects as part of his ministry—can't tell you how many times we have told the story of Isaac and Rebecca to houseguests. Anyway, when my mother came to stay with us she remarked on the fact that my great-grandmother, Sarah Jane, had a beautiful porcelain statue of Rebecca with the jug on her shoulder, gracing her mantle of her home. How about that?

I have never told my Uncle Richard that story, think I'll e-mail it to him.

What am I giving up for Lent? I don't always give something up, sometimes I add something like daily scripture study (Uh-oh, there's that subject again—I still have not gotten around to my study). I have not given it enough thought yet. Will let you know when I decide. I once gave up all sweets and my headaches disappeared for 40 days!

So, I take it your visit with your mom was kind of poopy...do you want to talk about it? (or maybe you'd rather eat a large bag of m&m's)

Well, enough fun! Must go fix lunch, I'm starving from all this talk about foods. Have a warm, cozy day, pal!
Love, Sal

Subj: Life
Date: 1/16/2001 8:47:11 PM Central Standard Time
From: debbiesb13@aol.com
To: sarahjf50@hotmail.com

Hi Again!!

My mother has called me three times to tell me that I don't care about her and that my dad has tried to phone her. My mom can still get to me like no one or nothing else.

You know Sal, the scariest part of this is there is no resolution. She is destined to be this sad and miserable for the rest of her days. Can't there be a limit on misery? I still can't help but feel the need to make things better some how.

On discipline vs. chaos—I don't think of you as chaos. I think of you as the more ethereal, creative one. A bit like a butterfly. As for me and discipline, maybe, but definitely obsessive at being organized, or perhaps the plodding turtle. It makes for a good balance don't you think? Though, I think I did see a new side of your personality in talking about your wisteria (sp?). There seemed to be a bit of a sadistic note in that "hee-hee-hee" about cutting it back and bringing it to submission!

The story of your interest in roses paralleling Sarah Jane's is intriguing. And the Rebecca sculpture also! Things like that make me wonder sometimes how much further God's plan for our lives goes beyond our imagination. How neat too that you have this relationship with your uncle who can keep the family stories alive. Would think your daughters also enjoy having this bit of history. There is an actual written history of my mom's family that goes back to the early 1700's, but I know nothing of my dad's history before their arrival here from Slovenia in 1914.

I thoroughly enjoyed your visions of our future in the nursing home!!!!! Loved the games especially and have a few to add:

- Life: all the squares are medical bills — doctor, hospitals, Rx; object is to get to the last square before your money runs out.
- Jeopardy: there are no questions but you have to negotiate an obstacle course with a walker.
- Clue: you try to remember who you are and which room you live in.
- Candyland: no sweets, just drugs. The men will fight for the Viagra card!

No they don't make pink and blue Depends. Some brands are color coded by size, and no one has thought of control top. In fact you will be interested to know the pull up ones in large are so hard to come by in our area, they are almost a black market item leaving store shelves often as soon as they are put out. (See the useless info your friend is storing in her brain!) So maybe that's a business for us as we await our retirements days — Colorful and control top Depends, maybe even control "bottom" for sagging butts — they should come with little disposal wrappers — and the packaging should have a disclaimer that says in bold letters, "I'M BUYING THESE FOR SOMEONE ELSE!"

Know you will enjoy seeing Tisa, Zachary and little Lyndsey tomorrow. Hope the weather will let up for a bit to keep the little ones warm and dry (then you can be warm and dry too!) I have many errands in Humble tomorrow. So I will be slogging in it along with you. Will go now and read for a while (escape, escape!) Love and Blessings, Deb

Subj: *Depend(s) on me!*
Date: *1/17/2001 10:07:32 PM Central Standard Time*
From: *sarahjf50@hotmail.com*
To: *debbiesb13@aol.com*

Dear Deb,

Oh my! I'm wiping the tears out of my eyes. Just read your paragraph on the Depends. Love the part about control butt and disclaimer about these being for someone else. Yes, we would really be good at creating ambiance for seniors! Weird games and control butt diapers. I like it!

Well, today was busy but okay. Gina and Stephen looked like Mr. & Mrs. GQ today: tall, blonde, slim, and graceful hosts. Mom and I went up to their apartment to deliver some stuffing for the turkey they were roasting. Julie, at age 9 days, is also tall and blonde. Rather like walking into a room full of Vikings.

Do you watch TV? What do you like to watch? I like the Weather Channel the best, next Home and Garden Channel, then Discovery Channel, classic old movies and the Food Channel and PBS.

Must keep this short (that's a new concept!—but not for long) as Anthony needs to get on the cyber spaceship. Will write more in the morning about your mother. I know it is a heart-wrencher, dealing with her.
Love, Sal

Subj: O-o-o-o-odin
Date: 1/18/2001 8:28:51 AM Central Standard Time
From: debbiesb13@aol.com
To: sarahjf50@hotmail.com

Dear Sal,

A family of Vikings (I loved that movie, weird kid). Hmmm… They could name their first boy Odin. Glad to hear they are doing so well. Which reminds me Nana, I still haven't seen a picture of little Julie.

In answer to your question on television, the only show I make it a point to watch is *JAG* about the military courts. Also like *Who Wants to be a Millionaire*, (really any game show), and will watch *Drew Carey* or *Whose Line is It Anyway?* with Austin sometimes. In the mornings, the *Today Show*. Other than that, I also like to check the weather channel often; from time to time, Animal Planet, PBS, CMT, and old movies. I mostly read in the evening. When baseball season starts, I will often have the Astros game on just to keep up with the score, but don't really watch the game.

I am having a little trouble again with anxiety for some reason. Not panicky, just tight chest, and feeling very on edge. Mary Jo thinks it is because I am moving to a new place in my mom thing — having more compassion because of her disease progression and coming to terms with the reality of losing her. She gave me a book to read on basically talking myself through it.

My mother and I are still struggling with the issue of my visits. I'm going more often now, 4-5 days a week. But she still feels I don't stay long enough and therefore don't care about her. Would like to hear your thoughts on what is a fair amount of time to stay.

On a further mental health note, my cousin called last night and is so happy she went to the psychiatrist. Doctor said she should go to therapy so she's going to find a therapist through her pastor. She's staying on the anti-depressant, which she's tolerating now. At any rate, I'm glad she feels better.

Hope you aren't freezing up there. It's another cold, wet one here and we are supposed to have another 2" of rain today. Tired of it.

261

Will close for now. Hope you have a warm, comfortable day. Is it still supposed to snow?
Love, Deb

VIII

Peace Be With You

*

Rising Above

Moving On

Heavenly Fathers and Friends

*

Candles in the Darkness

*

Rising Above

Subj: *br-r-r!*
Date: *1/18/2001 10:07:45 AM Central Standard Time*
From: *sarahjf50@hotmail.com*
To: *debbiesb13@aol.com*

Hello there!

It's a glorious, cold, wintry morning. I fed my little sparrows this morning. I call them my "breakfast club" as they will line up in a row on the fence, with their feathers all fluffed up. They look like little furry gray tennis balls. Some days there are upwards to 40 little birdies on the fence! In this cold weather they congregate in the photinia hedge next to the fence and make such a chirpy racket—sounds like the movie "the birds." But this is a cheerful sound. They also snuggle inside the slats on the fence and peek out, hoping for a space at the feeder. Of course they have their resident bullies, who, when feeding will chase away any other prospective diners. I can see all this from my kitchen window. I keep binoculars there as I will get some interesting birds sometimes.

Our new winter visitors, who flew in just for "the season," are the gray juncos from Canada (I also have four bird books). They have black hoods and wings accented with a light grey breast. Pretty little birds. There is a little wren, who is very talkative, her chirp much bigger than her size warrants. She hops around with her tail sticking up, complaining about the lack of good bugs this time of year. In the summer she sits on the back fence and talks to me, as long as I keep my distance. Beautiful little chirping.

Of course there are the royalty of the fence: the cardinals, who are very shy—except when the feeders are out of seed. For years, first in Houston and now in north Texas, I have noticed when I am out working in the yard, the cardinals will alight close by and make their chirping calls, eyeing me the whole time. More often than not, when I am graced with their nearby presence and song, the feeder is empty. It has happened to me many times and I accept this relationship with them and immediately go fill the feeders! I love the birds and am a very interested bird watcher in my own backyard. Bob keeps asking me how much the birdseed is costing us. I say, "Not enough to stop buying it!"

Your mom...Deb, I am sorry that she can take away your peace and joy. But I have to say you are not alone. I would think that in everyone's life there is at least one person who has that power over them. More often than not, I would think it is the mother, or the father, because these are the people we are programmed to please and desperately try to please all our lives. How many times have you heard a person say, "If only Mom (or Dad) had lived to see me do this."

I found an interesting reaction when Bob's mother died. I would always send her letters and tell her about the family and myself but it wasn't until she died that I realized that I was always trying to impress her so I could get the positive feedback. I felt this void when she was gone, that no longer did I have that relationship where I wrote to her with the express idea of telling her the triumphs we had, so I could hear how great I was, or my kids, or Bob.

I think people who are very critical and unhappy, push a button in people like you and me—it's a button from our childhood that says, "Your job is to make this person like you by pleasing them." So, we keep marching to this tune, no matter how our adult side will say, "This is futile, this is not necessary, this is an unhealthy relationship/focus." It is an addiction. I had it with my mother-in-law, and honestly, to a lesser degree, I have it with my family. Unfortunately, we have based our self worth on how these people react to our actions.

Read that last sentence of the paragraph again. We, in other words, have given these people the power to control our peace and happiness.

Why do you feel so good in scripture, why do you feel so at peace? Because at those times you acknowledge and give God the control over your life. You put Him in charge of your peace and happiness.

What to do about your mom? What do you want to do? I can tell you from my limited point of view how long you should tolerate her criticism. But, I think the place to go to find that answer is in your time with God. He will show you how to handle her, and where your focus should be. God is your FINAL ANSWER.

How long should your visits be? In my opinion, long enough to see to her physical needs and to tell her you love her. Then get the hell out of Dodge. (Sorry, Lord). Your focus (which realistically you won't always be able to hold on to) should be:

1) Serving her with honor, as she is your mother.
2) Keeping in mind any verbal abuse from her wounds the little girl inside of you, but it cannot touch the woman that you are who walks with God as her light.
3) Remember Philippians 4: 4-9. That is how we should live every day.

I love the term "rise above." To me it means to get a different perspective on a situation. To elevate yourself out of the "self" which wounds so easily, to the level where you can see the bigger picture. It also means, to me, becoming closer to God's vision.

How about practicing "rising above" when you are with your mom. She wants to address that little girl who snaps to attention. How about rising above to the godly woman who knows her mother is to be pitied and forgiven. The godly woman knows that no one can hurt her, if she brings her God into the relationship, if God is holding her hand and giving her a broader vision.

Must go, "the weather outside is frightful!" I love it. Have a warm, peaceful day. Rise above.
Love, Sal

Subj: Weather or not…
Date: 1/18/2001 4:58:32 PM Central Standard Time
From: debbiesb13@aol.com
To: sarahjf50@hotmail.com

Hi Sally Snowflake!

Couldn't help but be struck by this morning's e-mails and our different perspectives on weather. You are reveling in winter and I'm griping about the rain. Do you like it to be gray too or just enjoy the cold? Snow doesn't count because that is a special entity (sp?) unto itself. And yes, I think it is God's special gift.

In reading your ideas on my inner conflicts with my mom I am reminded of the scripture you sent me sometime back about focusing on the things above and not on the things of earth.

You are right that we strive, too often fruitlessly, to please those who cannot be pleased. And even though we know it, we still keep working at it a little like a hamster in a wheel trying to go somewhere. And, yes, there is a part of self worth that is attached to getting this approval. I had not actually translated that to letting them control our peace and happiness, but it does follow.

As to your answer to my question on how long my visits should be — that is basically what I do. (Some days I can't wait for the "get the hell out of Dodge" part). Usually I'm there about an hour to an hour and a half, which seems to max me out. I will confess this is less time than I would spend when Daddy was there, but it was different being with him; even she was different with him there. Another thought: If the visits were longer they still wouldn't be long enough. However, Mary Jo cautioned me not to put myself in a position where I had "regrets" later on.

Will strive with renewed vigor and no doubt needing occasional reminders to "rise above," to give this matter to God, and not let myself be so vulnerable; to remember strength lies in faith.

Hope your day was good. Maybe by now you are watching delicate, lacy little snowflakes drift down outside your window. Maybe a la Charlie Brown you are outside catching them on your tongue!
Love, Deb

Subj: snuggles
Date: 1/19/2001 10:35:51 AM Central Standard Time
From: sarahjf50@hotmail.com
To: debbiesb13@aol.com

Good Morning Deb!

I am sitting here with a cup of Constant Comment, Keoli is playing with her toy at my feet, and the breakfast club is dining on the fence. It's literally freezing outside but a bright, breezy and sunny day. The wind is coming down off the great plains and it is cold! You asked if I like the gray too: yes. I love most kinds of weather, I just realized. My favorites are rain, sleet and snow. I was in the parking lot at Blockbuster a few weeks ago, and it was snowing and before I knew it I had stuck out my tongue to catch a snowflake. I quickly glanced around to see if anyone saw this grandmother playing with the snow… I also love any weather that allows me to work outside in the yard. I can mow the lawn, even when it's 100 degrees outside, I have a good cooling system. But I guess my least favorite weather is very hot and humid. Yuck. But we combat that with the pool and pray for rain.

Winter babies: snugglers. Both Julie and Lyndsey curl up in little balls, about the size of a football, tuck their delicate hands under their chins, burrow their little noses into the hollow of your shoulder, and snuggle. They both enjoy sleeping on their moms and dads, as opposed to a chilly crib, and both sets of parents are very accommodating on a conditional agreement: the crib will become the main sleeping area when the babies are a little older and warmer—within the next couple of weeks.

I really do go back and forth on the idea of getting a job. I am a professional housewife, and full-time mom. I love to spend time with the family and they need me right now, all three generations around me: my mom, my daughters and my grandchildren. Right now most of my time is spent caring for my home and adorable male residents, and caring for my mom and helping the girls. In fact, I don't have enough time to do all that. If I go to work I'm not sure how I would handle my mom's affairs, let alone ever see the girls and their families. Plus I have this strong feeling that I would be deserting our home, if I went to work.

Because of Bob's schedule, especially with the master's program the past few years, which is still ongoing, he has absolutely no time to do anything at home. Not even take out the trash. When he comes home there are no chores for him to do. But it has been like that most of our marriage. In the years when our children were home, I would rather that he spent time with the kids when home, than doing chores. Plus I have always loved the outdoor chores, even washing the cars. Even the bills, he looks at them every month, but I do the budgeting. This is probably sort of a strange, rather lopsided way of handling the family homestead, but it has worked for us. I feel if I went to work, the home would crumble. Bob would like me to work, he feels I deserve some time doing something for myself. Plus, I know he would appreciate the income for our retirement. But I would have to pay people to clean the house and do the yard…Bob says he and Anthony will pull up the slack. If I only worked part time, I don't think I would clear enough money to pay for the house help. I often picture myself working someplace…I am so ambivalent about this. I will continue to pray about this.

A question I've been meaning to ask you: you mentioned you don't work in the yard. Is that because of your back?

A note on your mom: Let us remind ourselves that people who hurt us can only have power over us if we hold on to that hurt, and replay it in our minds. This makes us feel miserable all over again. We can respond to the hurt, deal with it if need be, but then move on…? Is that making these complex problems too simple? This sounds good "on paper," I'm going to see if it works in the real world.

Have a good weekend.

Sal

Subj: It's a Beautiful Day
Date: 1/19/2001 11:53:27 AM Central Standard Time
From: debbiesb13@aol.com
To: sarahjf50@hotmail.com

Hi Sal!

Well, finally we are having a beautiful day — meaning cold and a bit of sun. I'm definitely a sun person. Don't care what the temperature is, just let the sun shine! I do appreciate a rainy day now and then (apart from the obvious need for them) and like to get caught walking in the rain when it's warm, but weeks like this where the sun never shines are not my cup of tea.

Can just imagine your little granddaughters curled up to stay warm. Your description of them tucking in their hands under their chin...I have always found baby hands to be the most amazing thing!!!

Can tell you are very ambivalent on the work issue. I don't think your current arrangement is strange at all (perhaps because it's not too very different from ours with the exception of the outside chores). Are you thinking now that being a housewife and mom is a "lesser" job in some way? I wasn't sure. I don't see you as being motivated by the money, so I am assuming the conflict is within you to find what will give you the greatest happiness and personal fulfillment.

You didn't ask me, but I would say keep talking it through with yourself and with God. (And of course you know I will listen any time you want to share your thoughts). He will at some point reveal the answer to you. Perhaps it will be something along the way that gives you the best of all the worlds, or perhaps it will be something you have to wait a little longer to find. But I think when the right choice presents itself you will know immediately; there will not be any feelings of ambivalence; you will just know it is God's plan for YOU.

As to your question about me and yard work — I can't do much because of my back. I am able to water, sweep, and rake. Sometimes I just go out and watch Tom to offer moral support and be outdoors. Besides sitting and lifting, bending is also a problem. I find this frustrating with things in the house as I often have to wait for Tom to move or lift things that I'd much rather take care of myself. I don't say this by way of complaint, merely a statement of fact. Whatever my limitations, they are not as bad as they could be and for that I am grateful.

I was struck by your statement about not replaying the hurt so we feel miserable all over again. I am very guilty of that! It may sound simple on paper, but maybe with enough conscious thought to stop that cycle we would be able to then step away from the hurt easier.

The book I'm reading talks about a four step plan to changing your reaction process: re-label, re-attribute, re-focus, re-value. Sort of the same don't you think? Of course this doesn't mean we won't have days we fall off the wagon and have to give each other a friendly nudge (or swift kick in the butt).

Must go to my mom's. Have a wonderful, joyous weekend.

Love, Deb

Moving On

Subj: A day of rest?
Date: 1/21/2001 5:02:38 PM Central Standard Time
From: debbiesb13@aol.com
To: sarahjf50@hotmail.com

Dear Sal,

Don't know about you, but I'm looking forward to Monday for a day of rest! Can imagine your home today is full of all the little baby things and wonderful food as you described in your e-mail last week. What a blessing!

My home was strewn all weekend with visitors' things but they were all the remnants of 8 teenage boys and lacked the charm of pink blankets, booties etc. More like empty chip and cookie bags, coke bottles, dishes and glasses galore, and socks big enough for Paul Bunyon! I'm not really complaining. Actually I'm quite grateful that Travis and Austin feel comfortable bringing their friends to our home. Truth be told I will miss it when Travis leaves and the crowd is reduced by half.

So how was your weekend? Fun I hope! We have gone non-stop. Today Tom and I went to see my mom and then to Humble Trade Days which is a sort of flea market. We got this adorable little wishing well for the backyard, a couple of cookie tins and canisters for the kitchen decor. I'm using the canisters as bookends for my cookbooks. They're turquoise ball jars and I filled them with beans. Do you like to go to things like that? How about "antiquing"? Tom and I laughed on the way home…we decided in twenty years or so, he'd be retired and we'd be making the flea market circuit selling all this junk we couldn't live without!

Have to brag momentarily…I am now eight games ahead of Tom in Scrabble. He gets so mad when he loses. (Never mind that I struggled with losing for the last five years since we started keeping track of our scores.) Last night I even put back the "Q" when I drew it so as not to inflate the score further. Then I was wondering why do I have this need to protect him? OK it's not such an overwhelming need that I'll lose, just not win so big. He thinks it's the anti-depressant that's making me play better. Whatever works!

Well, will go for now to get started on dinner preparations.
Love, Deb

Subj: *Museday*
Date: *1/22/2001 10:43:17 AM Central Standard Time*
From: *sarahjf50@hotmail.com*
To: *debbiesb13@aol.com*

Hi Deb,

    Enjoy hearing about your home. Your kitchen is pictured in my mind as a warm but airy and cheerful place. It is full of your treasures that make you feel good and speak to your personality.

    As to: do I love to go antiquing—when it's furniture, yes. Knick-knacks I have had to stop buying, as my home was getting so full of stuff. I have been going through a more austere mood in this house. I really think some of that is attributed to "cleaning out" the children too—as when they have moved out (for good), I pack up their things and gradually send all of their stuff to them to treasure—I do not like having bedrooms which look like my children still live there. I now have guest rooms instead.

    Sounds rather cold, in thinking about it, but I am a firm believer in children creating their own home—at the appropriate time, of course. I love to have everyone come over and visit, to think of our place as a retreat, a place to feel our love and comfort, but their stuff is where their home is. Maybe this is my military/gypsy upbringing, where our home was where our things were. We did not have a home we lived in for more than four years, and there was no "hometown." Our belongings were our "home."

    Wow, where did all that come from? Anyway, I understand about your twinges about Travis leaving, his life changing—your life changing. I felt that acutely when my girls left home, one by one. It is a grief (ouch) and it is a new beginning. Life with them does not end, it becomes a different exercise—but the relationship continues and deepens. The old "empty nest" is a real adjustment. It is a rather sad, but liberating time. Life goes on!

    We, as housewives, have more of an adjustment to make than those who are working, I feel. Our days were designed around our children and now there is more time, more freedom—what to do? Volunteer more? Get a job? Do more projects around the house? So far my choice has been projects around the house.

    Does your back hurt all the time? Does it hurt when you move a certain way? You hide it so well, I never would have known you were in pain when I met you last summer. What is the prognosis? Can you ever have surgery to improve it or stop the progression?

    I like Mary Jo's advice on the "re's." I have often thought if I would just pause, take the time to think (and create some mental distance) before I react or answer, I would do something different from a different, better perspective. The pause is the part I have to work on.

    Go, Deb! The Scrabble Queen! Men are by nature competitive, and it never rests well when we beat them. Bob's reaction: he won't play certain games with me. Women are better at multitasking and Scrabble is good for our multilevel brains.

This Saturday the hordes descended on us. It was fun and I was constantly holding a baby. Gina is a little worn out, and not looking forward to Stephan going back to work today. I think she will find (I hope) that it is nicer to have some time to do her own thing, make her own schedules with Julie, without having to consider his needs. The living room was covered with baby paraphernalia and the girls like to put the babies down on a blanket by the fire. Keoli is very concerned when the baby cries, however, and she likes to lick their heads...something the mothers frown upon.

Well, my chat time is over, have a lovely day, enjoy the sun!
Love, Sal

Subj: Miles Russell Palmer
Date: 1/22/2001 5:13:29 PM Central Standard Time
From: debbiesb13@aol.com
To: sarahjf50@hotmail.com

Dear Kindred Spirit Sal,

Before going on to actually respond to your thoughts, I have a connection that will give you a bit of a chill with reference to your dad. Mary Jo's office is in her husband Mike's church. The church is on a street called Russell Palmer. When you sent the poem with your dad's full name, it really took me aback. Asked Mary Jo if she knew the origin of the street name but she doesn't. I am trusting you aren't involved with anything named Frank Zerjav.

Tom and I are good "collectors." But we are also good at cleaning out. Probably a semi-version of your gypsy thing. Since we have moved so many times (our 7th residence in 20 years, some stays were very short) we also get rid of things easily. My general rule of thumb when moving, if we didn't use it in this house, it's history. Another thing, which changed my perspective on "things," was our first flood in Beaumont. We lost all of our furniture except for 6 family pieces we wouldn't have given up short of total destruction. Although I do have certain things that have sentimental value, I also know only life has true value. Things are just that - things.

Since you have been the empty nest route ahead of me, you can keep me grounded. It is a mixed blessing though. I know I will miss Travis (and later Austin), but will also be proud to see him continue on his quest to become his own man. And even though the house will be more quiet, I really look forward to the days when Tom and I can travel places we would enjoy and pursue our interests. We do very little if any of this now, as we always feel the need to make the rare bit of free time he may have a family time.

You are right that as housewives we have more of an adjustment to make when our children leave home, but on the other hand I think we have reaped greater rewards.

Told my mom that this coming Friday, which is my dad's birthday, I would take her to the cemetery, and dinner. My dad would have been 86. Unlike my mom who still won't even admit to being 65, my dad took pride in his age. As soon as his birthday was past he'd start telling people, "On my next birthday I'll be..." This will be the first time she has been to the actual grave site itself since the marker was installed. I hope the presence of the marker will help her deal with the reality of his being gone.

In answer to your questions on my back: I have two discs that are degenerated to the point of being near flat. There is some arthritis and one disc has a slight bulge and from time to time puts pressure on a nerve (as has been the case since this past summer). Over the years I have controlled it with exercise, anti-inflammatories, and being careful. Though I never have pain free days, I used to go months without significant problems. This particular episode has been a long one and has been complicated by the interaction between the pain and the anxiety. Like you with your voice, sometimes it's embarrassing for me when I have to say I can't sit a long time. At some point it will become intolerable and I will have surgery, but am in no hurry to go there. Just keep plodding along.

Hope you have a blessed day and peaceful evening, my friend!!!! (Yes, I was glad to see the sun today by the way and get out to walk. It was wonderful!)
Love, Deb

Subj: Connections
Date: 1/23/2001 11:21:24 AM Central Standard Time
From: sarahjf50@hotmail.com
To: debbiesb13@aol.com

Good Tuesday to You, Deb!
      Yes, we certainly have many strange connections—some seem like obvious signposts. The Russell Palmer name on the church street is a message to me that Dad did make it into heaven...and maybe he's showing the way to a higher power???? Let me know if you see any 33's, as this number has many significances with my dad and when I see that number I always say, "Hi, Dad!" If the church has 33 in it's address, I would not be surprised, but that would really be Dad laying it on thick. Is it an Episcopalian church? He was Episcopalian—actually he was an agnostic but his family was Episcopalian.
      Today I am going to walk in earnest. I keep gaining weight and I am not overeating. I don't know if my hormones can be screwed up—would that make a difference? I have gained 10 pounds since Thanksgiving (when I had my last period). Fatty-fatty two-by-four: can't fit through the bathroom door. My face even looks pudgy. Mega exercise and really trimming the fat—hope that works—but already I don't eat a high fat diet. Kind of scary.
      Yes, moving does have its merits when it comes to "thinning!" I always like the fresh start...eternally a gypsy, am I.
      On your dad. Is his birthday this Friday, Jan. 26? I thought you had mentioned that. Also, if I could be so callously nosy, what day did he pass away last spring? I would like to keep these days in my heart for you, dear friend.

Your back, my voice: The apostle Paul also had an affliction, which God would not take away "a thorn in his side." I find that this kind of constant affliction does tend to make one more humble and more accountable to God for not only the suffering but also the blessings bestowed are much better appreciated. Pick up the cross...

On that rather heavy note, I will bid adieu and pick up my cross and get on with this day. Take care, dear Deb, and have a happy day!
Love, Sal

Subj: zip code
Date: 1/23/2001 7:03:21 PM Central Standard Time
From: debbiesb13@aol.com
To: sarahjf50@hotmail.com

Hi there Pal Sal!

Guess I will be saying hi to your dad for you and a little prayer whenever I cross Russell Palmer. The address for the church has a zip code 77339. I think it's a non-denominational church, definitely not Episcopalian, called Grace Church of Kingwood. This is really very amazing to me. I couldn't believe it when I read your e-mail and then found Mike's card for the address. Wow!!!!!

You would really like Mike and Mary Jo both, not that they are any relation to these coincidences. Whenever my dad would see Mike at their club at the apartment, he'd stick his hand in his pocket, pull out a hand full of change, and say, "If I had a dollar I'd give it to you." Of course, he never did because my mom always had the money. I think sometimes Mike tried to give him a dollar too. Anyway, for whatever time, 3 or 4 years this went on.

Mike visited my dad regularly at the hospital for months without me even knowing. At Tom's suggestion, I asked him to do my dad's funeral service with Nancy. He related a few funny stories including this one and in parting taped a dollar bill to the casket getting in the last laugh. Yes, this Friday, the 26th is his birthday and he died on April 6th. I appreciate that you asked. He would appreciate you having a glass of wine for him!

Here is my true confession, Sal. Only my immediate family knows this: I like to drink the milk out of the bowl when the cereal is gone. Tom is horrified by this (or at least pretends to be), but I never do it in public. It tastes so good with all the sugar in it, I cannot be bothered with spooning. So there you have it, my dark secret (even darker than domestic schizophrenia!). Can we still be friends?

On a more serious note, your metabolism must be changing if you've gained 10 real pounds (meaning not fluid) since Thanksgiving. That's something like an extra 35000 calories or an extra hamburger and milk shake every day for two months. The walking should help not just for burning calories but also for speeding up your metabolism. Yes, let's blame it on hormones!!!

As you were "picking up your cross" in parting today, I wondered if there is something bothering you, dear friend? (or maybe you were wanting the bag of m&m's?)
Love, Deb

Subj: *33*
Date: *1/24/2001 9:01:53 AM Central Standard Time*
From: *sarahjf50@hotmail.com*
To: *debbiesb13@aol.com*

You know, Deb, my dad had a great sense of humor. This just cracks me up that my bestest friend goes to counseling down Russell Palmer street (my dad had a master's degree in psychology, by the way) and there just had to be a 33 in there somewhere.

There are 33 years age difference between my father and me.

The first time I started noticing the number 33 was in the fall of 1999. Seemed like every time I looked at the clock in the car it was on 33. After a few dozen times, I decided 33 was supposed to mean something to me. Then I found out there were 33 years between me and Dad. Since he was, at the time, declining in mental health, I took this as a sign that I was to say a prayer for him every time I saw this number.

After Dad died, I was driving down the freeway and feeling very sad about the fact that he had not been a Christian when he died. I was listening to the Christian radio channel and Charles Stanley said, "If you have a question for God, ask it and He will answer." So, I asked God to give me a sign right then that Dad was in heaven. I started looking around as I was driving and not 20 seconds had gone by when I saw a huge sign saying, "Exit 33A." Since Dad had been a teacher (before the military) I thought to myself he left at the top of his class: "A": Heaven. Thanks Lord.

After Dad passed away, my mother gave their Taurus station wagon to Tisa and Dave. Dave and his father drove it out here from California. When it arrived, Tisa called me and said, "Did you know the number on the license plate?" I said, "No." Guess...33, what else.

I drink the milk out of the cereal bowl too! I eat Frosted Flakes or Captain Crunch—I think those are health foods, right? hee-hee

If that's the darkest confession you can make Deb, you are an angel in my book. Let's see, my darkest confession is...I sometimes sleep in my sweats when Bob is out of town. I just get so tired and fall on the bed. Then I get up in the morning and I am dressed for walking. Is this too gross? You should have seen me in college. What a mess. It's amazing I turned out to be such a neatnick. When Bob starts complaining about how sloppy Anthony is, I remind him of our slovenly habits when young and how we turned out to be so neat and tidy. My girls, also, have become neat and tidy in their old ages. My most favorite way of cleaning my room in high school was to rearrange the furniture—then I would pick everything up for a few days, then regress. Now you can blackmail me.

You asked if I was down—referring to my cross. Yes—I hate being chubby. I will trim down eventually with walking and working out at the club (if I would ever GO!) but I am enjoying feeling sorry for my fat self. Yuck, I don't think I've ever weighed this much. Don't ask me how much that it is, because I do not own a scale. I just know that in order to fit into my size 10 jeans, I have to stand on my head and suck in for five minutes. Last summer I could put on my jeans, tuck in my blouses and have room to spare. Now my underwear doesn't even want to be in there. I'm surprised the seams don't give way and all this fat would come blubbering out. My stomach is bigger than Gina's right now—and she just gave birth two weeks ago. On the other hand, my boobs are one tenth the size of hers...She looks like a Viking babe, I look like the hag who rolls the bones and tells the future—I saw "The Vikings" 50 times—remember that Norse witch who would howl, "O-o-o-din!" That's me. Eek! Except my teeth are in better shape. And my hair is shorter. I like that movie too.

So, I am depressed about fat. I'm even thinking I have more fat on my back, sticking out below my bra, than I have boobs to fill the front. I think I'll start wearing my bra backwards—it would fit better.

Don't come and see me—you'll take one look and scream, "Who are you and why did you eat my friend Sally!?"

One good thing: can't think of any good...oh, maybe this: My wrinkles on my face have stretched out and aren't so evident.

I will definitely toast to your dad on his birthday! I liked the story about Mike and your dad. It's so nice that you are near these people who were near to your dad. You can always share your memories. I'm not sure I will ever come across a street named after Frank Zerjav, but the church I go to is St. Francis— that's rather another coincidence! God is just full of little signs for us. How magical life is!

Maybe if I wiggle my nose I can lose 15 pounds. Maybe not.

Well, it's time to heft myself off the chair and go read—I may not change into my jammies, as Bob is gone...if I had some m&m's I would eat the whole bag- yum. Then I would moan and groan about being fat! I think my hormones made me do it.

Hope your Wednesday is fun-peaceful-warm-delicious-fragrant and pretty! Love, salthepal

Subj: Rockin' Robin
Date: 1/24/2001 2:53:01 PM Central Standard Time
From: debbiesb13@aol.com
To: sarahjf50@hotmail.com

Hi Sal !!!!

Exclamation points should never be directly next to an "I"; too hard to tell where one stops and the other starts.

How very interesting about all the 33's and your dad!! You said before he enjoyed music. Did he listen to lots of albums? They're "33's" too. You know now I will think of you and your dad every time I come across that number.

It is such an absolutely gorgeous day here!!! The dogs and I are sunning on the deck. Back door and windows are open. And all this week there have been robins everywhere in the greenbelt (haven't seen any in our yard though). Our yard is looking a bit more winter worn. Days like this tend to put me in the ready for spring mode.

It is amazing how 5 or 10 extra pounds can make such a big difference in how clothes fit. Seems you should be able to direct the weight gain a little more judiciously. Why do the stomach and butt get 99% and the boobs not even 1%? But if you lose weight, the boobs seem to deflate 99%. However, Sal (and this will be my LAST and final confession) I must tell you I would give something (but not sure what) to wear size 10 anything on my bottom half!

At least you were not graced with the "Smith" butt. All the women on my mom's side have it — large and square — only good for child birth, with no other redeeming features. My mom was the only sister with big boobs, but she had to pass on the butt instead (typical). Even when I lost all that weight recently (which of course is coming back) the waist was roomier, but the hips stayed the same...the classic "pear." So what does all this mean? Well, let's see...I can sympathize with how depressing it feels to gain weight; you and I are destined to never be Viking babes; and anything that smoothes out wrinkles can't be all bad (OK, that last one may be a little weak). By the way, is the nose wiggling thing working?

Went to see my mom. She is so looking forward to Friday. Please pray with me that she doesn't think she's actually going to see my dad. She's still in denial about his death, and I am hesitant to ask her if she is expecting to see him. He will greatly appreciate the toast. He would always say this Slovenian thing (which I have no idea how to spell) "nas dravia" which is basically cheers.

His mom's name was Frances and he was named for her, so maybe there is that "Francis" connection. Nothing would surprise me at this point. (Scary—my mom wanted to name me Fran Irene and call me FIZ! Thank God they saw *Singing in the Rain* starring Debbie Reynolds).

Well, must go and do something productive (not that our e-mails aren't productive to us). I haven't even picked up this house yet today. Hope your day was fun rather than stressful (there's always wine!). Have a peaceful, restful evening.
Love, Deb

Subj: *good evening*
Date: *1/24/2001 9:07:06 PM Central Standard Time*
From: *sarahjf50@hotmail.com*
To: *debbiesb13@aol.com*

Hi!
    No, I have not started walking. I am still sitting on my blobby butt. I think I am rebelling. Will get to it tomorrow. As Scarlet says, "Tomorrah's ahnothah day." Got her through the Civil War, will get me through the fat crisis.
    Had fun with girls and kids today. It was nice for Tisa and Gina to sit and talk and feed their babies. Zachary and I went up in the window seat and snuggled and read books. When I told him it was time for he and Mommy to go home, he looked at me and yelled,"NEVER!!!" I told Tisa I liked his style: he had taken the classic two-year-old response, "NO!" to a higher level: "Never!"
    Well, will write you tomorrow AFTER I WALK...take care, pal, sweet dreams.
Love, Sal

Subj: *morning rose song*
Date: *1/25/2001 8:48:32 AM Central Standard Time*
From: *sarahjf50@hotmail.com*
To: *debbiesb13@aol.com*

Hello there!
    It's in the 30's here this morning, crisp and sunny. I am looking longingly at my yard, mentally doing inventory on all the items I have planned to plant, transplant, etc. I could just picture you on that lovely, warm day, enjoying the balmy weather that Houston enjoys most spring, fall, and frequent days in winter.
    Don't forget, on Valentine's Day to cut back your roses to four of the strongest canes that grow outward, away from center of plant. Cut them 12-18 in. high—I know it seems brutal, and there has been many a V-Day when I was living in Houston that my roses had already put on some lovely new growth—Cut it off. Your bush will thank you for it this summer, when it is a healthy shape with strong canes that grow in the right direction.
    By Easter you will have your first roses.
    Once I get my arbor built, my newest addition to my rose garden will be four climbers.
    On to more current topics, my prayers are with you tomorrow that your mother will not have some kind of negative reaction over your father. Aside from the task of trying to comfort her, you are most likely feeling some tender thoughts about your dad and may not be able to share those with her on his birthday. I want you to know that I am here, you can talk to me anytime about your very special dad.
    On a coincidental note, don't you find it rather odd that the church where you go for comfort and guidance is on Russell Palmer Dr. and the church where I

go for comfort and solace is St. Francis, which is Italian for Frank? I find it rather prophetic, as if our dads are helping us to continue our candle light ministry and connection to one another.

Well, it's finally time: I'm going to put on my walking shoes this morning, after I do some chores. Taking my mom shopping later, she needs 50 rolls of toilet paper from Target. She likes to stockpile her pantry—child of the depression thing?

Do you have resale shop today? Have fun with your lady friends.

Love, Sal

Heavenly Fathers and Friends

Subj: brain dead
Date: 1/25/2001 3:17:42 PM Central Standard Time
From: debbiesb13@aol.com
To: sarahjf50@hotmail.com

Hi There!!!!
    Think I'm brain dead. Was trying to think of some rose song or something for subject and can only think of "Second Hand Rose" which was not at all what I was looking for. So just consider this a rose e-mail anyway. You know, thought that counts...
    My life: got home to catch up on a few things and had a message from my mom. Must digress...how is your mom with answer machines? Have discussed this with people working at the Rosemont. Seems many elderly, my mom included, get confused and think they are actually talking to who ever is on the recording or that you somehow get the message instantly. This has caused many irate messages in the past.
    Anyway, called her and she tells me she is in bed, never had breakfast or got dressed and her wedding ring is gone. I tried to sort this out on the phone but couldn't, so went over to find all this information was false. Hope this is not going to be a new ongoing thing for us. Her watch however, is gone. I find this sort of thing still has a tendency to stress me.
    It is so interesting that we have that connection between the street-churches-names. Things like that are more than just coincidence.
    Loved your story of Zachary saying "Never!" What a cutie!!!! How fun to have that cozy place to share a story and make him feel so special and well loved.
    Well, Scarlet, how was walking? It's probably still a little cold there to walk first thing in the morning. I usually will pass if the temps are below 38 or if the wind chill is really low. But find that if I don't go before 8:00 it isn't going to happen that day.
    Will keep your instructions for the roses handy and have marked my calendar to cut them on Valentine's Day. One of them is still growing and blooming despite the cold. But I will just tell her my friend Sal said I must be "heartless" and cut her back.
    Hope you have had a blessed day.
Love, Deb

Subj: Happy Day!
Date: 1/25/2001 9:03:28 PM Central Standard Time
From: debbiesb13@aol.com
To: sarahjf50@hotmail.com

Hey Sal !!!!!!
    Guess what…Travis got an acceptance letter from Texas Tech today! He was so excited (this means he smiled and even let me hug him). This was a good confidence booster for him and will get him moving forward on actually visiting before deciding.
    The Rosemont just called. Their elevator broke down and my mom has been stuck upstairs since she went to the beauty shop at 2:30. Evidently she's not being very nice about it so they had me talk to her to settle her down. For now all is well, but I may have to go up there if they don't get it fixed soon. Can't blame her for being mad. Don't understand why they built this building with space for 60 residents upstairs and only one elevator.
    Do have one more story about my dad I'd like to share with you. My dad loved to go places. Didn't matter where: post office, store, restaurant, gas station, just wanted to go. On one of Mike's visits he talked to him about going home to be with God. Mike says Daddy told him he was ready. I'm not really sure he understood the significance of the question. I could see him hearing the word "go" and just agreeing on general principle. My greater wish, is that he meant it. This thought made your story of seeing the "33A" sign all the more meaningful to me.
    Will say "Hi" tomorrow, but don't know if I'll get to e-mail you on the weekend as we have so much going on. Need to get Travis a present tomorrow. Tracey, David and Tristan are coming Saturday afternoon. Travis wants me to make him a spice cake and do his birthday with us Sunday lunch as he's doing something with his friends for Super Bowl in the evening. Austin wants to have his own Super Bowl party here and sometime Saturday his ensemble group is coming over to practice. Is there no balance? Our weekends are either rigormortis (sp?) or chaos, no happy medium.
    Well, I will close this for tonight and wish you pleasant dreams.
Love, Deb

Subj: Lo, How the rose ere blooming
Date: 1/26/2001 9:28:19 AM Central Standard Time
From: sarahjf50@hotmail.com
To: debbiesb13@aol.com

Dear Deb,
    One of my favorite hymns/carols: Lo…blooming.
    I think it's appropriate to mark today and give you a little balance to this birthday of your dad.

First, happy birthday, Frank, wherever you are! Thank you for arranging things after your death so that your daughter would meet someone with whom she could share both her joy and sadness about you. You and my father knew that your daughters would need someone to help them fill the void left by both of you on your entrances into heaven. Also, thank you for providing yet another holy connection with your daughter in that our fathers' names are prominently visible with our churches. How obvious, how fun! May the grace of God bless your spirit through eternity.

Now, for a little balance—and something a little coincidental and of course a signpost: Today, January 26 is the birthday of my dear friend, Anne who is Gina's Godmother. When I began the process to enter the Catholic Church, Anne was already my dear friend. She belonged to the church where we were receiving our pre-baptismal education. She is a great source of spirituality, education, and sisterhood for me. We asked her to be Gina's godmother and they have shared a special bond. Anne, coincidentally, is going to be visiting me this week. She will see her goddaughter's daughter! A special moment for us all.

So, as you think of January 26, think of these two good people born on this day, and how they have spread their goodness to others. Thank you, Lord, for the gift of these two people, Frank and Anne, who entered the world on this date. They have touched our lives.

Have a good day, Deb. Know that your love for your father was a holy, sacred grace: a bit of God within you.
Love, Sal

Subj: *yippee-skippee*
Date: *1/26/2001 10:32:41 AM Central Standard Time*
From: *sarahjf50@hotmail.com*
To: *debbiesb13@aol.com*

Dear Deb,
Hurray for Travis!! What an exciting time for him. And what an accomplishment! His perspective on life probably changed when he got that letter. Congratulations to him on preparing for a successful future.

After my walk yesterday I came in and just lied on the floor! Boy, am I out of shape...Will have to be good about either going to the club on inclement days or doing my dancing (I turn on my favorite CD's, get out my tiny weights and dance for 30 min—great fun, but not something I would let anyone witness, as I hop around and wiggle—my kids would really die).

Was your mom's watch stolen? I guess it's a problem in every facility, but a little aggravating that these helpless people are so open to this opportunity for robbery. Was her fear that all those items had been stolen a manifestation of the initial realization that her watch had been stolen? It must be frustrating for you not to be able to know what is really going on with her and her things. Is it possible she gives things to others? One nursing home administrator told us they will find patients wearing each other's clothes as they wander from room to room at times picking up things that don't belong to them.

Well, I have just got to go! I'd much rather chat with you but chores await. Hope your day has been a good one with your mom and with your dad's birthday. My prayers are with you to "Rise Above."
Love, Sal

Subj: Amazing Grace
Date: 1/26/2001 11:14:49 AM Central Standard Time
From: debbiesb13@aol.com
To: sarahjf50@hotmail.com

Good Morning!!!

Don't you kind of wonder if maybe our dad's have met up in heaven somewhere and are smiling down that we have each other for comfort in their loss?

This morning was a little sad, but as I walked and prayed I felt more at peace and can now actually be happy with my memories. How nice you have a special friend who shares his birthday! Someone who has obviously played a very important role in your life and your family's.

My prayer of late for my mother is that she find faith. I ask God every day to come into her heart so that she might have some happiness in her life. Evidently, her heart is a hard nut to crack.

My mom finally got down stairs last night courtesy of the fire department. She'll probably never have her hair done again. Don't know if her watch was stolen or went to the laundry or what. There are a few wanderers. So far she's only had perfume and hand cream missing, and she leaves her door open all the time. Mostly the things there have only sentimental value except her wedding and engagement ring and she doesn't take those off, so I'm not too worried. Will get her a new watch.

Do you get Victoria's Secret catalogs? Got the bathing suit one yesterday. What a joke! I thought why are they sending this to my fat butt? Think I will just leave it out for Travis and Austin. It's more skimpy than the *Sports Illustrated* swimsuit issue.

Know you will have a great visit with Anne and she will be so happy to see all your new additions! Be sure to wish her a happy birthday for me.
Love, Deb

Subj: a new day
Date: 1/29/2001 9:37:18 AM Central Standard Time
From: debbiesb13@aol.com
To: sarahjf50@hotmail.com

Good Morning!

Can imagine you are enjoying a cup of coffee or maybe tea with your visitors. Know you will be having a wonderful time catching up and sharing time with your girls and their little ones. It looks like you had some fairly wet weather all weekend; hope this didn't put a damper on your festivities!!

Seems like ages ago since Friday. Everything went well for our little trip to the cemetery. When we got there to pick up my mom she was waiting outside with one of her favorite pictures of her and my dad from the 40's tucked neatly in her lap. It really made me feel sorry for her and guilty at how maybe sometimes I do not give her enough credit for her sorrow. She only commented once on her disappointment at not being able to talk to my dad directly. She is much more open and talkative about her feelings with Tom, so it was nice he was there to give her some comfort. All in all that part went much better than expected.

To celebrate his turning 18, Travis bought his first lottery ticket (not something I would have even thought about). Think he was a little disappointed they didn't ask for his ID. Will let you know if he's a rich man on Wednesday.

The landscaper did a great job on the plants. The oak tree for my dad is small, but in a nice place in the back yard.

Will close for now. Need to run a few errands and visit my mom. I have no energy this morning; may be starting a period. How are you doing in that regard? Are the hot flashes still getting you? Are you eating your tofu? Wishing you a happy, fun day filled with the blessing of family and friends!
Love, Deb

Candles in the Darkness

Subj: one of life's mysteries
Date: 1/29/2001 8:23:02 PM Central Standard Time
From: debbiesb13@aol.com
To: sarahjf50@hotmail.com

Dear Sal,

After going to see my mom today, I am thinking about life's many mysteries. Like why is it sometimes we can get along so much better with "strangers" than with the ones we love the most. My mom was actually in quite a good mood today and we had a nice visit. But the truth of the matter is, sometimes I have a more enjoyable visit with some of the other people living there.

Wish you could meet Mayme, the lady that reminds me so much of Miss Sadie. She's 95 and eats at the same table with my mom. Recently when I had lunch with them, she was just chatting away about her mother making pickled tomatoes. She is almost blind, only able to make out shapes and colors. She told me the lady next to her has been putting the food she doesn't want on her (Mayme's) plate. She said with a robust little laugh, "I'm blind, but not that blind!!" There is another lady who lives there named Helen who is 82, has sky blue sparkling eyes, will dance any time she hears music, and is always happy. I really enjoy talking to her, and she loves to flirt with Tom when he comes. She told us yesterday she's moving to Arizona as her daughter's husband is being transferred. She was saying how much she'll miss us, and I will really miss her too.

Anyway, in thinking this over, I think the whole root to enjoying their company is these women are happy. They're old and have their infirmities, but they are happy at heart. They are both of them grateful for the blessings they have had in life, not complaining about what went wrong. Gosh, I wish my mom could be like that!!! What a difference it makes not only for them but for those around them. We'll have to remember this in our old age when we have our adjoining suites at the nursing home: with God's grace, be cheerful at heart! I think perhaps it is a key to avoiding loneliness (that and a good pair of tweezers!).

Hope you had a great weekend and a fun visit with Anne and your girls.

Love, Deb

Subj: *It is well with my soul*
Date: *1/31/2001 9:44:30 AM Central Standard Time*
From: *sarahjf50@hotmail.com*
To: *debbiesb13@aol.com*

Good morning!

I had a whirlwind, fun few days with family and friend. Put Anne on the plane yesterday afternoon, we were both exhausted from our in-depth conversations—Anne and I used to run into each other in the parking lot somewhere and stand and talk for hours. We just like to mull over everything. It was so nice to have the girls over to visit with her. She remembers the girls, Gina at age 5 and Tisa at age 16, and watched them grow up—she was amazed to sit and watch them feed their babies.

I was very touched by your description of your mom holding the picture of your dad and her. I can see how your heart would have softened and become more understanding. That's one of those moments when God gives you an opportunity to see a different perspective.

My friend Anne was in Dallas to see her dad who is in a nursing home. He has always been a very difficult man. This last visit with him was not good, he was again very abusive to her and actually threatened her physically (she could have knocked the frail man over with a feather) and for the first time ever, she stood up to him and told him not to speak to her like that ever again. Then she really let him have it, a lot of pent up anger, which took the form of a declaration to him that she was no longer going to tolerate any abusive language from him. It took a lot for her to do this. But when she was staying with me, she said she felt like her anger for her father had left her, she felt relieved and more at peace with him than she ever has.

I've told you this because I know you understand the kind of pain she has endured over the years and endures now that the parent is rather senile. It is a hard situation, given the physical and mental frailty of these people. They have remained abusive, and maybe become even more so, now that their senility prevents them from hiding emotions. This is what causes "domestic schizophrenia": anger, hurt, sympathy, compassion. A tennis match, watching your emotions bounce back and forth, into one emotional court, then another. Let us all pray for the strength to rise above, get out of the game and into the commentary box! There are no winners in this game.

Another yucky period, you said you're having. It isn't fair that we have to suffer for Eve's indiscretion—but I guess God knew what he was doing—I still haven't had a period since Thanksgiving. I told Bob the other day maybe the dam will break and I will have a horrendous flow—he said he didn't want to talk about it...this is why men don't have periods and give birth. It's way too unpleasant for them.

Your comments on how you enjoy visiting with the other people at the nursing home, rather than with your mom, was so understandable! I, as well, admire elderly women who have maintained an upbeat personality.

Please say a prayer for my son, he's a bit lost right now. In turn, I will pray for Travis, that the choice he makes for a college brings him success and wisdom.
Love, Sal

Subj: a light in the window
Date: 1/31/2001 5:59:32 PM Central Standard Time
From: debbiesb13@aol.com
To: sarahjf50@hotmail.com

Reading your e-mail earlier it was like a quick drink of water as I jogged through the day. Now that I'm taking time to reply, don't expect anything too mental. I just tried to sign on when the laptop is literally in my lap but not plugged into anything. I'm lying on the heating pad, as I still have not started that period but have been spotting and cramping for three days. (May chew on a stick next!) Have seen an ad on TV several times recently for some natural estrogen soy thing that's supposed to help hot flashes and night sweats. Will have to remember the name to give you.

Glad to hear you had a fun visit with Anne. Can imagine how amazing it was for her seeing Tisa and Gina with their babies.

Can also imagine the cleansing feeling she had at expressing her frustrations to her father. Even if she doesn't realize it yet, I would think this was incredibly important for her to have accomplished this before he dies so she is not left with all these unresolved, unexpressed feelings and no one to express them to. Liked your analogy to the tennis match. With you and I at least I think we do have days we get in the commentator's box, but it is still a struggle.

Will be praying for Anthony to find peace. Being a teenager is harder today I think than when we were that age. Harder for them and for us as parents. It is especially hard when they don't open up a lot to your questions and efforts to help.

I'm here anytime you want to unload your parenting fears, frustrations whatever. I don't have any answers, only common concerns: Wondering every time something is out of sorts if it's drugs (even though it never has been, thank God); disagreeing over who sets the rules; and thinking where did I go wrong as a parent to get to this point. In truth though, you and I both know we have taught them well, and they will inevitably make some bad choices. We can only pray for them, pray their mistakes aren't too bad, and be there the second they want us.

This has been a busy week so far. The manager of the place where my mom lives asked me to be part of a panel on marriages for his Kiwanis club. He wants me to talk about how my parents' marriage was successful for so many years. I was reluctant at first, not thinking of them as the "poster children" for the idyllic relationship; plus I was concerned about having major anxiety. Tom told me to do it as it was a wonderful way to honor them. I asked God for an opinion, and came to the realization He would not have given me this opportunity if I weren't supposed to do it.

Also went back to the psychiatrist today, as I still seem to float through a lot of days with sort of low-level physical symptoms of anxiety. She upped the anti-depressant dose.

Will go for now and let you have a rest from the eye strain.

Love, Deb

287

Subj: candle in the dark
Date: 2/1/2001 10:10:27 AM Central Standard Time
From: sarahjf50@hotmail.com
To: debbiesb13@aol.com

Dear Deb,

Sense a little melancholy from you! Keep talking to me, and you will work through it. One of the things I love and dearly need is to "hear myself speak" when I am writing to you. I learn things about myself. Do you also notice this when you write to me? It occasionally brings me to an epiphany (Father Tim's "aha").

Recovering from the past year and your depression is still an ongoing process and you are managing it well by consulting your psychiatrist for the drug therapy and continuing counseling with Mary Jo. And let's face it, it's not like you live a stress-free life on a daily basis! Two teenagers, a difficult terminally-ill mother, a hormonal upheaval—which reminds me of something I discovered about myself—maybe this would help you as well:

I have been noticing my mood changes and I have a new culprit! My menopausal hormones. As you are continuing to suffer from some anxiety and depression, HELLO, it could be your feminine hormones acting up as well.

Now, what do you do about this? How do you distinguish between the two causes? Do you make charts? Do you eat seaweed? Do you rage uncontrolled because it's a normal woman thing? Do you become a Zen Buddhist (sp?)? Do you order straight jackets from the JC Penney catalogue? Do you read every book on menopause? Do you read every book on depression? Do you get a hysterectomy? Do you get a lobotomy? Do you tell your husband it's all his fault? Well, I have a solution—I really do! And it will help.

Get ready, this is a religious infomercial…

You have to demote the power of your feelings to run your life. Do not trust your feelings as truth. They are a reaction to either a belief or a chemical. In the case of a belief, a lot of times the belief you have does not have all the facts and may not be totally correct. In the case of a chemical causing you to feel a certain way, the emotion it induces is definitely an untruth.

You know how people say, "trust your feelings." DON'T. What do you trust? God. He tells you fear and anxiety are not from Him. They are an absence of faith.

FEELINGS ARE A REACTION—NOT A TRUTH.

Try this: Picture your mind in two parts.

One part is the God, higher spirit, adult, "rise above," you.

The other part is the ME, self, child, emotional, you.

When you are feeling anxious let the "child" express its feelings. Then take your adult side, your higher spirit, and talk to that child. Validate that the child has these feelings. Then think what would the adult/God say to the child about those feelings. Are they based on infallible truth? Look for the truth in the cause of those feelings.

If you find a truthful feeling, act on it in a godly way, pray for guidance, then let the feeling go, it is in God's hands until he sends you an answer.

If this feeling is not based on truth (a chemical or gossip or supposition) then this feeling is not valid, and it needs to be let go of. It needs no further action other than to see it as a bothersome cold that will subside on its own.

I once heard Charles Stanley talk about the unreliability of feelings. He says don't trust them. See them as a reaction to a stressor. Your job is to discern if the cause of those feelings is a truth, then pray for guidance.

I never said this was easy, I struggle with it every day. Bottom line: Let God, rather than your emotions, rule your life and actions. It takes practice, it takes faith. Amen.

Your panel discussion on marriage. Who is going to speak from your lips? The spirit of faith or the spirit of fear? Which do you want to control you? Then tell God to use you and concentrate on his will—search your holy spirit—you will have so much to say and have joy! Oh, and don't think their marriage has to be a rosy picture! Tell the truth, tell how they compensated for a not so perfect marriage— that is reality! Who has a perfect marriage? Tell how even after decades of marital conflicts, your mother took a picture of the two of them to honor their marriage, to his grave on Jan. 26. Love has many parts. Give the listeners God's perspective on your parents' marriage, not just your daughter's perspective.

Briefly, Anne, yes, she does realize her recent experience with her father was a profound, life changing moment. She is still surprised at her strength and ability to break out of the role she has assumed with her father for so many years. Not to be redundant, but she "rose above" the situation, and took on a new perspective.

I, too, saw that soy supplement commercial and came up out of my commercial time blahs enough to take note. However, all I remember was it was by the makers of Monistat…our memories are really not doing their jobs these days…I need brain food, big time.

Have a "loverly" day, friend, and enjoy the first day of February!
Love, Sal

Subj: Danger: radioactive
Date: 2/1/2001 5:10:47 PM Central Standard Time
From: debbiesb13@aol.com
To: sarahjf50@hotmail.com

Dear Sal,
    Salmon is brain food.
    Yes, I do learn things about myself when I write to you. Sometimes I find myself telling you things I haven't even admitted to myself yet. Sometimes like today, I learn them from reading your response because you see things I didn't even know I said.

Your thoughts on hormonal cycles are probably very accurate. Perhaps perimenopause is nothing but one long extended megadose of PMS.

If you thought yesterday was melancholy, I hate to think what you will say about today. Perhaps, I shouldn't even be writing to you now, as I am FULL of feelings. You are going to think, "Why did I waste my time?" You didn't really. It is really more like you foresaw the future. I know all the things you said are right, but I am finding it hard to comply at this moment.

My day started out good enough: Went to resale and listened to a lecture tape by Patsy Clairmont along the way, which incidentally, covered your theories on feelings. Listened to tape on way home. There was one part about panty hose that had me laughing so hard I was crying and could barely see to drive. Then I got home.

First thing, Travis hits me with when I walk in the door, "I want to buy a Camaro convertible." We argued, of course. Tom and I have no control here as he has the money, and since he just turned 18, he can do this without parental supervision.

Shit! Shit! And Double Shit!!!! Those are my feelings on that subject.

And why? Because I have fear. I have an absence of faith when it comes to my son wrapping a fast car around a tree somewhere. So there it is, right out in the open, I lack faith on this issue. Right at this moment, I cannot rise above, or be an adult, or completely let go and lay this at the cross. At some point I will, but for now I just want to cry.

So that should be enough self-absorption for one e-mail.

The only thing I remembered also about the estrogen stuff was, "It's made by the makers of Monistat." Now we're even having parallel memory shortages. Yikes!

Are you doing anything fun tomorrow? I promise I will be in a better mood and will write you something cheery. Must go now: meeting Tom for a company thing at the horse races. Thanks for letting me unload. Thanks for lighting the candle.

Love, Deb

Subj: the cool down
Date: 2/1/2001 11:09:34 PM Central Standard Time
From: debbiesb13@aol.com
To: sarahjf50@hotmail.com

Hey—

Well, the horse race thing was fun and a nice diversion to get out of the house to another world. But it's nice now to come home to the quiet, a fire, and a little time to unwind before slipping off to bed. Have to admit to feeling a bit contrite about unloading to you earlier.

You are correct in everything you said about prayer; and that feelings are a reaction (exhibit A: earlier e-mail, child expresses feelings). Know the candle is burning, if I just open my eyes to see it, and hold out my hands to feel its warmth.

Perhaps Jupiter will align with Mars tomorrow — which means brain chemistry, hormones, and life will move towards a peaceful coexistence. In the meantime, think I will check on the straightjackets and lobotomy.

Want to give thanks tonight Lord, for my dear friend Sal, who keeps me grounded and is always there to remind me of your word, holding the lamp up to guide my way even as I am so easily blinded by my fears. I pray for our sons... that You will guide them along the path You have laid out for them. Thank you for giving us this connection in prayer and in You. Amen

Good Night and God bless you, Sal.

Love, Deb

Subj: cool down is right
Date: 2/2/2001 10:35:27 AM Central Standard Time
From: sarahjf50@hotmail.com
To: debbiesb13@aol.com

Oh Deb,

Even if we are hormonal misfits—we have such a connection it is eerie. Your e-mail to me entitled "cool down": I just did my exercises and sat down to cool down and read your e-mails!

On your son wanting a Camaro convertible, maybe my experience with fearless teenagers of my own will help a tiny bit: I have learned that children only listen to the first 20 seconds of anything you are going to say to them. So take advantage of that window and do your worst!

Now, Deb, the big news is he won't pay attention to most of what you tell him.

Realistically, some guys never get over the car thing—this may be the first in a long line of cars/toys he enjoys over the span of 80 years. And you know what? It's out of your hands once you have given him advice and counsel.

I always compare motherhood moments like this to a scenario where you are standing on the side of the freeway with your 5 year old child, and you put a blindfold on yourself and say to the child, "Go ahead, honey, try to get across the highway." That's how I feel when the kids are making decisions that you cannot prevent—all you can do is pray they get to the other side.

Thanks for praying for Anthony. Boy, does he need everybody's prayers. He is going with a bunch of friends to the winter formal tomorrow night. My prayer is that he enjoy the fun of friends and find peace in just being himself—and to take good care of the life he has been given. And for dear Travis: I pray he will find his worth not in what kind of car he has or even what school he goes to, but in a life which reflects the love and care that has been given to him by his parents — and also, Lord, keep him safe, for his mom's sake.

Have a great weekend, Deb! I think the weather is going to be pretty nice down your way! Think Bob and Dave will get some tennis in tomorrow, while Tisa and I push babies around the park. Sunday Gina has promised to help Bob with his algebra—he has a GRE test on Monday as part of his Master's program. Gina is a brain in math, and actually likes calculus...wants to become a math teacher!

Saturday we are having roast turkey and celebrating our two sons-in-law and their new jobs. Both begin this month. I know my mom will come because I'm making turkey!

Speaking of calories, did I tell you I dance/exercise/lift weights to Aretha Franklin? My favorite songs are "Respect," "Chain of Fools," and "Think"—assertiveness training—talk about getting rid of some bothersome feelings: just dance to Aretha—but I don't let anybody see me do it, it probably looks pretty funny, leaping around and hefting my tiny weights, waving and shimmying my blubber all around the living room. I have to force myself to stop—it's too fun.

Now, back to you and me: PUHLEEEEEEZ don't apologize for feeling down, bad, mad, scared or any of a number of emotions you (or I) may have every day. The beauty is we can talk about it, and help ourselves to discern how serious the situation really is. Sometimes we may put it on the list to talk to a professional about, or sometimes we may just have a glass of wine and decide "whatever, Lord." The point is that you can feel anything, it's what you do with that feeling that you and I can talk about ANYTIME!

Deb, we are fighting a battle, did you know that? It's the battle against aging bodies, unfaithful hormones and the darkness. We need to encourage each other to care for our bodies, which are a gift from God, eat the healthy foods, laugh at the hormones, and pray for strength against our negative emotions.

God bless you, dear friend, and thanks for being my undying, faithful candle, burning bright, every time I look for you.
Love, Sal

Epilogue

*

Enjoy the Ride — August 10, 2001

*

Epilogue

Response to Prologue:
Subj: enjoy the ride
Date: 08/10/2001 7:05:11 PM Central Daylight Time
From: debbiesb13@aol.com
To: sarahjf50@hotmail.com

Hi—

I hate this! Just lost the reply to you about compiling our e-mails into a book. Oh well, will try again. As to which of us is the more sane, I thought we established that a long time ago! Or are we taking turns?

Lets start with the end: Can we help readers get through their own daily trials? "No. But God can." Exactly!!!! That's the message I felt in my heart. When we first playfully mentioned this book idea last October, the "message," if there even was one then, seemed completely different.

Do I marvel at divine intervention? Absolutely!! Our friendship is a product of it no doubt: that we were thrown together only briefly, that from the very beginning we trusted to share our thoughts so openly, and that so often we seem to know inexplicably when the other one needs a word of cheer or encouragement.

Would we have been friends without e-mail? As neighbors? Maybe, but surely with more caution. As pen pals? Not if you were depending on me! As wives meeting every two years at a company conference? Pleeeeease!!!!! Too many obstacles, but it happened! Don't think God invented e-mail just for us (Al Gore invented e-mail!), but do think He guided you to ask for all those e-mail addresses. He opened that door, and we went in.

So what can we give other women? We can show them the possibilities when they, as you so eloquently put it, open the eyes of their heart. They'll find humor in daily life; they'll find similar frustrations; they'll find rewards in friendship where they may least expect it; they'll find amazing growth can come from the most devastating events in their life; they'll find God loves them, if they only learn to listen as you have taught me.

Cannot tell you how many times I was embarrassed by reading the things I'd written to you. But rereading your e-mails never embarrassed me. As always I found what you had to say warm and filled with an engaging sense of humor. We're always our own worst critics! So sit back and enjoy the ride. The stuff that makes us blush is what "delete" is for.

Your comment on roses and negotiating the thorns brought to mind something I saw on a bookmark at Wal-Mart recently. It said something to the effect that some people look at a rose and think the thorns detract from it. Others look at the rose and see the beauty the bloom lends the thorns. That's how our e-mails have been, they're the roses that give beauty to the thorns of daily life. We're gonna put together one heck of a book!

Your sister in Him, Deb

An Ongoing Mission

When we decided to compile our e-mails into book form we chose a date on which to begin this seemingly monumental task. It was Tuesday, September 11, 2001. Our phone appointment (we live in different cities) was for 1 pm. By noon on that day, it was apparent that everyone's life had changed, and we were not certain what tomorrow would bring.

However, when we talked about how to proceed, we decided to carry on with our plan to begin editing. Our thought being that on this tragic day, the spirit of being a "candle in the darkness" was needed more than ever. Our hope was, that some day, in some way, that spirit would shine a light for others.

In honor of the people who died on that day, in honor of their friends and family, in honor of our sons & daughters who fight for our freedom, we are committed to keeping the spirit of *Candles in the Darkness* alive long after our book may have left the shelves:

Our website

www.candlesinthedarkness.com

is our way of adding some light to your day.

Join us there and e-mail us, as well.

Acknowledgements

Thanks from both of us
- *Mary Jo: For being our cheerleader before we even knew we had a team*
- *Nancy Ellis, our agent: For taking two nobodies under your wing*
- *1stBooks Staff: For bringing our dream to fruition*
- *Anne: Who understands about Foul Weather Friends*
- *Jan: For laughing in all the right places*
- *Liz: For looking past the typos to the value of the message*
- *Lynda: For taking time to call a famous friend: thank you*
- *Susan Drake: For professional advice and encouragement*

Thanks from Deb
- Travis: For giving up the computer and understanding writing "for fun"
- Austin: For being patient when mom was on the phone for HOURS!
- Tracey: For truly taking an interest and understanding kindred spirits
- Tiffany: For asking, "You're still working on that book?!"
- Mother: For being strong and loving
- Daddy: For teaching me the value of contentment
- Mary Jo: For your friendship, your light, your guidance, for Isaiah 41:10
- Tom: For being by my side every step of the way, for always: SD
- Sal: For asking for my e-mail address, for making everything a "fun time"

Thanks from Sal
- *Tisa: For allowing Mom to share your life with our readers*
- *Andrea: For always being a soft voice of reason*
- *Gina: For being such a wonderful support to a mother in a new job*
- *Anthony: For offering to "speak" to anyone who didn't like this book*
- *Nonny: For showing us women that it's never too late to start over*
- *Papa: For instilling an appreciation of writing in his daughter*
- *Elaine: Who was Sal's candle in the darkness in 1990*
- *Bob: For believing I could be the Scarecrow, the Tinman, and the Lion*
- *Deb: If you hadn't worked inside the box, we never would have made it*

Sources

The Book of Common Prayer, according to the use of The Episcopal Church. Seabury Press, Sept. 1979.

Frankl, Viktor. *Man's Search for Meaning.* Boston: Beacon Press, 1984.

The Holy Bible, authorized King James Version. Cleveland: The World Publishing Company.

The New American Bible. Nashville: Catholic Bible Press a division of Thomas Nelson Publishers, 1987.

New American Standard New Testament with Psalms and Proverbs. La Habra, CA: The Lockman Foundation, 1997.

Ortlund, Ann. "Finding Good in Every Circumstance." *Joy for the Journey.* Ed. Terri Gibbs. Nashville: Word Publishing, 1997.

Books We Discussed:

Barkman, Alma. *Rise and Shine.* Chicago: Moody Press, 1987.

Barnes, Emilie. *15 Minutes Alone with God.* Eugene: Harvest House, 1994.

Breathnach, Sarah Ban. *Simple Abundance.* New York: Warner Books, 1995.

Heatherley, Joyce Landorf. *Balcony People.* Austin: Balcony Publishing, 1984.

Karon, Jan. *At Home in Mitford* (and series sequels), New York: Penguin, 1994.

Rowling, J.K. *Harry Potter and the Sorcerer's Stone* (and series sequels). New York: Scholastic, 1997.

Stolz, Karen. *World of Pies.* New York: Hyperion, 2000.

A NEW BOOK FROM SALLY FUGAZI AND DEBBIE HARWELL

STORIES OF STRENGTH AND TRIUMPH

Waging War on the Battle-ax

In this collection of non-fiction tales, domineering divas face defeat by everyday heroines. Armed with strengths such as wisdom, humor, spirituality, and friendship, it is possible to overcome this meddlesome female once and for all.

TRUE STORIES

Authors Sally Fugazi and Debbie Harwell have gathered these inspiring tales from a series of interviews they have conducted with women from all walks of life. Each story is a unique struggle for power between two women: The Positive (our heroine) vs. the Negative (her battle-ax). In the characteristic writing style of their previous works, the authors spice up the stories with a bit of irreverent humor aimed at the Battle-ax. Let's face it: the dominatrix deserves it.

EMPOWERING ADVICE

Learn how to evolve from victim to victor. The last page of each story is devoted to the heroine's savvy advice for the reader.

WISDOM OF THE AGES

Each tale is enhanced with quotations of wisdom spanning three millenniums.

A SATISFYING "YES !!!" READING EXPERIENCE

Some battles are won quickly, others may last a lifetime. However, in every story the heroine discovers a way to survive and become victorious over the battle-ax, thus living "happily ever after."

WE WOULD LIKE TO THANK THE COURAGEOUS WOMEN WHO HAVE TRIUMPHED IN THEIR BATTLE, AND WERE BRAVE ENOUGH TO RETELL THEIR STORY IN ORDER TO HELP OTHERS.

THIS IS THEIR BOOK.

Coming Soon

About the Authors

Two Different Voices – One Harmonious Duo
Sally Fugazi and Debbie Harwell come from totally opposite backgrounds (Deb is a native Texan, Sal is an Air Force brat; Sal is a butterfly, Deb is the worker bee*), but they merge their life experiences into a story of midlife that is both heartwarming and inspiring.

Both women have racked up the miles as wives, mothers, grandmothers, and daughters. They have been housewives and working moms, corporate wives and volunteers. Both have mothered and mentored a houseful of children, been caregivers to their elderly parents, are survivors of clinical depression, and determined to battle menopause without the benefit of HRT.

Between them they have over 100 years of fieldwork as real women! It is with this unique set of life experiences that they reach out to other women with compassion and understanding through their quirky senses of humor and can-do attitude.

* Or: Deb is discipline, Sal is chaos

Printed in the United States
19118LVS00002B/112-117

9 781414 051246